CANCEL

Catherine Cri

A DEADLY KIND OF LOVE

**The intense story of the twisted
love which drove Susan Polk to stab
her husband to death**

JB

JOHN BLAKE

Published by John Blake Publishing Ltd,
3 Bramber Court, 2 Bramber Road,
London W14 9PB, England

www.blake.co.uk

First published in paperback in 2008

ISBN: 978 1 84454 601 5

All rights reserved. No part of this publication may be reproduced, stored in a retrieval
system, or in any form or by any means, without the prior permission in writing of the
publisher, nor be otherwise circulated in any form of binding or cover other than that in
which it is published and without a similar condition including this condition being
imposed on the subsequent publisher.

British Library Cataloguing-in-Publication Data:

A catalogue record for this book is available from the British Library.

Design by www.envydesign.co.uk

Printed and bound in Great Britain by CPD Group, Blaina, Abertillery, Wales

1 3 5 7 9 10 8 6 4 2

Copyright © 2008 by Crier Communications Inc.
Published by arrangement with William Morrow, an imprint of HarperCollins
Publishers, New York, USA. All rights reserved.

Papers used by John Blake Publishing are natural, recyclable products made from wood
grown in sustainable forests. The manufacturing processes conform to the
environmental regulations of the country of origin.

Every attempt has been made to contact the relevant copyright-holders, but some were
unobtainable. We would be grateful if the appropriate people could contact us.

Pictures in section 2 on pages, 1, 4 (bottom), 5, 6, 7 and 8 courtesy of Cole Thompson.

For my family, especially my parents, Ann and Bill.
Our first, best teachers.

NORTH AYRSHIRE LIBRARIES	
05045134	
Bertrams	30/07/2008
364.152	£7.99
BO	

CONTENTS

FOREWORD

With all the talk about living in the moment and the power of *now*, how easy it is for some to pretend that complicated, stressful, or traumatic events we live through as children and adolescents have little to do with the way we come to live as adults – that early chapters in our life stories don't really influence the chapters we are writing today, much less those we will pen tomorrow. We are, the most zealous behaviourists would argue, masters of our own destinies, with only bad habits to break, unfettered by unconscious psychological conflicts and dynamics.

Yet the story of every individual I have evaluated in fifteen years as a psychiatrist, several of them while specialising in forensic psychiatry, belies that sort of pure here-and-now reasoning. In every instance, from cases of major depression and panic disorder to those involving seemingly inexplicable and horrifying violence, I have been able to 'connect the dots' back to complicated, stressful, traumatic, or catastrophic events in a person's recent or much more distant past.

When I offered my views on Scott Peterson's psychological makeup on *Catherine Crier Live*, for example, I didn't limit my exploration of Peterson's psyche to the events of 24 December 2002, the day he killed his wife Laci and her unborn son Conner. I didn't restrict it to the five years he and Laci had been married. I looked all the way back to the barren psychological landscape of his childhood, a childhood that included severe emotional deprivation that rendered him unable to form genuine human connections or feel real empathy for anyone. Making sense of Scott Peterson's monstrous deeds required unearthing the ways in which he, himself, was psychologically murdered.

It is no different, in the case of Susan Polk, who murdered her husband Dr. Felix Polk. Because, as Catherine makes so clear and compelling in the pages that follow, the story of that murder has roots not only in the couple's tumultuous marriage and impending divorce, but deep in their pasts as well.

Susan Polk was only fifteen years old when her mother took her to Felix, a psychologist, for treatment, but already she bore the psychological scars of being abandoned by her father and alleged abuse as a child.

Felix Polk had travelled his own rocky psychological terrain. He bore scars, including debilitating anxiety and depression. He had tried to take his own life.

How did Felix Polk – who many describe as a very intelligent and insightful man – miss the way in which his desire to be safe from critical and controlling women led him to romance his vulnerable, teenage patient? How could he not see the perfect storm gathering from the day he first met her and imagined her as his lover? Didn't he wonder whether prior trauma, not genuine affection, was the reason she didn't object to his request that she sit on his lap in later sessions? Did he really believe that, as a slight, average-looking man in his forties, he was the lucky recipient of pure love from a pretty teenager? How could he not see that in having sex with her and marrying her he was violating the most sacred boundary between doctor and patient, that he would be the rightful heir to all the repressed, primitive, churning rage she harbored toward the controlling and abusive men in her life? Was he so narcissistic as to believe he could contain it, rather than be destroyed by it?

And how did Susan Polk, with all her intellect and familiarity with psychological lingo, miss the fact that the murderous intent building inside her was not only meant for Felix, but for her father and her brother and for God knows who else? How did she not realize that the stabbing of her husband was the culmination of her fury at those forces she believed had deprived her of personal freedom? How did she not see it would lead to the ultimate surrender of her liberty – to life in prison? How did she miss the fact that her three sons would be effectively orphaned, left without a father (as she had been), abandoned by their mother (as, in many ways, she was).

How did Felix and Susan Polk not see all of this?

The answer is that they were lost in a drama neither really understood nor controlled. It was a drama that, like so many, was built on powerful and painful events and themes from the past, about to seep into and commandeer the present. It was bigger than either of them, a juggernaut.

So it takes Catherine Crier, possessed of fierce intellect and unbridled curiosity about human emotion and behaviour, to reconstruct and tell the tale for us, to take us into a murder investigation and find a story not only of violence, but of desperation, passion, and betrayal. How lucky that the work should fall to her. For no viewer of Court TV could hope for a better host, and no reader of true crime could hope for a better guide.

This is Catherine Crier at her best. In these pages, she delivers what I and so many others have come to rely on her for: her trademark legal and psychological insight into the human condition, and how it can turn deadly in an instant.

—KEITH ABLOW, MD

PROLOGUE

'Mom fuckin' shot dad with a shotgun!' fifteen-year-old Gabriel Polk shouted into the receiver. His older brother, Adam, was on the other end of the phone line. 'Yeah, fucking crazy bitch! We still have an apartment house. We still have an apartment. We get income. We are [inaudible]. We can keep it, I think. Dad left us a pile of [inaudible]. That's for sure.'

Gabriel had been up all night, speaking with police after finding his seventy-year-old father dead, bathed in blood on the floor of the family's pool house, about 50 feet from their home in Orinda, California. It was 10.15am on 15 October 2002, and the teen had just completed a lengthy interview with detectives from the Contra Costa Sheriff's Office when he was told that Adam was on the phone.

'Yeah. Fuckin' crazy bitch! I stumbled in on dad,' he explained. 'No, no. She just shot him in the fuckin' chest. Fucking crazy bitch. I had to call 911 and shit. They have like our whole house under police inspection or something.

'What the hell is wrong with her? I hope they give her the fucking death penalty . . . [inaudible].'

The sound of footsteps prompted the boy to end his conversation abruptly.

Peering into the cramped interrogation room, an investigator asked, 'Are you still on the phone?'

'No,' Gabriel shot back. He was naked from the waist up. He had been so upset at the sight of his dead father in the pool house that he had left the residence barefoot, wearing only a pair of shorts. His usually bright brown eyes were bloodshot and framed by dark circles.

'Did the trauma guy say what we are going to do?' the officer asked.

'Just bring a sleeping bag,' Gabriel shrugged.

'Yeah, for right now . . . We are going to have to get you a sleeping bag and a pillow. And we will resolve this as soon as we can.'

'I would like to know what is going to happen to us financially,' Gabriel said.

'Financially?' the officer repeated. 'What do you mean?' It seemed an odd question coming from a boy who'd just discovered his father murdered – particularly when the boy's own mother was the prime suspect.

Gabriel then brought up an apartment complex the family owned in San Francisco's East Bay. 'I don't know what is going to happen right now, but I would like to hold onto that because we need a source of income.'

Twelve hours earlier, it had been a very different Gabriel that police encountered at the family's sprawling hillside compound on Miner Road. Then, he was a nervous wreck, out in the street with a phone and a flashlight, afraid that his own mother might come after him.

As the sheriff's officers arrived at the scene, he was unable to answer many of the officers' questions. All he knew was that his father, Frank Felix Polk, was dead, and he was certain his mother had killed him.

PART I

A DEATH ON MINER ROAD

CHAPTER ONE

UNETHICAL
BEGINNINGS

Susan sat quietly in the passenger seat as her mother parked the car in front of the yellow clapboard house on the corner of Ashby Avenue in downtown Berkeley, California. She and her mom were right on time for her first session with Frank Felix Polk, the Alameda County psychologist that school officials had ordered her to see.

For several months in the autumn of 1972, Susan Mae Bolling had been skiving from Clayton Valley High School in neighbouring Contra Costa County. At fifteen, the willowy brunette did not fit the profile of a truant. Recently, she had been called to the principal's office, not to be admonished, but to be congratulated for her score on the IQ test.

The principal was so excited he could barely contain himself. It was almost embarrassing how he gushed over the student with the 'genius' IQ. News that the quiet new girl with the long, curly hair and hazel eyes was the school's top scorer spread quickly through the student body, and Susan soon found herself a celebrity of sorts. Being the centre of attention was not something she was comfortable with; she was awkward, reserved, and even a bit withdrawn. Being hailed as 'gifted', however, made her feel powerful. Suddenly, she was recognised as a person with superior qualities, and everyone at school was making a fuss over her. She felt extraordinary, even a bit conceited.

Susan decided she no longer needed to study. Why waste time when she was a genius? Instead of homework, she spent her after-school hours doing what she really enjoyed – reading, looking up words in the dictionary, doing crafts, and watching *Dialing for Dollars*, a fast-paced television game show.

Then she simply stopped going to school.

It was not something she planned. It just sort of happened. It all began the day of her ninth grade maths test. She had not studied and could not bear the thought of tarnishing her genius reputation – so she just skipped school that day.

Things snowballed from there. At first, she attended classes intermittently, but soon she was falling behind. Being a genius wasn't enough if she didn't attend classes.

Then it happened. She received an 'F' on a maths test.

Realising she was in trouble, Susan went to her teacher. He was kind and attentive, immediately offering her extra help. Their impromptu session was helpful, and the teacher told her to come back. But Susan didn't follow through. All of a sudden, everything seemed too hard.

The walk to school was too long, especially on the days that the neighbourhood bully and his buddies were on the street. At the time, Susan was living with her mother and older brother, David, in a two-bedroom apartment in Concord, an area of the East Bay about forty-five minutes outside San Francisco. She didn't feel safe in their blue-collar neighbourhood, where gunshots were not uncommon, and there'd been several murders in the hills behind her house. The little girl who lived next door had been struck in the head by a stray bullet and needed surgery to have it removed. Susan had babysat for the child several times and was horrified when her father came by to share the news. It made her nervous to pass the older boy and his friends, and she didn't like the way they looked at her.

Even at school, she didn't feel safe. During her first week at Clayton, a girl jumped her, and then several others joined in, shoving her repeatedly, until a teacher intervened. Susan was convinced the attack was racially motivated, and that the girls at the mostly black and Hispanic high school were jealous that some boys had taken a liking to her. She was trim and attractive in a natural sort of way, with porcelain skin, hazel eyes, and long curly hair the colour of dark chocolate.

Staying home with her books and visiting the imaginary world of David Copperfield was infinitely preferable to the anxiety of traveling to school and the realisation that she was falling behind in class.

It wasn't that Susan didn't want to go to school; she loved to learn. She just couldn't muster the courage to leave the house anymore. When she did, she felt physically ill, as if she would faint from heart palpitations and shortness of breath. She wanted the feeling to stop.

For more than a month, Susan intercepted letters from the high school attendance office, enquiring about her excessive absences. When her mother finally learned that she had been skipping school, she didn't ask why. Helen Bolling simply followed the recommendation of the school guidance counsellor to have her daughter evaluated by Frank 'Felix' Polk, a licenced clinical psychologist who specialised in the treatment of adolescents and families.

Susan's stomach was aflutter as she trailed her mother up the steps of Dr. Polk's clapboard house. His office was to the left of a small waiting area; the double doors were ajar, but there was no one inside and no receptionist to greet them. After waiting for some time, Susan and her mother returned to the car. The psychologist was apologetic when Mrs. Bolling phoned to question his absence, and another appointment was scheduled.

On the second visit, Susan was just as uncomfortable, but as it turned out, she was off the hook again. Polk, who went by the name 'Felix', seemed more amused than sorry that he'd double-booked for their new time slot and asked Mrs. Bolling to reschedule once more. Susan didn't really have much choice; because of her truancy, the school required that she be evaluated by this doctor.

Her mother didn't even park the car on their third visit to the Berkeley office. She double-parked on Ashby Avenue until she was sure the therapist was available. A million thoughts ran through Susan's mind as she climbed the steps of the yellow house for a third time. What if the psychologist is really handsome, she worried. She would not be able to speak to him. She would be too shy to open up.

Dr. Polk requested to speak privately with Mrs. Bolling before meeting with the teen. Susan waited anxiously in the small reception area as her mother disappeared behind the office's heavy double doors. It was a long fifteen minutes before her mother summoned her to join the conversation.

The sparsely furnished room was dim with only one window located high on the wall, almost to the ceiling. There was a small kitchenette in the rear of the space. Standing awkwardly near one of the dark leather chairs, Susan remained silent as the psychologist and her mother continued their discussion. She felt relieved at the sight of the fortyish and not so handsome doctor. He was not particularly tall, about 5'9", 160 pounds, and his prominent nose, kinky brown hair, and thick lips were not what she had envisioned.

'No problem,' she mused to herself. She could never be attracted to such a person.

Her mother finally left the room. Feeling awkward and insecure, Susan glanced around, and then focused on the casually dressed professional. She didn't like the way he was looking at her.

At fifteen, Susan realised that boys were eyeing her differently. They seemed interested in a way she had not experienced. Yet a flirtatious look from one of her male teenage friends was one thing, while a similar look from her new psychologist was quite another. He looked more than twice her age.

Susan stared blankly at the tanned, older man when he asked if she had anything she wanted to discuss. 'I don't feel like talking.'

'That's okay,' the psychologist soothed. 'I'll talk for you.'

Felix Polk spoke in a slow, deliberate tone. His gravelly voice had a faint accent, almost like a lisp, that was more pronounced when he said certain words.

Susan sat, watching his movements and listening to him speak. There was something about this man that caught her interest. He seemed to know how to pay attention to a young person. Slowly, she began to feel at ease in his presence.

'What do you like to do at home?' he asked.

'I like to read,' Susan told him.

Her response seemed to intrigue the psychologist. Dr. Polk appeared genuinely impressed that Susan was currently reading Dostoevsky, Chekhov, and Tolstoy, and his interest appeared sincere. She felt flattered when this successful, professional man who was much older, and certainly wiser than she, gave her compliments. Suddenly, Susan felt important and smart. Dr. Polk was twenty-five years her senior, yet she felt the two had made a connection.

Their subsequent sessions were better. Talking about books was easy for Susan. Reading had always been a passion, a way to escape the drudgery of life, and the pain of her absent father, her working mother, and her frustrated, rageful older brother.

Just like her truancy, Susan kept her sessions with Dr. Polk a secret. The therapist had instructed her not to disclose their discussions, and she agreed. She liked the idea of knowing things that nobody else knew – not even her mother.

Already, Dr. Polk had told Susan that she was a lot like him. She was shy, withdrawn, and self-conscious. She wasn't crazy, just quiet.

It was her mother who was 'crazy' and a 'bitch', he announced.

Polk's assessment had huge appeal to Susan. She had been protective of her mother and had defended her vehemently to her father. Her parents had divorced when she was five years old. But at fifteen, she began blaming her mother, Helen, for the way her life was going.

Susan was angry that they didn't have more money and that she didn't have better clothes. Their tiny apartment was furnished with items her mother purchased at Good Will, while her closet was full of old clothes and other items from a secondhand boutique. Susan wanted to live in a nicer house and go to a better school with people who were smarter, people who were more like her. Faulting her mother for her unhappiness, as Dr. Polk suggested, was a good tactic, and Susan latched on to the idea. Her new therapist would often speak aloud what she was thinking, as if he could read her mind.

Susan's resentment of her mother ran deeper than that of a typical teenager toward a parent. Her feelings were heightened by her mother's lack of understanding and her constant excuses for her brother's erratic behaviour. Helen Avanzato Bolling was a no-nonsense type. The fiery, tiny-boned woman stood barely five feet tall. On her own since she was fourteen, she was extremely street savvy. She had supported herself for several years before marrying Theodore Dickson Bolling Jr., an undergraduate student at San Francisco State University in downtown San Francisco.

In February of 1956, not long after the couple married, Helen gave birth to a son, David. The following year, on 25 November 1957, Susan was born. At first, life was agreeable, and Helen stayed at home to raise the two children. But everything changed shortly after Susan's father announced a desire to attend law school. When they married, Susan's mother made herself a promise not to interfere with her husband's aspirations. Faced with this decision, Helen didn't stand in his way.

The choice was a costly one. Theodore Bolling was hardly ever home. His day job, followed by his studies at Southwestern University in downtown Los Angeles, ate up all of his time. His absence was difficult for Susan, who adored her father and his rare but sweet attention.

To soothe her children, Helen Bolling made promises. 'Someday daddy will be out of school, and things will be different,' she assured them. 'Then you'll have a real daddy.'

But that time never came. As Helen soon learned, her husband had begun an affair that progressed rapidly. Upon completing his studies, Theodore Bolling asked for a divorce. On 28 August 1962, he was admitted to the State Bar of California, and his final departure came shortly thereafter.

Helen was devastated, but little Susan was inconsolable.

The divorce destroyed Susan and, according to her mother, the child 'was left with an empty hole she could never seem to fill.' After the split, Helen quickly rented out the small house she'd won in the divorce settlement, relocating her children to a cheaper apartment in East Oakland. It was the first of several moves, each of which forced Susan and David to disconnect from their peers and start over.

Instead, Susan turned to books. 'They are my friends,' she told her mother. When Susan did finally fall in with a group of girls in junior high school, Helen Bolling let it be known that she did not approve of one of the teens. Her criticism sparked additional friction between mother and daughter.

Like Susan, David had also been labelled as 'gifted', Yet he, too, had stopped attending school. When he wasn't locked away in his room reading science magazines or building homemade rockets in the basement, he was taunting Susan, threatening her and pushing her around.

David fell in with a bad crowd while the family was living in Concord. Susan's mother tried to intervene and, at one point, even sublet their apartment and moved her children to a better area in downtown Oakland to get him away from the rough neighbourhood. To Susan it appeared that her mother was pacifying her brother despite his bad behaviour, while punishing her for trying to escape his persecution. With her mother at work much of the day, Susan was an unprotected target for David's rage.

Susan tried to tell her mother what was going on, but her cries for help seemed to go unnoticed; after all, it was the Dr. Spock era when hands-off parenting was encouraged. Nevertheless this method was backfiring. What Susan really needed was strong parental supervision and intervention, but Helen Bolling was not capable of such discipline. With Susan's dad now raising his new family in Sacramento, the kids had no other role model, and his presence in their lives was inconsistent and fleeting.

As the torment with her brother escalated, Susan could no longer bear the burden that home life placed on her. With nowhere else to turn, she ran away from home. Her mother was furious and reported Susan as a 'runaway'. She allowed authorities to place the twelve-year-old in juvenile hall to teach her a lesson. More than two years later, Susan still hadn't forgiven her mother.

On her fourth therapy session with Dr. Polk, the therapist asked Susan if she'd be willing to try something new and radical.

'Would you consent to be hypnotised?' he asked. 'I think you have various memories of trauma in your past. Do you want to dig those up?'

Cool, Susan thought. The idea of being hypnotised sounded intriguing.

Even if she wanted to say no, she didn't feel she could. Dr. Polk was a psychologist. He knew what was best for her, and besides she had read that it wasn't really possible to put someone under hypnosis. Regardless, she would do whatever he asked.

Susan watched eagerly as Dr. Polk strode to the small kitchen in the rear of the office and poured something into a teacup.

'This will relax you,' he said in a nurturing voice, handing Susan the steaming liquid.

The scent was hauntingly familiar. Yet as she drew her first sip, she didn't recognise the taste. Feeling very mature, Susan relaxed into the big leather chair. Sipping from the cup, she felt a warm sensation and began to feel sleepy.

Dr. Polk's gravelly voice sounded like a dull hum. He instructed her to count backward from ten.

She methodically followed along. 'Ten . . . nine . . . eight . . . seven . . . six . . .'

'Susan!' the psychologist's raspy voice startled her awake. It felt as if only seconds had passed since she'd sipped from her teacup. Yet the office clock had advanced forty-five minutes. Glancing over at the coffee table, Susan observed that her teacup was empty, and her mouth had a funny taste.

Uneasiness swept over her as she struggled to recall what had taken place. The last thing she remembered was counting backward. Now it was time to leave.

'What happened? What did we talk about?' she asked, feeling a sudden pang of mistrust. 'How come I can't remember anything?'

Dr. Polk appeared nervous and avoided her gaze. Rising from his chair, he escorted her to the door.

He would see her again in two days.

Susan still does not know what occurred during the hypnotic session. She later claimed that, from that day forward, she felt afraid whenever Felix Polk was around.

Not long after Susan began her therapy, she was arrested for shoplifting some clothing from a local store. The probation officer assigned to her case took an instant liking to her but also recognised the signs of an adolescent at risk: delicate and frail, the girl appeared in need of mothering.

It was clear that the teen was troubled but punishment was not the answer. What Susan needed was mental health counselling, and her probation officer told the judge as much. This girl was too fragile for the juvenile detention centre, the officer argued, not to mention the fact that there were some pretty tough kids in there. But her opposition did nothing to change his mind, and the judge sentenced Susan to one month in the Martinez lock-down facility, a place filled with delinquents, mostly teenage runaways.

During her time there, Felix Polk went to visit Susan, and his visit upset her. Seeing him reminded her of their hypnosis sessions. It was unsettling that she could not recall many of the details, and she believed there were things going on that were highly irregular.

She had been sent to Dr. Polk for an evaluation. He was supposed to help her anxiety, the panic she was feeling every morning before leaving for school; but now, she was locked away with a bunch of degenerate runaways. All her life, she tried to be a good girl. She primped to look pretty and remembered her manners, yet here she was in a place for delinquent youths.

How had her life become so unmanageable?

The only thing she could do now was run away again. She wanted to be free of Felix, her mother, and everything else in her teenage life. One afternoon, she escaped from the juvenile facility. It wasn't hard; a number of kids had done it. Susan simply hitched a ride with someone in the parking lot. She went to a friend's apartment in Trestle Glenn, a nice Oakland neighbourhood.

It was fun staying with her girlfriend who was engaged to a navy man. The two never made her feel like a third wheel when she joined them on their dates. To the contrary, she felt part of a unit, something she had never experienced. The apartment was peaceful, and Susan felt 'normal' for the first time. She had companionship, someone to share meals with, to talk to. It was the happiest she had been in a long time.

After a month on her own, Susan decided to return home and placed a call to her mother. Helen Bolling was now living in a small house she purchased for twelve thousand dollars in a community south of Concord. With its large homesteads and centuries-old eucalyptus trees dotting the rolling green hillsides, the unincorporated city of Orinda was a definite step up for the family. At the time, Orinda was still a farming town with orchards covering much of the landscape and no main shopping district. The home Helen had purchased was in the 'low-rent' section of town, across the tracks from fancier, more expensive homes nestled in the hills.

Helen was surprised to hear from her daughter. Uncertain how to proceed with Susan's desire to return home, Helen immediately called Dr. Polk to find out if her daughter could come back without being rearrested.

There were indications that Helen was aware Dr. Polk was employing some unusual techniques during the sessions with her teenage daughter. Susan had confided that she'd sat on Dr. Polk's lap during one appointment. The approach sounded a bit unorthodox, but it was the early 1970s in Berkeley, California. Things were pretty fast and loose. For Helen, the doctor's behaviour could well be part of a new trend in adolescent therapy. In the back of her mind, she may have sensed that something was going on between Dr. Polk and her daughter, but for whatever reason she did nothing about it.

Dr. Polk said he would take care of everything.

As promised, Felix Polk wrote a letter to the court explaining why Susan Bolling had run away and received permission for her to come home. In exchange, the court mandated that Susan return to her therapy with Dr. Polk and attend a continuation school to complete her ninth grade studies.

Ironically, the psychologist whom Susan had been sent to see for a simple evaluation had somehow become the person responsible for her freedom.

Felix Polk, it seemed, was going to be a powerful force in Susan's life.

CHAPTER TWO

MORTAL COMBAT

O n the night of 13 October 2002, floodlights broke the darkness and illuminated chunks of the brick walkway that led to the guesthouse of the Polk's rambling Orinda residence. Set high in the hills on a steep slope, the house had several levels – with two bedrooms, including the master suite, on the top floor. Another bedroom and a laundry area were one floor below. The main living area and a home office were situated on the first floor.

It was sometime after 10pm when forty-four-year-old Susan Bolling Polk climbed the flagstone steps to the guesthouse, built adjacent to a free-form swimming pool. Flashlight in hand, she entered the small redwood cottage through the living room door. Inside, her husband of twenty-one years sat reclined in an oversized leather chair. It was a brisk night, yet Felix was clad only in a pair of black briefs, seemingly engrossed in a novel, *The Company*, about the CIA.

At seventy, the doctor was still in decent shape; he was tanned and toned from the long jogs that were part of his regular routine. Tired and worn from his nearly 800-mile roundtrip drive to Los Angeles that day, remarkably he was still awake when Susan came to speak to him that night. Aside from the redwood panelling, the rectangular living room of the pool house looked somewhat like Felix's old Berkeley office on Ashby Avenue, with a couple of leather chairs and a busy tapestry rug of reds and blues. The couple had done little to update the sprawling property since purchasing it for nearly $2 million eighteen months earlier. In an attempt to realise Felix's dream of living in the now-wealthy suburb of Orinda, the family had overextended themselves financially and the monetary pressure was adding to the already stressful home life.

Within minutes of Susan's entry into the cottage, the couple was arguing – a common occurrence ever since Susan announced four years earlier that she wanted to leave the marriage.

'You'd better think of the consequences,' Felix had warned her in an annoyed voice at the time. 'You'll never get the kids! You're not fit!'

Her husband's angry retort hit a nerve with Susan. His words were like an assault. Felix had always been a kind of Svengali to Susan, and she believed everything he told her. She thought that he had the power to commit her if he wanted to, and for Susan, there was nothing scarier than being put in a mental institution. She had already been committed once to the Kaiser mental facility when she was fifteen – and she'd never go back again.

Susan had spent much of her life trying to keep her anxiety and panic under control. She had managed to run a household, raise three boys, and take care of the family's personal finances, yet throughout their marriage, Felix repeatedly threatened to play his trump card – to proclaim that she had a mental illness and have her locked up. It was never clear to Susan that she was sick, but she was unwilling to take the chance that such a diagnosis might be believed.

The Polks' oldest son, Adam, who was currently a sophomore at the University of California in Los Angeles, had been in high school when the fighting began. To him, the solution was obvious – his parents were a mismatch and should separate. As far as he was concerned, the two fed off each other like children who both wanted to be right. Things were not as clear-cut for the couple's middle child. Initially, Eli had inserted himself into the melee in hopes of mediating a settlement, but he soon found himself over his head, and the constant bickering began to take a toll on the teen. While his loyalties to each parent shifted constantly, Eli frequently found himself drawn into his parents' routine altercations. During one fight, he'd intervened to defend his dad from what he perceived as unwarranted behaviour by

Susan. He became so angry that he hauled off and punched Susan in the face, leaving a scar on her lip that remains to this day. On that October night, he was at the Byron Boys' Ranch, a juvenile, minimum security facility about thirty minutes away in the hills of the East Bay, where he was serving time for a parole violation.

The youngest son, Gabe, was ten years old when the craziness began. He was the most vulnerable of the three boys. Almost immediately, he aligned himself with his mother, probably because she was the parent most often at home. His dad worked long hours, and when he was around, he would read or spend time in his bedroom. Gabe agreed with his mother's assessment that his father was a 'monster' and not stable enough to care for Gabe and his brothers. Now Gabe stood 5'9", with almond-shaped brown eyes and close-cropped dark hair. He was muscular, yet significantly leaner than his two older brothers.

When she first broached the topic of divorce four years earlier, Susan told Felix that she would strike a compromise with him: She would remain in the marriage until the boys reached eighteen. This was unacceptable to Felix, who protested that Susan was the centre of the family, and without her, everything would fall apart. Nevertheless his words rang hollow because his behaviour demonstrated that he saw himself at the centre of it all, with everyone walking on eggshells around him. Soon after rejecting the compromise, Felix made his hypocrisy clear when he confided to his youngest son that he didn't want the marriage to end, not only because he loved his wife, but more important, because he didn't want to be alone in his golden years.

In truth, Susan loved him in her own way. He was her saviour, a man who knew everything and whose word was law. For over twenty years, he had controlled her decisions, dictated her behaviour, and micromanaged every aspect of her life. Though his actions were often overbearing, they seemed to be undertaken to help and potentially heal her. It was for this reason that he supported her education and funded her college degree, but despite this encouragement, he did not want her working outside the house once she received a diploma. Susan cared for the children, while cooking, cleaning, and managing the couple's finances. Like his first wife, she even kept the books for Felix's practice. After the couple wed in 1981, she also cared for Felix's daughter, Jennifer, from his first marriage, while Jennifer's mother completed her doctoral studies at Northwestern University.

By the time she was thirty-five, Susan had had enough. She wanted to go out into the world – to break free of his controlling grasp. She was tired of being told what to do and wanted to make her own decisions, to find her own friends. For too long her social world consisted primarily of Felix's patients, relationships that most therapists would have avoided, yet Felix encouraged. In fact, Susan found it odd that Felix had no real friends, only patients and colleagues.

She was increasingly intolerant of his close friendship with a former patient. What had started out as twice-weekly counselling had morphed into an affair-like relationship, with the patient an invited guest to family birthdays and holidays at the Miner Road compound. It was not immediately clear why her husband had taken such a fancy to this woman; she was older than Susan and not particularly pretty. Nevertheless, she put Felix on a pedestal, Susan thought, even going so far as to enroll in courses at a local college to be a psychologist, just like her doctor.

In her new role as therapist, the woman joined Felix in deciding that Susan's mother Helen was 'crazy' and not fit to share in the family's holiday festivities. That Felix's former patient, also a tenant in one of the Polk's Berkeley apartment complexes, was making decisions for the family angered Susan.

Then there were the gifts. Sheila was spending an inordinate amount of money on presents for Felix, with a pair of expensive gold cufflinks that cost upwards of $1,000 among the offerings. Unfortunately, these lavish gifts were not the most disturbing aspect of their relationship. A few years earlier, Susan had supposedly walked in on the two embracing in a way that was 'not a hug' but a kiss that spoke volumes to Susan about the possible nature of their friendship.

But Felix's former patient was not the topic of their pool house argument that October night.

Susan was enraged that Felix had slyly gained control of the Orinda property – and won temporary custody of their fifteen-year-old son, Gabriel – while she was out of state looking for a place to relocate. Also, he had succeeded in getting her monthly alimony payments reduced from $7,000 to $1,700, a sum too low to live on, and certainly not enough to afford the condo she had just put a deposit on in

Bozeman, Montana. Additionally, Felix had filed papers several months earlier that demanded Susan get a job to help support her and Gabriel, although she hadn't worked since 1979 when she did part-time bookkeeping for his burgeoning private practice.

Once inside the pool house that Sunday night, it wasn't long before Susan and Felix were exchanging heated words once again. But this fight would end quite differently from the others.

CHAPTER THREE

THE MORNING AFTER

On Monday 14 October, Susan began her morning routine as if it were just another day. The forty-four-year-old mother possessed the rare ability to disguise troubling thoughts, a point reinforced by Gabriel's later statements that she appeared calm and relaxed when she drove him to school in nearby Walnut Creek that morning. Like his mom, the teen had been ordered to attend a continuation school after he'd stopped attending the ninth grade at the public high school in Orinda.

After dropping him off at Del Oro High School, Susan claimed she went directly home and spent the remainder of the morning chasing down the family's yellow Labrador, Dusty, who was loose in the neighbourhood. In fact, she had the dog in the car with her when she returned to pick up Gabe at school around 12.30 that afternoon. The dog even joined them for lunch at Baja Fresh Mexican Grill in the neighbouring town of Lafayette.

As far as Gabe was concerned, his mother was acting 'perfectly normal' during their meal at the fast-food grill. They stopped at a local drugstore to buy some acne medication for his teenage complexion. It wasn't until they returned home, and Susan promptly announced that she needed to run another errand, that the teen grew suspicious.

It didn't make sense to Gabe. Why didn't she complete her chores while they were out?

The car keys jingled in her hand as Susan ran back out to the silver Volvo and took off down the driveway. She later told police that she went to Blockbuster Video to return an overdue movie and pick up another film, *Scooby Doo*, for Gabe. As Susan left for town, Gabe went to the home gym the family had set up in a small outbuilding adjacent to the pool house. He planned to attend a baseball game with his father that night, a date made the night before during their drive back from Los Angeles. Though it was Columbus Day, Felix was going to see a few patients that morning, but he assured Gabe that he would be home by 3pm, in time to make it to Pac Bell Stadium for the playoff game between the San Francisco Giants and the St. Louis Cardinals.

By late afternoon, Gabe began to worry. Though Susan had returned home just before 3pm, Felix had not returned or even called to say he was running late. In addition, there was something odd about the way his mother was acting. She was doing housework and preparing dinner as usual, but despite the normality of it all, her behaviour just didn't feel right.

Gabe placed a call to his dad's office. There was no answer. By seven-thirty, he had made at least a half-dozen calls to his father's phone numbers with no success. It was time to go downstairs and find his mother.

'Mom, where's Dad?'

'I don't know,' Susan replied coolly.

Gabriel didn't like the way she answered the question. She fluttered her eyelids – something he had seen a million times. This reaction usually accompanied a lie. Gabe repeated the question to see if she would do it again. She did. Now he was certain that something was wrong, but he wasn't sure what to do, so he decided to go back upstairs and wait one more hour. If his dad didn't turn up, he would call the police.

Just before 9pm, Gabriel questioned his mother once again. 'Where's Dad?' he demanded.

'I don't know,' Susan's eyelids flickered.

'Where's my dad?' Gabriel barked at her. 'Where is my dad?'

'I don't know. Have you seen him? Have you talked to him?'

His mother's odd responses were annoying him. She had been

acting strangely for a long while, ever since a family trip to Disneyland five years earlier during which she had an emotional breakdown, Gabriel thought to himself. It had all started at dinner one night, as she cried and told the whole family she suddenly remembered that her father abused her as a child. With everyone seated around the table, she recounted the events in some detail, insisting that her mother and older brother had abused her as well.

That same evening she claimed to recall that her parents had murdered a police officer and buried his body beneath their home. The stuff she was saying sounded crazy, and Gabe had looked to his dad for answers. Felix excused her behaviour, explaining to his sons that their mother may have been molested as a child and was experiencing what he termed 'repressed memories' of the events. These allegations have never been substantiated and have been denied by all parties.

After the Disney trip, Gabriel was told that a doctor examined his mother and had deemed her 'sane'. This seemed to be the case; Susan appeared perfectly normal most of the time. Yet, '20 percent of the time,' to quote Gabe's older brother, Adam, she was just nonsensical, even scary. Gabriel had seen more of that behaviour of late. In fact, just five days earlier she threatened to kill his father if he didn't transfer $20 million into her bank account, a sum he most certainly did not have. She had promised to blow his brains out if he didn't give her the money.

Gabe heard these threats by eavesdropping on a call Susan placed to his father during her drive back from Montana on Monday, 7 October. She threatened to shoot Felix with a shotgun if he didn't move into the pool house and let her live in the main house with Gabriel, a warning that sounded real enough to the teen.

The warning also sounded real enough to Felix. Eventually he became so frightened that he called the police, arranging to have them come to the house for Susan's return, but after hours of waiting, the officers left the property, instructing Felix to call if trouble arose.

It was after 11pm when Susan pulled into the driveway in Eli's Dodge Ram truck. Gabe and his dad were on the couch watching TV when his mother strode into the living room.

After a brief discussion with Felix, Susan slept in the master bedroom, and Felix stayed in the spare bedroom/office on the first floor. Things seemed okay until Wednesday, 9 October, when Felix returned home to find that Susan had enlisted Gabriel to help her move all of Felix's belongings to the redwood guest cottage. The first few minutes after Felix entered the house were riddled with tension, and Gabe had no idea what would happen. He began to relax when his parents sat down and engaged in a reasonably civilized conversation. Susan told his father that she did not want him to stay in the main house, and shortly thereafter their discussion turned to the recent court hearing while she was in Montana in which his father had won custody of him and control over the Orinda house. A Superior Court judge signed the order on 27 September 2002.

Not surprising, things quickly heated up, and at one point, Susan asked that Gabe leave the room. He didn't move; he just stayed on the couch watching a programme on the giant-screen TV his mom had bought when his dad had first moved out in November 2001. It was one of the first big purchases she made on her own without Felix's approval, since he had long opposed the idea of an entertainment centre in the living room. Still, Felix enjoyed it in Susan's absence.

Gabe grew worried as his parents' voices began to rise. He heard his father tell Susan that if she threatened him, he would call the police. Suddenly, his dad began yelling, then grabbed the phone. But he returned the handset to its receiver and tried to speak calmly to Susan. Still, the threats continued. When Susan whispered something in Felix's ear, he jumped up and dialled for help. Gabe was too far away to hear what she said, but it was clear from the look on his father's face that it was serious.

Gabe watched his father enter 9-1-1 on the phone.

'Can I talk to somebody about a domestic dispute, please?' Felix said.

'Okay, what's going on?' the dispatcher on the other end of the line enquired.

'I've been residing at 728 Miner Road with my son. And my wife came and kicked me out of the house, and I am not interested in being kicked out of the house.'

'Okay sir, is your wife there at the house with you?'

'She's right here.'

'Okay, is it physical?'

'No, it's not physical but it's . . .'

The dispatcher jumped in, 'but she's kicked you out the house.'

'Well I'm standing in the house, but she says I have to leave, which I'm not going to do.'

'Was there a reason that she gave why you have to leave?'

Felix responded curtly. There was annoyance in his voice, as if he expected the dispatcher to know the problem and understand the urgency. The mere fact that he was dialing 911 was sufficient. 'She was living away, she decided to come back,' he blurted. 'I have custody of the kids, I have legal custody of the kids and . . .'

'Okay, do you live there?' the dispatcher didn't need the particulars, just the reason why this man felt he needed emergency personnel at his home. 'Are you guys still married or are you separated?'

'We're still married.'

'So you both live there?'

'No, she vacated, and I took over the house, and take care of Gabriel the kid here, and we've been living here.'

'Have either of you been drinking? Using drugs?'

'No.'

'Are there any weapons in the house?'

'I don't know. You'd have to ask my wife. She has a shotgun,' Felix replied matter-of-factly.

The dispatcher's tone took on a new urgency. 'Your wife has a shotgun – as in she's holding a shotgun?'

'No.' Felix replied with no further explanation.

'She's got one in the house?' the dispatcher pressed on for information.

'I don't know where it is. Probably in the car.'

'You don't know if it's locked up or not then?'

'I don't know anything about it. You'll have to ask her. But I feel at risk.'

As patrol units were dispatched to the scene, the operator continued to question Felix about what seemed to be a potentially threatening situation at 728 Miner Road. 'So you said she vacated? Now did she move back in?'

Felix's responses were brief, perhaps because Susan was standing beside him. 'She moved to Montana, and she came back, actually to pick up her things and move back to Montana, and while I was at work, she moved me out of the house.'

When police arrived, they found Felix and Susan seated at the granite breakfast bar in the main house having a quiet conversation. Both parties appeared calm, yet Felix was annoyed that his wife had moved him out of the house. He insisted the officers ask Susan to leave and provided a copy of the signed order giving him sole custody of the Orinda residence. At one point, he told the officers that his wife had a shotgun, a claim that she immediately denied. In response to the officers' questions, she explained she had been in Montana and recently returned to be with her sons, Gabriel and Eli. But after an argument with her husband, she had moved his belongings to the pool house, where she insisted he remain.

To the officers, the situation appeared to be under control. Even the teenage boy who had witnessed his parents' fight assured them that there had been no physical contact or threats made. It was almost midnight when police advised Felix to find another place to sleep that night. He didn't have the *right* paperwork to force his wife to leave, and it would be best for him to stay elsewhere until he and his wife could sort things out with the court.

Shortly thereafter, Gabriel and Felix left for the nearby Lafayette Park Hotel. Gabriel insisted on joining his father, who had been a frequent guest of the hotel, visits which led to rumours – albeit unsubstantiated – that he entertained women friends there while married to Susan.

The following morning, Felix drove Gabriel to school in the family's beat-up blue Volvo sedan. That afternoon he called police from his hotel room, determined to regain control of the house.

'I was living there, and the officer [who'd come to the house the previous night] said that unless I had a court order indicating that I had use of the house, I couldn't continue to live in the house,' he calmly explained to the operator. 'I do have that court order now and I want to talk about implementing that court order.'

It was after 7pm Thursday evening when Felix phoned police for a second time, requesting an officer be present while he and Gabriel went inside the Miner Road residence to fetch some of their belongings. Questions over Felix's paperwork remained and it appeared he and his son would be spending a second night in Room 304 of the posh, hillside hotel, a standard room with two queen-size beds, French furnishings, and ample books on the shelves.

When officers met Felix at the base of the driveway after 7.30pm, they informed him that he would need to be prepared to make a 'citizen's arrest' if his wife refused to leave the premises. Felix was visibly hesitant and asked if they would be able to speak to his wife first, but, in the end, it didn't matter. As it turned out, Susan was not at home when Felix went to the front door with the police. Instead, he found a note posted there. It read:

> Dear Felix,
> You do not have a signed court order. By law, I have 10 days to respond from date of receipt of proposed order. I received it today. Adam and I are at the movies.
> Susan
> PS You are welcome to stay in cottage tonight.

The police watched as Felix tried to enter the residence only to find that Susan had changed the locks, leading them to advise Felix to follow up with his attorney in the morning. In the meantime, Felix returned to the Lafayette Park where he spent the remainder of the night.

While he should have remained at the hotel until things with Susan were resolved, he opted for the cottage. Despite his fears and the repeated advice of his attorney, Felix moved back into the pool house that Friday morning. Meanwhile Adam and Gabriel stayed in the main house with their mother. Though it was a risk that could lead to confrontation, Felix felt it was necessary so that he could spend time with Adam who was home from UCLA for the weekend.

It was yet another decision he would regret. In fact, in a letter dated 23 September 2002, his attorney, Steve Landes, had expressed frustration with Felix's inability to protect himself. For more than a year, he fought to get Felix to proceed with the divorce. 'Getting actual financial information out of you is like pulling teeth,' Landes wrote in the letter. 'I don't know why you call me and tell me you need to be protected and yet you ignore the most basic stuff I need to give you this protection.

'You give me the impression that you feel I'm harassing you when I ask for this stuff, but I can't really proceed without it. How well we do in this case depends on both our efforts. I won't even raise the issue of how often you have ignored my advice.'

On the evening of Saturday 12 October, Felix took his sons to a horror film, *The Ring*, and afterwards, he spent a second night in the Miner Road guesthouse. At the crack of dawn the next morning, Felix drove Adam back to UCLA and Gabe went along for the ride.

Felix and Gabe stayed to watch the Sunday afternoon Oakland Raiders football game on TV before beginning the four-hundred-mile drive back to Orinda sometime after 3pm. During the trip, Gabriel sensed his dad was worried about his mother's repeated threats, but these concerns were not strong enough to entice Felix to find alternate accommodations. Distracting each other with idle talk about sports, they decided to attend the Giants' playoff game the following night.

It was almost 8pm on Monday, 14 October, and still, there had been no word from his dad. As Gabriel climbed the steps to the guesthouse, the darkness enveloped him. There were three entrances to the cottage, but he was hesitant to go in, scared of what he might find. The door he tried – the one everyone used – was locked, and he didn't check the other doors. Besides, there were too many light switches and he could never figure out which switch worked which light. He returned to the main house and went back upstairs to his room where he stayed for about an hour, trying to figure out what to do; he was beginning to think that he would need the police if his dad didn't turn up in the next hour.

It was exactly 9pm when Gabriel dialed 911 to get the number of the Orinda police department's nonemergency line. Even though his gut told him something was wrong, he didn't want to make a fool of himself by calling authorities if there was nothing to report. He would try to locate the officer who had come to the house several days earlier to see if he'd heard anything. Perhaps his dad had been in a car crash, he thought.

'Nine-one-one,' said the female dispatcher who answered the call.

'Hi, can I get the nonemergency number for the police department?'

'What is it that you're reporting?'

'Um, I just need to talk to an officer there,' Gabe said.

'Okay, about what, sir,' the dispatcher asked.

'Do I need to tell you?'

'Yes, you do. You called me on 911. We don't give out numbers on 911. It's for emergencies only, and I can maybe help you on this line depending on what you need to report.'

'Fine, I'll just call the police department,' Gabe said.

'Okay, thank you.'

Grabbing a flashlight, the teen went back downstairs with the phone number for the Orinda police department tucked in his dark-coloured shorts. On his way out the door, his mother stopped him.

'Why did you call the police?' she asked.

'I didn't call the police!' Gabriel snapped, and continued outside to the upper carport where his mom kept her car. The house had two driveways; Susan preferred the one at the top of the property that was reached by a neighbouring street, while Eli and Felix used the lower one that was accessible from Miner Road. Gabe wanted to check Susan's Volvo wagon for any traces of his father. A grisly thought had crossed his mind: maybe his mother had used the car to transport his dad's dead body somewhere. But upon inspection, the car yielded nothing out of the ordinary.

'What are you doing?' his mother yelled out to him.

'Nothing,' he called back. Gabriel was barefoot and shirtless as he walked down the steps to the cottage in an attempt to hide from his mother. With the main door locked, he went to another door that faced the house, entering through the galley kitchen and proceeding down the narrow darkened hallway to the balcony area that overlooked the living room. Shining his flashlight into the blackened space, he saw his father lying on the ground with blood covering his near naked body.

The sight was too much for the fifteen-year-old boy, who quickly left the cottage and shut the door behind him.

Gabriel's heart raced as he returned to the main house. Without saying a word to his mother, he rushed to the bedroom, grabbed the cordless phone and ran back outside, sprinting up the path that led to a hidden area of the property where the family kept the trashcans. He could hear his mother calling as he ducked behind the wooden carport that housed her Volvo. He dialed 911.

Barely seven minutes had passed since he first called that number. He recognised the female dispatcher's voice when she answered.

'Uh, murder,' he blurted out.

There was a moment's hesitation, as if the dispatcher was processing the declaration. 'Where at?'

'At 728 Miner Road.'

'Okay, what happened?' she asked, switching on the police radio to alert units in the field. Orinda is one of five unincorporated cities in the county that contracts patrol services from the Contra Costa Sheriff's Department.

'Um, I think my mom . . . my mom shot my dad.'

'You think your mom shot your dad?' the dispatcher repeated.

'Yeah.'

'Okay, stay on the phone, I'm going to connect you to the fire department. Do not hang up,' the officer instructed.

There were several beeps, and then ringing, as the call was transferred to the fire department's emergency line.

'It's a possible shooting,' the sheriff's dispatcher said, briefing her counterpart at the Contra Costa Fire Department.

'Okay, what's your name, sir?' the fire dispatcher asked Gabe.

The teen spelled it twice.

'Where's your mom at now?'

'She's still in the house,' the teen responded breathlessly.

'Does she still have the gun?'

'I believe so.'

'Where is your dad at?'

'He's dead,' Gabe shot back.

'Where is he at, do you know?'

'He's in my cottage.'

'In your cottage?'

'Yeah.'

'Does your mom still have the gun?'

'I believe so.'

'Do you know when this happened?'

'No, no idea.'

'Do you know where your mom is in the house?'

'No, I don't.'

'How do you know she's still in the house?'

'Because I was just in the fuckin' house,' the teen's voice was beginning to waver, as though he was fighting back tears.

'Okay, where are you now?'

'I'm outside,' Gabe's voice grew softer.

'Okay, what's your mom's name?'

'Susan. She's got a mental illness.'

'What's her last name?'

'Polk.'

'How old is your mom?'

There was no response.

'Gabe. Gabe? Are you still there?' The dispatcher asked.

The line went dead.

Gabriel's attention had shifted to the sound of a door opening. He could tell it wasn't coming from the main house. Peering around the carport, he was certain that it was his mother opening then closing the door to the guesthouse.

'Hey, did you see that?' she yelled up to him.

Gabe didn't respond. He wanted to get as far away as possible. Bolting down the hill and onto Miner Road, he flagged down an arriving fire truck. Panting furiously, he remained with the firemen until police units arrived just after 10.15pm.

CHAPTER FOUR
'SHE'S CRAZY'

It was after 1am on the morning of Tuesday, 15 October 2002, when Contra Costa Sheriff's officers Jeff Moule and Jeffrey Hebel finally sat down with Gabriel Polk in a small interview room at the Field Operation's Bureau in Martinez. They had left the teen alone in the tiny space for nearly thirty minutes, watching and recording his movements on the hidden video camera in the ceiling. Gabriel still had no shirt on.

The officers who would be interviewing him were members of the county's Criminal Investigative Division (CID). They were responsible for follow-up investigation of all reported felony offences in the 521 square miles of the unincorporated areas in the county. Before placing the visibly shaken teenager in a patrol car, they performed a gunshot residue test on him to determine whether he had recently discharged a firearm. The test was negative, and now they needed some answers from the distraught teen.

Gabe told the officers that his mother was 'crazy and delusional', and that she had tried to buy a shotgun after threatening Felix during the Montana trip. Although Gabriel was pointing the finger at his mother, the officers were reserving judgment. It was standard protocol to look at everyone in a homicide investigation, and the teenager was no exception. He was not under arrest, but he remained under scrutiny.

Officer Moule took the lead role in questioning the boy. He started with some background information.

'Right now, you are going to, what's the name of the school you are going to?' The teen was sitting hunched in a chair with his elbows resting on a small round table; his head cradled in his hands. Without making eye contact, he explained that he was currently attending the Del Oro continuation school in Walnut Creek.

'Did you go to Del Oro the whole time you lived in Orinda?'

'No, I went to Miramonte,' the teen replied, referring to the city's public high school.

'How come you dropped out?'

'My mom encouraged me to stay home from school,' Gabe replied in a mumble.

'Why did she want you to stay home from school?'

'She is crazy, and so she thought that all the teachers were like, against me, or something. And so I missed a month and a half at the end of the year.'

Taken aback, Officer Moule repeated the boy's explanation. 'She kept you home?'

'Yeah.'

'All right,' the officer said, shooting his partner a look. 'Have you been in trouble with the law?'

'No,' Gabriel replied. Officers would later learn that the teen was not being completely truthful. While he had never been arrested, Gabriel, like his two older brothers, had been in his share of trouble over the years.

'Okay, you say your mom is crazy,' Officer Moule prefaced. 'Tell me about your growing up, things that she has done that justify you saying that she is crazy.'

'My mom was fine up until about five years ago, when – I don't really – I am not clear on what happened, but she had memories of her childhood. And her parents were real scumbags.'

Gabriel repeated Susan's allegations about being abused as a child. 'Apparently, at that time, and she was put on medication for a few months. And after that, I don't know the name of that medication. But it was for, to stop her from being so delusional and paranoid,' the teen explained, while staring blankly at the table.

'I think her and my dad went to a bunch of psychologists and she eventually stopped taking the medication. And then, in a few years, she, like, directed all of her delusions, and paranoia toward my dad.

'And what my dad said is that she got him confused . . . with her father. So she had all this anger towards my dad, which was actually the anger towards her father, which was probably pretty scary for my dad. And so these last four years have been really, just, arguing, just at each other's throats.'

'Five years ago, when she had these memories about her father, did she tell you herself?' Officer Moule asked.

'Yes.'

'She told you about that?'

'Mm-hmm.'

'You were about ten years old?'

Gabriel paused, and stared at the ceiling as if recalling the exchange. 'No, I was older.'

'You were a little bit older?'

'And when was the last time she told you about it?'

'She told me about it up until today.'

The officer wore an astonished look. 'She's been telling you about it?'

'She told me about it up until today . . . not today, but like the present day, she talks about it often.'

Officer Moule again glanced at his partner, 'So for the last five years she's been acting out? Would you tell me what kind of stuff she does do?'

'Ah, it's crazy shit,' Gabriel replied, readjusting his slender frame in the simple wood chair. 'Do you want to know stuff she says about her father?'

'Sure, what does she say about her father?' Officer Moule prodded.

'Well my dad is like . . . I don't know . . . I don't really know a lot of stuff,' Gabriel replied, before hesitating. 'I don't know too much about her family and everything.'

'What does your dad do for a living?'

'He is a psychologist.'

'Has he ever hit you, or anything like that?'

'No,' the teen answered.

'Did you ever see your dad hit your mom?'

Gabriel paused. 'Um-um. I have seen my dad, like, slap my mom. It's like, she's totally out of her mind, and I could see a reason for it. She can act perfectly normal, too. And she does for the most part. But she just has a distorted reality.'

'You use some pretty good-sized words for a fifteen-year-old man.'

'Mm-hmm.'

'All relative to psychological stuff.'

'Mm-hmm.'

'Is that because you're . . . why is that, you have a good vocabulary, but it's just kind of unusual,' Officer Moule solicited. 'Are those terms that you discussed with your father about your mom's condition?'

'I have discussed it with my father, I have discussed it with my brothers, and I have discussed it with a psychologist.'

'You go to a psychologist to help you out dealing with your mom? Or do you have . . .'

Gabriel jumped in. 'I did for a while, for like a few weeks. I didn't like the psychologist, though. So I quit.'

'So, you've had this, this has been going for about, everything was okay for the most part until five years ago?'

'My mom and dad loved each other.'

As the conversation continued, Moule prompted the teen to discuss his parents disintegrating relationship, leading Gabriel to recount the story of the family's tumultuous trip to Disneyland and the memories that his mother uncovered during the vacation.

Officer Moule sat back in his chair. 'Has your mom ever been hospitalised?'

'No. Well . . . she tried to kill herself in Yosemite,' Gabriel replied dryly, recalling his mother's trip to the national park in central California.

The officer leaned in closer to the teen. 'Well how long ago did that happen? Two years, three years?'

'Actually, no, it was after our other house, so it was one and a half to two years ago.' Gabriel was speaking about the family's move from Piedmont to their current, more expansive Orinda address.

'Were you there when she tried?'

'I was at home when she called.'

'So, who was with her in Yosemite?'

'She went by herself.'

'She just drove there? By herself?' Officer Moule asked.

'She didn't drive there by herself. She just took a bus and tried to kill herself,' Gabriel casually replied, as if attempting suicide in the national park at the base of the Sierra Nevada Mountains was an ordinary occurrence.

'Well, how did she try to kill herself?'

'Overdosed on pills.'

'And then she called home and told you guys what she did?'

'She called home and wanted to talk to my dad, and this is, like, supposedly, what she told my dad. And she says that she loves him and that she's really sorry that she tried to kill herself, and that she's, like, dying, or whatever.'

Officer Moule stared at the teen. A veteran at concealing his reactions, he remained stone-faced. 'So, then what happened?'

'My dad called the police,' Gabriel casually explained. 'And they picked her up, and she was put in a . . . she was at the hospital, and they were interviewing her for a . . . just a mental examination. And they felt like she was perfectly sensible. Like I said, she can act perfectly sane most of the time.'

'Have the police ever been out to your house?'

'Hmm-mm. Many times,' the teen replied without hesitation.

'Well, when was the first time?'

'I don't remember.'

'Was it in the house at Piedmont?' Officer Moule asked.

'Yeah, for stuff like . . . mostly for my brothers to try and break up parties and shit.'

'Did Piedmont PD ever go to your house because your parents were arguing or your mother was acting strangely?'

Gabriel shook his head, indicating no.

'How about Orinda PD?'

'Orinda PD, definitely,' Gabriel nodded.

'How many times?'

'Three to five.'

'What happened the first time, if you know.'

'Oh, there were just so many complications, I can't really remember.'

'Just pick one out,' Officer Moule nudged. 'When was the last time they came out?'

'The last time they came out was last week.' Gabriel was referring to the call his father had made to 911 on 9 October, when Susan moved him from the main house to the guest cottage.

'Last week?'

Gabriel went on to tell Moule the story of the previous Wednesday when he had helped his mother move his father's belongings to the guesthouse, and the ensuing argument that led Felix to call 911. As he told the tale, his feelings toward his mother became more and more apparent, with Gabriel describing his mother as 'nuts' and referring to his own life as 'pretty unstable'.

As the interview progressed, Gabriel displayed signs of stress. He had difficulty sitting still in his chair and avoided direct eye contact with the officers. At times, he seemed close to tears, and other moments he appeared detached and spoke in a monotone.

'Did she talk about killing him while she was in Montana?' Officer Moule inquired.

Cupping his forehead with his hands, Gabe paused for a moment as if to think. 'I'm not sure,' he uttered. 'She said she was taking care of business. It sounded like it was about dad. She wanted to handle dad, I don't know how . . . To get money and stuff.'

Gabriel went on to say that his mother had actually spoken of killing his father.

'Did she say how she would kill him?' the detective asked.

The teen sat back in his chair. 'Drugging him, and drowning him in the pool,' he replied. 'Maybe run him over, or tampering with his car.'

'Why was she telling you all this?'

'I don't know. She thought that, like, I agreed with her or whatever, when I was going along with what she was saying, or that, I don't really know why she told me. She just trusted me, trusted me.'

'Did you kind of agree with her?' Officer Moule asked.

'No.'

'Did you and your dad get along all right?'

Gabriel paused. 'Fairly well.'

Gabriel claimed his mother had been talking about murdering his father on and off for weeks, most recently when he was eavesdropping on the 7 October phone conversation between them during his mother's return trip from Montana. 'When she was coming back from Montana, she actually called my dad and told him what she was going to do. She threatened to shoot him with a shotgun.'

'So how did she phrase, what did she say?'

'She just said that, oh yeah, that if he didn't let her stay in the house with me – she wanted him to be out in the cottage, and if he didn't let that happen, let her in the house, she would kill him.'

The teen's eyes grew wet as he recounted his father's fear. Gabriel said his father had been so frightened by the conversation with Susan that he arranged to have police waiting at Miner Road in anticipation of her return, but after several hours, it grew too late in the evening and the officers left the property. When his mother finally arrived, 'She walked right in the house. They had a nice talk. Not a nice talk, but they were calm. I was there for the whole thing,' he said.

'What were they talking about?'

'Money. And that she thought it was not fair that they had a court hearing without her.'

'And what did your dad say to that?'

'I don't know, but it was calm. Then my dad was just trying to deal with her.'

Two days later, however, it was a different story. It was then, after Susan had Gabriel move all of Felix's belongings to the guesthouse, that she threatened to kill him.

'What did she say? How did she phrase that?'

'She whispered something in his ear. I didn't hear it, but . . . my dad got excited and called the police.'

'How do you know that she threatened to kill him?'

'Because my dad isn't alive.'

CHAPTER FIVE

SUSAN'S DENIAL

As fifteen-year-old Gabriel Polk talked with the officers, his mother was in an adjacent interrogation room, giving a completely different account of the past forty-eight hours to sheriff's investigators.

Contra Costa Sheriff's officer Kenneth Hansen had taken Susan into custody as soon as she answered the front door that night. He had been alerted over the police radio that she had long suffered from mental illness and could be in possession of a weapon. Not about to take any chances, he watched her cross the living room through the home's expansive windows as he ascended the stone steps to the front of the house with his gun at the ready.

By the time Officer Hansen reached the landing, Susan was already standing in the doorway. Pulling a pair of handcuffs from his belt, he immediately closed them around her thin wrists and sat her down on a small wood bench just outside the front door. Directing his partner, Shannon Kelly, to keep a watch on the suspect while he inspected the property, Hansen left to locate and secure the pool house, where the victim was supposed to be. Flashlight in hand, he climbed the brick steps to the pool and adjacent cottage. After only a few minutes, he returned and apologetically advised Susan that her husband was dead, apparently from 'unnatural causes'. He didn't elaborate or reveal that he had just observed Felix Polk covered in blood on the floor of the pool house. Most of the blood appeared to be dry, an indication that he'd been dead for some time.

He noticed that Susan did not react to his pronouncement. She sat on the bench and said nothing. At one point, he removed her handcuffs and asked that she sign a consent form to search all four buildings on the property, which she did without hesitation.

It was after 11pm when Officer Kelly escorted Susan Polk to the Field Operations Bureau in Martinez.

'Where is my son?' Susan asked repeatedly during the twenty-minute ride to Martinez. 'Is he okay?'

Officer Kelly did not know the answer.

'Are you sure it's my husband?' Susan prodded. 'Did my son identify the body? Because his car isn't here,' referring to Felix's 1999 Saab.

Officers securing the Miner Road house had located four cars during their initial search of the property, but the Saab was not among them.

'Are you comfortable?' Officer Kelly inquired, thinking about the patrol car's temperature, not the handcuffs around Susan's wrists.

'I'm not too comfortable being in the back of a police car,' Susan responded. 'My husband was killed, and I didn't do anything.'

'Excuse me, do you have a blanket, or a jacket or something?' Susan asked Detective Mike Costa as he entered the sterile interrogation room some time after midnight on 15 October. Dressed in shorts and a polo shirt, Susan felt chilled in the small, air-conditioned room, and Costa offered her an official police jacket.

The stocky, moustached detective had introduced himself to Susan earlier in the night at the crime scene, where he had been assigned lead investigator status. He had been on the force for twenty-six years and had responded to more than a hundred homicides since joining the Criminal Investigations Division. Now, having been briefed about Susan's arrest and her statements to police while in route to the field operations office, he was prepared to question her.

'Okay. Like I said at the house, Susan, my name is Mike,' the investigator began, taking a seat at the room's small round table. 'I'm a detective with the Sheriff's Office, okay? We are going to be looking at what happened to your husband tonight. I assume it's your husband in the . . .what you guys call the pool house out there.'

'The guesthouse,' Susan corrected, wrapping the jacket with the official police emblem around her shoulders. 'I didn't hear any shots. I don't own a firearm right now.'

'Okay, because you're in custody here, and you're not under arrest. I want you to understand that. But you're not free to leave, okay. The law says I have to admonish you of your rights, okay.'

'Uh, huh.'

'Do you want to talk to me about what happened?'

'I do, and I am very, very tired,' Susan told the detective, unaware that she was being secretly recorded by a camera hidden in the ceiling.

'So am I. I haven't been to bed all day either, but we have to do this.'

Susan looked directly at the officer. 'What did happen?'

'Well, that's what I'm hoping you can tell me.'

'I did not hear any gunshots, and I do not own a firearm.'

'Okay, you've been occupying the main house.'

'I didn't see him all day today, so I don't know.'

'Okay, what time did you wake up today?' the detective inquired.

'I woke up at around seven.'

'7am, this morning?'

'Uh, huh. I took my son to school.'

'Which son?'

'Gabe.' Susan said, as she began retracing her steps during the day. She busied herself with housework and cooking after picking Gabe up from school on Monday afternoon. Around 8.30 that night, she took a bath.

'And during this time, didn't you wonder where Felix was?'

'Yeah, I did wonder,' she replied dryly. 'In fact, Gabe and I talked about it in the morning. Gabe thought they were going to a game together.'

Susan repeated that she hadn't seen her husband at all that day. 'And I didn't see his car this morning.'

'Does he park it in the garage?'

'He parks it in the lower driveway.'

Detective Costa jotted something on a notepad. 'How long have you guys been married?'

'It would be twenty-one years in December.'

'How long has the marriage not been going well?'

'Well, there have been times off and on throughout the marriage when I've brought up getting a divorce. And particularly five years ago, I said that I couldn't see living with him any longer.'

'That was five years ago.' The detective pointed out that the couple was still together and had moved to a new house in Orinda just eighteen months earlier.

'Well, he said, you know, that he would never let me go and that kind of thing . . . And he was really, it was just very difficult. I don't have a job, and you know he is my source of income.

'And we do have some apartments, and we get income from those, too. But I just, you know, couldn't, and I was very attached to him, too . . . So, I mean it was like, you know, yeah, I wanted a divorce but then he would say things, and then it would be hard to go through with it.'

'So the past five years, it's been particularly bad? Is that what you are saying?'

'Five years ago, it was very, very clear that I wanted a divorce. . . . And I backed off of it . . . pretty quickly.'

'Where is this marriage, as far as from a legal standpoint right now? The officers out there told me that you both have attorneys.'

'I fired my attorney, I don't have an attorney right now.'

'How long ago?'

'Just a few days ago . . . I had the house, I was given exclusive use of the house and custody of Gabriel . . . but then there were proceedings in juvenile court,' Susan explained. She claimed that initially she had been granted custody of Gabe and the Miner Road residence. But she said that difficulties arose that past winter when the judge wanted to grant Felix custody of the couple's middle child, Eli.

Eli had been in trouble with the law. He was arrested in February 2002 for possession of marijuana and for assaulting a fellow student with a weapon. Further complicating matters, Susan had encouraged her son to remove the ankle monitor he wore as part of his sentence, leave his father's home against court orders, and join her and Gabriel in Montana for an extended holiday that summer.

Even though Susan took full responsibility for her son's violation, the judge had sentenced Eli earlier in the month to time at the sixty-acre juvenile camp, Byron Boys' Ranch.

'And it was just really upsetting for me,' Susan continued. 'It was just, you know, I couldn't see living around here anymore. Gabe and I and Eli had lived in Montana for a few months last year in the fall of 2001. And it was just really great. So I decided I would head for Montana and find a place to live.'

Launching into the story of the court order and the reduction of her spousal support payments, Susan made no attempt to hide her dissatisfaction with the court decisions that had been made in her absence, eventually telling her side of the events that had occurred that past Wednesday, which resulted in Felix's call to 911. Informing Costa of how her trip to Montana had impacted her relationship with Gabriel, Susan tried to demonstrate her son's bias, telling Costa that Gabriel had 'turned loyal to his dad' without her around.

While she was trying her best to appear sympathetic to the officer, Susan was doing little for her case. Her tale was winding and disjointed, laden with tangential stories. On one hand she managed to control her anger when she discussed Felix, but on the other, she did not apear convincingly affected by her husband's death. As she answered questions, she opened herself to increasing scrutiny, showing the investigators that she had both the motive and opportunity to kill her husband.

The detective continued to take notes, and at some point tried to steer the interview back to the events preceding the murder. 'So getting back to this morning, you said you woke up at 7am. Never saw Felix the whole day?'

'No. But I mean it was unusual because it's a holiday, and Gabe said he was going to be around. And usually he makes an appearance at the house. But since I've been back in the house, I've said not to just walk into the house. To knock at the door.'

'Didn't you see him yesterday?'

'Oh, yeah, I did. Yesterday was Sunday. He and Adam got up around five to leave for UCLA with Gabe. And he was marching around the house, so I went down and said, 'You know, you're not supposed to be in the house.' '

'So, at some point, Adam came back from UCLA?' the detective asked.

'Yeah, Adam flew back on Friday.'

'This past Friday?'

'Uh, huh.'

'And Sunday you're saying they all left to go back to UCLA?'

'Right. To drive Adam with the dog, 'cause Adam wanted his dog at UCLA.'

'And when did they get back, Gabe and your husband?'

Susan paused. 'I'm not sure, I think Gabe walked in around nine or ten or something.'

'So they went down and back in one day?'

'Yeah, pretty miserable, but yeah.'

'Well okay, let me ask you this? When is the last time you saw your husband?'

'Sunday morning around five or five thirty when I came downstairs and chewed him out for just roaming around the house.'

'And then Gabe and your husband came back that night, Sunday night.'

'Yeah, Gabe walked in around ten probably and said, "Hi, Mom." I was in my bed.'

'Okay. Do you own any firearms?'

'Well, a number of years ago, probably sixteen, seventeen years . . . my husband had a patient who was an ATF agent and he took me out and helped me purchase a revolver . . . I don't remember, I think it's like Smith and Wesson, something revolver.'

'Okay, so you bought a revolver?'

'Yes . . . But I have not had that gun for a long time. He has had it. Since we separated, at least.'

'Where is the gun now?'

'He took it to his office, I don't know.'

'Your husband took it?'

'Yeah.'

'How long ago did he take it?'

'A few years . . . maybe two years. I said I didn't want to have a gun around the house.'

'So what's all this about a shotgun that I heard about?' Detective Costa asked. 'You supposedly said you were gonna get a shotgun.'

'No,' Susan replied, closing the shiny black police jacket tightly around her.

'You never had a shotgun?' the officer asked emphatically.

While Susan's son, Gabriel, was in the adjacent room telling officers that he was certain his mother had a shotgun, and had used it to kill his father, Susan was insisting that it was Gabriel who had enquired about obtaining a gun.

'In fact, my son was talking to me today about how he wanted to have . . . have some gun that he had his heart set on,' Susan claimed. 'And I was like, no, because it's just not a good idea. And he was asking me what the gun laws were, and whether he could . . .

'So I said, "If you want a gun, go into the military and then you can, you know, get into all of that,"' Susan rambled on. "But no, you know, I don't think you should."

'Did he indicate that he already had one?' Detective Costa asked.

'Oh, God, no . . . He's a good boy. He's going to continuation school, not because he's been in, you know, trouble or anything. It's mainly the divorce, divorce issues.'

It was then that Costa returned his attention to Susan's actions after Gabriel found the body, asking Susan to recount the sequence of events once Gabriel made his gruesome discovery. Telling the detective of Gabriel's assertion that she had murdered his father, Susan did not appear the least bit distraught that her son would make such a painful accusation. As she walked him through her activities leading up to the police officers' arrival, Susan finished by telling him about how the officer that handcuffed her was the one to tell her that it appeared her husband had been killed.

'And what did you say to that?'

'I don't remember exactly.'

'Okay, I mean if somebody gets told her husband was killed, I would expect some reaction, some sort of response.'

For nearly an hour, he had listened as the forty-four-year-old housewife rambled on about her life, her financial arrangements, and the details of her crumbling marriage. Her husband was dead, and yet she had not exhibited one iota of grief. How could she remain so stoic, or was she just cold? The detective was incredulous.

Trying to better understand the situation, Costa dug into Felix's personal life, soliciting answers about whether Felix engaged in extra marital affairs or gambling that might generate enemies. While she said that Felix had had affairs in the past, he was not a man to owe money to loan sharks, and both of these questions led nowhere.

Costa began to explore the nature of the family dynamic, questioning Susan about Felix's deceased parents and the whereabouts of Felix's twin brother and his sister who both lived on the East Coast. Probing the relationship with her own parents, Costa found Susan unhelpful as she repeatedly described her father as a 'paedophile' and her mother as 'perverted', while informing Costa that neither had any contact with the family in years.

As the questioning continued, it became apparent to Costa that Susan was the only immediate person with motive and opportunity, and he tried to convince her that the evidence was mounting against her.

'You have the motive, you know, the marital problems going on,' he said. 'I'm sure tempers are not good between you, you know, as in any divorce.'

'He's my sole source of income . . . There is no life insurance. He makes – he grosses about $18,000 a month from his practice – and his teaching. I would not kill my husband. I can't pay the bills.'

Costa wasn't convinced, and the detective pressed the idea that Susan was the only person other than Gabriel who had the opportunity to kill Felix. Stepping back, he tried a different tactic.

'It only takes a split moment to get angry enough to do something like that. It happens all the time.'

'That's why I don't own firearms,' Susan replied coolly.

'Maybe, you know, like I said, maybe there's a self-defence issue here. We're not gonna know about it.'

'I didn't do it,' Susan insisted. 'I did not kill my husband!'

Despite her remonstrations, Costa remained skeptical. It wasn't just her words that didn't ring true, it was her unflinchingly stoic reaction. Only once, when the detective said definitively that the body in the cottage was that of her husband, did she display any emotion.

Detective Costa sighed aloud. 'I got to tell you, the other thing, you're sitting here, you know, we've been together for an hour now or so, and you don't seem really choked up. You don't seem really upset that he's gone. I find that kind of, I mean granted . . .'

Susan interjected. 'I'm very, very, very upset.'

'You do well at not showing it.'

'Well, you know, I can't defend myself against an accusation like that,' she huffed.

'Well,' the detective shrugged, 'It's an observation that I'm making.'

'I'm not in love with my husband anymore,' Susan offered. 'But I'm horrified. Particularly for my son that he found his body . . . but as for tears, you know.'

Detective Costa decided to take the questioning in another direction. 'Was Felix under any professional care himself?'

'Yes,' Susan said.

'Was he seeing anybody?'

'He was seeing Justin Simon,' she said, referring to the psychiatrist who owned the Berkeley complex where Felix leased office space. According to Susan, Simon also prescribed Felix with antianxiety drugs. Though she was uncertain of the precise name, she indicated that it was a 'valium derivative'. Susan was quick to point out the hypocrisy of it all — that Felix pointed the finger at her for being crazy, while never considering his own pharmaceutical dependency.

As the detective looked over his notes, he restated his theory yet again. 'I've got to tell you, you know, something happened between you and Felix today that got out of hand.'

'No way!' Susan insisted.

'Well, that's my feeling.'

'Did not!' Susan sniped back like a child in a tiff with a fellow classmate.

'I guess we just have to disagree, because something happened obviously. And I think it was between you and him. And you're sitting over there, and you're probably just dying to spill out what happened. And you can't, for whatever reason. I don't know, afraid of going to jail or . . .'

Susan jumped in. 'No!'

'You know, we've had quite a few of these in this county recently, where wives have killed their husbands. One got off with manslaughter because of his past.'

'I did not kill my husband. I'm not that kind of person . . . I don't know what kind of a crime it was. You know, I wasn't there. I don't know what happened.'

'Well, they call it murder,' the detective replied before rising to his feet. He informed Susan that he needed to check on the status of the crime scene investigation and exited the room, returning a few minutes later with a second detective in tow. 'This is Detective Jeff Moule, my partner.'

'How are you doing?' the second investigator said, nodding at Susan. Outside the interrogation room, Detective Moule had updated

Costa on the crime scene findings and the information gathered from Susan's youngest son. Moule had been on the force for eight years, and during that time, he had worked ten homicides, four of them as lead investigator.

Susan looked up at the other detective, but before she could reply to his question, Detective Costa jumped in. 'What's this about you believed your husband was with the Mossad, he had like millions stashed in a Cayman Islands account somewhere? Why would your son think that?'

As with many of her previous responses, Susan's explanation was long-winded and contradictory. It appeared she truly believed her husband was an Israeli agent, and she explained how this belief was based on the fact that Felix had insisted she sign a prenuptial agreement when they married in 1972.

'And usually when people sign a prenup it's because there's something to protect, right?' she insisted. 'And over the years, I mean he sort of had a way of talking about things that was kind of like, not straight out, but it was kind of like hinting around and under the surface and, you know, a lot of just, it was double talk. And he sort of would talk about having assets, it seemed like to me, that I would always be provided for and the kids would. But now that we're getting divorced, I've asked him, you know, about that. He's like, "no." '

Susan spoke in circles for nearly twenty minutes, citing various reasons why she believed her husband was a member of the Israeli Intelligence Agency. Another central component to her theory were statements allegedly made by Felix at the time of his ex-wife's wedding that raised suspicions in Susan that Sharon's new husband was a Mossad agent, too. Though Susan repeated them on many occasions, these allegations are unfounded.

'We like to keep it in the family,' Felix had allegedly joked to her.

Susan claimed that her husband's offhanded comments were meant to telegraph certain information that he could not divulge for security reasons. Another clue was that Felix had treated CIA, ATF, and IRS agents in his practice, as well as several judges. She argued that he had to have some sort of high-level security clearance in order to care for such individuals, claiming he had hinted his affiliation with the Mossad enabled him to be 'connected', she said.

'And I went and told someone, and he was like, "Oh, my God",' that

I had a "big mouth". And so I just speculated that his real loyalties, even if he is, or was, a government employee, are really with Israel because of statements that he's made. So yeah, I did think . . .'

Detective Costa pointed out that Felix had no family in Israel. 'Has he ever travelled there?' he asked.

'No, but his cousin who's older goes back and forth quite a bit. And a lot of his, you know, clients do, and close family, friends type of thing.'

At some point, Susan did an about face. She explained that while she once believed her husband's connections to be real, her pronouncements of late had been more a tool to enrage him. Felix, she said, hated it when she accused him of such an association.

Regardless, it was becoming clear that Susan's diatribe was not advancing the investigation.

'This is your time to tell us what happened and why,' Detective Costa directed.

'But I didn't see him today. I've told you what I know.'

'Mrs. Polk, we know otherwise,' Detective Moule jumped in, and with an air of annoyance, he laid out the facts, as he saw them. 'I've been talking to your son, Gabe, for a long time. And I know about the background and some problems that started about five years ago with memories about your father and all that. I know it's personal. I'm not trying to embarrass you, but I know about that, know problems with, you know, keeping the boys out of school and taking the anklet off your son, he had to go to Byron and all that.

'You know, you've had some problems around the house. We know about that. You probably saw all the people standing around, there's a whole bunch of detectives with Detective Costa and I. And there's other detectives, and we all have little jobs. And one of our jobs here is to interview you and interview Gabe. There's other people processing the scene. There's judges that are being contacted. And there's scientists that are arriving at your house right now and they're gonna go through that entire house. They vacuum every little particle.'

'Well, that's good,' Susan agreed.

'Yeah. And there's some evidence found that you're probably aware of, there's evidence that's already been found that is putting you right up there,' Detective Moule offered.

'Susan, your boys know that you did it,' he continued. 'There's not a doubt in their minds. They know. They go, "My mom did this, I know she did it." '

'I love my children,' Susan insisted.

They know you did it. You know what, I think you can do them a favour and let them know why, this is why it happened.'

'I love my children even though you're . . .'

Detective Moule did not permit Susan to complete her thought. 'A lie,' he interjected, his voice rising. 'You might as well be spitting in their faces right now.'

'I didn't do it, no way, that's ridiculous.'

'You think they're gonna think that you didn't do this? They know you did it. Explain why. Tell Detective Costa why and he can document, this is why, this is what's going on, this is the background, these are the problems.

'You're going, "I didn't do that." They're going, "Bull shit, my mom just killed my father." '

Detective Costa cut in. 'Susan, you're obviously a smart woman. You have a nice background and everything. Think this through. You're not gonna get away with this. It's a done deal.

'We know about how you went up and cleaned up. It's all figured out. There's scientists collecting that stuff. You're not gonna beat this. You're done. You're caught up.'

'I didn't kill my husband. And I would think that nowadays, you know, that you would rely on more than guesswork or, you know, what children in the middle of a divorce would say. I mean you do have technological expertise and I'm sure you'll figure it out. But I didn't do it.'

'Well, we've already figured out enough to know that you were involved.'

'I was not involved.'

'Your family is a lot more involved than just an argument here and there.'

'Pardon me?' Susan was indignant.

'There's a lot more going on in your family than just an argument here and there between a couple,' Detective Moule repeated.

'My husband really loved me and the kids, you know, I know that, and he just, you know, I was very fond . . .'

'I'm sure he did,' Moule interjected. 'Did you love him?'

Susan hesitated. 'I was very fond . . .'

The detective looked directly at Susan and demanded, 'Did you love him?'

'I did for many years.'

'But not lately.'

'No, I didn't love him anymore.'

'Did you hate him?' Detective Moule asked.

'No.'

With the progression of the questions, it became clear that the detectives were not going to obtain a confession. Though the evidence was mounting, investigators could not convince Susan to confess to the crime. Costa insisted that she free herself from the 'dream world' in which she was living.

'I've been living in a dream world for many years,' Susan replied.

'Well, it's time to get out of that world, and let's face reality here.'

'No, I didn't kill him,' Susan insisted.

'Yeah, you did.'

'No, I didn't.'

Detective Costa continued to push. 'This is how you want to leave it, just deny, deny, deny, lie, lie, lie, let me live in my little fantasy world and say I wasn't involved, when everything is going to certainly tell us you were. I'm confident of that. I have no doubts about that.'

Susan looked up. 'Well, apparently you seem pretty sure that I did it, so there's nothing that I can really say that's gonna dissuade you, it seems like.'

'The truth is always good.'

'So maybe the scientific evidence will help,' Susan said.

'I'm sure it will,' Detective Costa nodded. 'That's how you want to leave it, huh?'

'I didn't do it . . . I'm very, very tired,' Susan declared. 'If you're gonna put me in jail, put me in jail, so I can go to sleep, okay?'

Detective Costa smirked. 'We're taking care of that.'

CHAPTER SIX

A GRISLY SCENE

It was just before 7.30am on Tuesday, 15 October, when Alex Taflya and Song Wicks of the Contra Costa Sheriff's Office pulled up the steep driveway at 728 Miner Road. Rays of early morning sun streamed through the branches of the soaring oak trees surrounding the home. The residence felt more like an expansive tree house than a million dollar estate with its hilltop location, tangle of lofty trees and thick foliage. Detectives Jeff Moule and Mike Costa were waiting on the large wood deck between the main house and cottage to brief the criminalists.

When he was first summoned to the scene the previous night, Costa performed a preliminary investigation of the main house where he observed damp washcloths in the shower stall of the master bathroom. It made sense, since Susan told him she had showered around 8pm that night. During his search, he also located a steak knife with its tip slightly bent and a small piece of unidentified material stuck to it in the dishwasher. Despite these items from the main house, he was convinced that the crime scene did not extend beyond the redwood cottage where the seventy-year-old victim lay in a pool of his own blood.

On this return trip, Costa and his team focused on the cottage in their search for bloody clothing; expended bullet casings; unfired cartridges; trace evidence on the floors, walls, countertops, and drains; any evidence that might be linked to the homicide. Upon arrival, the investigators agreed with the initial assessment that there was no forced entry into the cottage. The door located on the north side of the pool house was open, and the entire house was dark. In fact, the blinds were drawn throughout the cottage, including those on the sliding glass doors on the west side of the living room near the victim's body and those on the south side of the bedroom in the rear of the house. In the kitchen, the windows were closed but not locked, and the blinds were shut so that only cracks of sunlight were visible.

The kitchen was small, with barely enough room for the small, café-like wood table set beneath the bay window. The cabinetry was worn, with white paint chipping in spots. A delicate set of plates and saucers of blue and white bone china was displayed on one wall. While there was nothing of interest on the linoleum countertops, investigators noticed a partial bloody shoe print on the small, multicolour rug beneath the sink. More bloody shoe prints were observed on the wood floor in the hallway leading to the living area, as well as on the landing to the north of the living room, and again on the terra cotta tile on the living room floor, creating a trail that most likely indicated the killer's path around the cottage.

A foul smell grew stronger as the officers neared the body that lay face up on the living room floor. More than thirty hours had passed since Susan and her husband had engaged in what would be their final argument, and Felix's body had been left in the sealed cottage. Standing over the corpse, police carefully documented and photographed its position. Felix Polk was lying on his back, with his legs pointing towards the kitchen and his arms outstretched at a forty-five-degree angle as if he'd fallen backward when he died. His eyes were wide open, and there were rivulets of blood on the front and right side of his face. His head was facing the bedroom at the rear of the cottage, and there was blood on the leather chair directly behind the victim's head.

The scene was grisly, with 'a great deal' of blood on and around the victim's body, the investigators noted in their report. Blood smears and spatter revealed that a violent struggle had taken place. An ottoman had been turned upside down, and an open book lay next to Felix's left foot. Police observed that there was blood on one side of the ottoman but not on the top, which led them to conclude that it was knocked over early in the struggle, before any blood was spilled. There was also blood of a 'medium velocity' found on the book, indicating that the victim had most likely been stabbed and/or beaten.

While there had been much talk about a shotgun, there was no indication that a gun of any kind had been used in this murder. In fact, all signs pointed to a blunt force trauma and multiple stab wounds. The way Felix's body was positioned on the floor indicated that he was sitting in a chair reading at the time of the attack and was most likely struck in the head, as indicated by the blood that had flowed from his head and pooled along the south wall of the living room.

Investigators also noted that the blood on Felix's chest and abdomen had smeared, suggesting he had been on his stomach at some point during the struggle. Police observed apparent stab wounds on the front and sides of his abdomen and chest area, and the rivulets of blood on the right side of his stomach suggested that his heart had still been pumping while he was lying on his back. Blood found on the bottom of Felix's feet indicated he had been standing at some point during the struggle and had stepped in his own blood. Cuts were also apparent on the index fingers of his left and right hands, as well as the bottoms of his feet, indicating that he had tried to defend himself from attack. Upon closer examination of Felix's hands, police observed several hairs wrapped around the fingers of his right hand and another hair on the back of his left hand.

Moving to the cottage's tiny bathroom, police collected blood from the counter near the sink and from the linoleum tile floor. They also observed a substance that looked like diluted blood on the cabinet door handle in front of the sink. A hairbrush, toothbrush, toothpaste, and three bottles of prescriptive medication for 'Felix Polk' were among the items on the windowsill above the sink, investigators wrote in their report. Lorazepam and Clonazepam, two drugs widely prescribed for the treatment of panic disorder, were among the medications that police collected from the bathroom.

Police also removed a hair from the right faucet handle of the sink and two blue towels on the floor in front of the shower stall, which had apparent bloodstains. Additional forensic testing performed on the bloody shoeprints leading from the kitchen to the living room showed that 'all of the shoeprints appeared to have the same sole pattern consisting of various multiple geometric shapes.'

Once they had finished examining the cottage, the investigators went on to the main house for a more in-depth exploration that yielded additional evidence for the forensic team. Inside the small office on the first floor were handwritten letters to family members from the couple's middle son, Eli, mailed from the Byron Boys' Ranch, the 100-bed minimum-security facility, where he was currently serving time for his probation violation.

It appeared from Gabriel's interview with detectives earlier that morning that he had a good relationship with his father, yet Eli's letters seemed to indicate another side to Felix Polk. 'He basically writes how he hates it there in Byron Boys' Ranch,' police noted in the report. 'It's apparent from these writings that Eli distrusts his father and even warns Gabe at one point to be careful of what he eats at home, especially if given to him by dad.'

'Nothing indicating that Eli had any prior knowledge that this incident would occur,' the report stated.

On a desk in the office was an Apple Macintosh laptop computer, and a check of the hard drive revealed some lengthy documents apparently created by Susan Polk that showed she agreed with her middle son's views of his father. One document, dated 16 March 2001, which was submitted as evidence at her trial, outlined what Susan believed was Felix's 'unethical conduct' and spoke of abuse 'throughout their marriage'.

'She claims that her husband has drugged her in the past and has even struck her,' investigators noted.

The purpose of this letter is to document the unethical conduct of Felix Polk, a Licenced Clinical Psychologist in private practice in Berkeley. I was referred to Felix Polk in 1972 when I was a student at Clayton Valley High School in Concord. During the course of therapy, I was drugged by Felix and coerced into having a sexual relationship with him. We married in 1982. We have three children together, Adam, Eli, and Gabriel, aged 18, 15, and 14.

Throughout our marriage, Felix has been psychologically and physically abusive. He has punched me on numerous occasions, and threatened to kill me if I ever left him. He has also hit the children. On one occasion, he punched Eli who was twelve years old at the time in the face with a closed fist, knocking him to the floor where he lay stunned and unable to stand up. The violence, psychological and physical, has escalated as I have become more and more convinced that a separation was necessary.

The psychological abuse has taken several forms. Felix has threatened to withdraw financial support from me as well as the children ... When I have stated that I would be willing to leave without receiving a division of our property, he has threatened to kill me or, in his words, drive me crazy. Felix has throughout our marriage told me that I am crazy and told our children that I am crazy. He states that I come from a crazy family and that the dynamics in our family reflect my family dynamic rather than his ... Felix tells me that I am bad, ugly, evil, and destructive. At these times, I cannot help but being reminded of the family scene in which I was raised. As Felix knows, my mother subjected me to harsh criticism. The adjectives Felix chooses to employ are identical to those employed by my mother.

In October of last year, in order to avoid another violent scene, I informed Felix that I was going to spend the day at the beach. Felix responded by hitting me in the face. When I burst into tears, he told me to leave the house and not come back. Felix told the children that I was crazy and destroying the family. He then ordered me: 'go to your room.' He dragged me up the stairs and shoved me into our room. He said that he felt like hitting me because I was so provocative. One of my sons then stepped forward and punched me in the face ... These family scenes do indeed remind me of the way in which I was brought up. As Felix knew, there were constant violent confrontations in which my mother goaded my older brother into beating me up. It was part of my motivation to escape from my family that I submitted to Felix and agreed to marry him. While the despair that I feel in response to Felix's violence is reminiscent of the despair I felt growing up in an abusive family, it is not just transference as Felix states. When Felix threatens to destroy me, to kill me, to leave me with nothing if I leave him, I do feel hopeless. After the last violent scene, I attempted suicide despite the fact that apart from my marriage, I love life.

During the course of our marriage, Felix has at times drugged me. Almost four years ago, when I talked of getting a divorce, Felix employed hallucinogens. Felix then hired a psychiatrist to evaluate me for antipsychotic medication while I was experiencing flashbacks. He refers to this period of my life as a psychotic episode. He denies the use of drugs in therapy, and would most certainly deny using hallucinogens. I know of no other way to account for the flashbacks, which I experienced during that time period. I have never willingly used LSD or hallucinogens. I do not drink excessively or use drugs.

Also on the computer's desktop was a document 'My diary'. During her interview at headquarters, Susan had mentioned that she kept a diary, and suspecting this was it, investigators confiscated the laptop for further examination. Continuing their search of the office, police recovered a receipt from the Best Western Hotel in Bozeman, Montana, for the dates that Susan had given during her interview with Detective Costa, and a Blockbuster Video rental receipt dated 12 October 2002, at 2.34pm. There was also a piece of paper listing the residence at 1530 Arch Street, Berkeley, the five-unit apartment complex jointly owned by Felix and Susan Polk. According to the paper, Felix occupied Unit 1532. Gabriel claimed that his father vacated the unit prior to his murder, and the apartment was currently empty.

Other paperwork showed that the couple had nearly $5 million in real estate assets, including the Miner Road home, the Arch Street apartment complex, and a third building with four units on Linda Avenue in nearby Piedmont. The papers indicated that their debts totalled just under $1 million, and it seemed there was substantial money at stake in the divorce proceedings.

Officers observed an unusual number of books throughout the house. On the mantel in the living room above the stone fireplace were collections of Charles Dickens and William Makepeace Thackeray. Biographies of Europe's master painters sat on a coffee table near the room's enormous flat-screen TV. The glossy red and white cover of *The Joy of Cooking* stood out among the myriad cookbooks stacked on a counter in the kitchen.

On the second level of the home was a small laundry room. Inside the washing machine, police found a wet area rug, and the dryer held several towels, but a check of all the items revealed no visible bloodstains. No blood was detected on any of the clothing in the hamper near the appliances.

The master bedroom suite was up one more flight of stairs. The expansive room was tastefully decorated in soft earth tones and bathed in natural light from oversized windows. A queen-size bed with a wood headboard jutted out from one wall. Soft carpeting, an ample master bath, and an enormous walk-in closet gave the space a luxurious feel. In the bathroom, police collected the three blue hand towels that Costa had seen the night before and then searched the walk-in closet for bloody shoes. None were found.

Across the hall from the master suite on the north side of the staircase, there was a second bedroom and bathroom used by Gabriel. Between the two bedrooms, there was a third door that led out to the covered carport where Gabriel had hidden the previous night while he called the police. That carport, used mostly by Susan, was reached from the higher of the two driveways and provided access to the uppermost living quarters. Susan's silver Volvo station wagon was still there, along with two additional cars parked farther down the driveway – another Volvo and Eli's Dodge Ram 1500 pick-up truck that Susan had driven to Montana. The guesthouse where police were collecting fingerprints was south of the main residence and west of the small structure that contained a bathroom and the family's home gym.

At 5pm on Tuesday, 15 October, the coroner's van made its way to the cottage to remove Felix's dead body, clearing the way for additional examination of the immediate crime scene. The forensic team remained there for several more hours to gather fingerprints and collect other potential evidence.

It was after 9pm when Detective Costa and the others wrapped up their work at the Polk house, now encircled in bright yellow police tape. They returned to the Main Detention Facility at 1000 Ward Street in Martinez, where Susan Polk had been transported during the early morning hours after her interrogation. After being processed at the jail, Susan had been booked for the murder of her husband, Felix Polk. She knew both the routine and the facility, since she was processed at the same location eighteen months earlier on charges of 'battery' after an argument with her husband had turned physical.

Once she was secure at the jail, the investigators conducted a second interview with Susan during which they observed several injuries on her body, prompting officials to undertake a full forensic examination of Susan's hands, face, and body. Among other things, the examination uncovered bruising and redness on her right eye, and small red cuts on her hands and upper arms. 'The injuries were consistent with someone who was involved in a physical confrontation in the recent past,' one of the detectives jotted in his report. 'I asked Susan if she would consent to providing hair samples and photos of her injuries. Susan permitted the hair samples, but denied consent to the photos due to modesty.'

Her refusal prompted police to obtain a search warrant.

Detective Costa was on hand that night to supervise the photographing of the slight reddish discolourations around Susan's eyes and the small healing wounds on her hands. He also stood by as an officer plucked a dark brown hair sample from her scalp. He was certain it would be a positive match to the strands found clenched in Felix Polk's bloody right fist.

CHAPTER SEVEN

THE DOCTOR'S DISEASE

Frank 'Felix' Polk had been a well-respected therapist and esteemed member of the faculty at Argosy University, where he taught psychology for more than a decade. His faint accent and formal attire reflected his wealthy European upbringing. His intuitive approach ingratiated him to others, from his superiors right down to the Argosy librarian.

Born in Vienna, Austria, on 30 June 1932, Felix had enjoyed a privileged childhood. His father, Eric Ernst Polk, was a wealthy clothing manufacturer, who was born a Jew in Czechoslovakia and later emigrated to Austria, where he met and married Johanna Hahn. The couple's daughter, Evelyn, was two years old when Felix and his fraternal twin, John, were born. The children were reared by a nanny and led a charmed life for several years, but all that came to a sudden end in 1938 when SS officers came for Felix's father. Young Felix could do nothing but hide as the men dragged the elder Polk away. It was a terrifying scene; large men in uniforms and helmets brutalising his father and carting him away as the boy stood by, unable to help.

He wanted to run after them, to save his father, but the little six-year-old could do nothing. Losing his father that way changed Felix forever. He would never be comfortable in the real world again.

With Eric Polk gone, the family was forced to flee the German invasion and abandon their majestic stone house in the country's capital.

'We had to keep one step ahead of the Nazis,' Felix recalled many years later.

He claimed the family headed to the French countryside, where for nearly a year, they secretly lived in the attic of a farmhouse used regularly by German troops. It was a kind of Anne Frank existence in which no one dared speak for fear of being discovered, Felix said. To pass the time, he retreated to an imaginary world – a world in which he was able to save his father.

While Felix would later say the terrifying experience gave him a 'built-in sense of survival', this knowledge carried a high price. Children who are separated from their parents early in life often do not recover from the trauma. Six is a critical age for a developing boy to lose his father to what the family believed was certain death. For Felix, there was also a powerful belief that he had failed his dad. He had stood idle, his heart pounding in his chest, as the men with the big guns carted away his beloved father.

In his heart, Felix believed he should have done something. But what?

The act of hiding and the psychological impact of believing that people are out to get you – because they are – can leave profound and lifelong scars on a young mind. As an adult, Felix would suffer from bouts of severe depression, marked by dark moods, anxiety, and panic attacks.

At some point, Felix's father escaped captivity at a concentration camp and rejoined the family for a time, but he soon left to fight alongside the British Expeditionary Forces. This voluntary departure was almost worse than the first. Good fathers weren't supposed to leave their families, and without his dad, Felix felt lost and unprotected once again.

Years later, the family was reunited in Marseilles, thanks to an ad Felix's father had run in a French newspaper seeking their whereabouts. For a brief time, Felix attended boarding school in France before crossing into Spain with his family, where they converted to Catholicism to gain entry. From Spain, they travelled to Portugal and eventually boarded a ship bound for the United States.

It's not known what effect, if any, the involuntary change of religion had on young Felix. An autopsy revealed that, despite his Jewish heritage, he had never been circumcised, possibly to protect him from persecution in war-ravaged Europe. Years later, he would joke of his conversion with friends, who described the psychologist as 'culturally Jewish'.

In 1941, the Polks landed in America and eventually settled in Harrison, New York, where Felix's father set up a retail business that quickly succeeded. Throughout his life, Eric Polk exhibited a remarkable ability to rebound from tragedy, and America was the perfect venue for his resilience, as he quickly established two profitable five-and-dime stores in Rockland County.

Despite his father's success, Felix, who was nine when the family made the transatlantic voyage, proved least able to adjust to life in the land of opportunity. He resented that his family no longer enjoyed the financial status they enjoyed in Austria. He had no time for play because his father expected Felix to work in the family business. His was a Victorian upbringing; crying was not allowed in the Polk home.

In 1949, at the age of seventeen, Felix left the comfort of his parents' New York home for St. John's College in Annapolis, Maryland, where he had earned a scholarship. Even though Felix started high school late, he still managed to graduate with his class. Nevertheless his parents weren't satisfied with his academic performance, and they constantly held up the achievements of his twin brother, John, as the example to follow. Felix resented the comparison and John's ease in forming many friendships. Neither came naturally to Felix. He was plagued by a foreboding he couldn't explain.

Once at college, Felix's academic interests flourished. Philosophy became his passion, and he immersed himself in his studies to the point of obsession. While the work was invigorating, his constant self-analysis seemed to alienate his classmates, and Felix made few friends on campus. Similarly, family members reported that Felix's dark letters home were filled with 'marked preoccupations' and 'esoteric discussions', and that he exhibited 'fluctuating moods of unhappiness' during his visits home.

Upon graduation from St. John's with a bachelor of arts degree in 1953, Felix enlisted as an officer in the US Navy to meet his military obligations. That summer, he was sent to Officer Candidate School (OCS) at the US Naval Reserve Station in Newport, Rhode Island. Within walking distance of the sandy ocean beaches and the hopping downtown, it was a grand place to be stationed in July and August.

However, Felix rarely enjoyed these surroundings. According to US Naval records, the twenty-two-year-old officer-in-training was 'under greater strain than other students' at OCS. 'He disliked the routine, but got through the program,' records stated.

After amphibious training at a base in Little Creek, Virginia, Felix was assigned to a Landing Ship Tank (LST) on the West Coast and cruised to Japan. An LST carries supplies and troops and has a top speed of ten knots, slower than a champion woman marathoner, and the four-week crossing seemed endless. Aboard ship, Felix held the rank of Lieutenant Junior Grade (JG) and served as a stores officer. Though not always content, he adjusted well, according to the naval records.

But still, something wasn't right.

Felix was 'moody and depressed' according to family members who advised him to seek help. While on leave from the navy in December of 1954, Felix went to see a psychiatrist named Kurt Goldstein, but he was only able to meet with Dr. Goldstein once before deploying back to the West Coast that month.

His parents, Eric and Johanna Polk, were aware that their son was troubled. He had always been the 'maladjusted' member of the family they reported, but the couple remained aloof, according to naval records, 'because of his treatment'. It was the 1950s, and mental illness was something that people feared. Felix was seeking help – that was all his parents would acknowledge. Discussion of any emotion – love, fear, or sadness – was not encouraged in the Polk house. After all, Felix's father had been a war hero, and he was a man with high expectations. Weakness was not to be tolerated.

But Felix felt weak. He tried to function as best he could, completing high school and even meeting with some success in college, but enlisting in the navy proved emotionally difficult. Though he made it through boot camp, he had a difficult time. Wearing a uniform and training for combat went against everything he believed in. Uniforms signified guns, blood, and death. He had seen more than his share as a youngster.

Once in the navy, that panicky, pulsating anxiety he felt as a child hiding in a farmhouse returned. While at sea, Felix documented his emotional difficulties in a diary. In one entry, dated 21 January 1955, he recounted his disappointment and anger at a letter he received from a woman named Adele that he courted with little success:

Despite the general stupidity of the letter, there were several thoughts which caused me real anguish. I was accused of being unrealistic, of living in a world which does not exist. I deny that my world is unrealistic, and yet I am tormented by my inability to communicate in the 'real' world.

The entry described a double date the couple attended with Felix's twin brother, John, and a woman named Evelyn B. The four had gone to Manhattan to see *The Saint of Bleecker Street*:

I felt beforehand that I would be self-conscious. This turned out to be the case. I couldn't speak. I was terribly uncomfortable at the concert. The more I tried to relax, the more self-conscious I became, until it became almost unbearable. When we left . . . I was near collapse. Of course, she [Adele] must have noticed that something was wrong. The first two times that we met I had the good fortune of having had several drinks beforehand. Alcohol is usually very helpful in subduing my consciousness.

I wonder what she [Adele] thought when my letter came. Her answer took a motherly and, at the same time, destructive attitude. I resent the motherly, and resent even more the fact that Adele believes she knows enough about me after such a short acquaintance to be able to call my way of life 'moral tragedy'.

Whether it really is or not is not the important question. In my letter, I tried my best to stem mounting anger. I fear that she will not write again. Although I hope against hope that she will. I need desperately to write to someone other than my sister and mother. The familiarity of what they say in every letter is becoming monotonous and is not in the least helpful. I am always disappointed when the letters I receive bear the familiar writing of my father's or Evelyn's green ink. And yet, I need their letters desperately.

In another entry, dated 1 February 1955, Felix further described his 'self-consciousness' in social settings.

'A dream about dignity, it escapes me,' the notation begins. 'The past few days I have been unable to concentrate on my dreams upon awakening although I know that I have dreamt. All the officers went to a dance tonight. I wanted to go, but knew that the evening would have been painful.'

Two weeks later, on 15 February, Felix wrote again of his social anxiety. This time, it prevented him from attending a surprise party being thrown for the captain of his naval unit. According to the notation, Felix had accepted an offer by a friend named Dean to get him a date for the winter affair, knowing full well that he would not attend the event.

'This evening I told Dean with a smile that I would not be able to come,' Felix wrote. 'I told him that there was an important reason, and he of course, misunderstood me.

'How can I tell anyone what the real reason is? Can I say to my friend, "Sorry, Dean, I cannot go because of my self-consciousness." It would make me utterly miserable. The girl would think I was crazy. I would have to laugh, and it would simply be too painful for me. This is what I would have had to say. How impossible my existence is.'

Felix also wrote about a letter he sent to his older sister, Evelyn, in which he tried to explain his state of being.

In this letter, I expressed what has long been turned over in my mind, i.e., the anger and guilt which I direct towards my parents for having made me what I am, a helpless, utterly self-conscious and miserable individual.

Instead of the closeness I once felt for my parents, there is now anger and resentment. The guilt, which I once felt for their sake, I have emplanted [sic] in them. Mother's letters now leave me with a cruel kind of coldness. In the letter, I announced my determination to sever, although not entirely, relations with Harrison [Felix's hometown in New York].

Perhaps this sounds dramatic, yet it must be so. I also told EV [Evelyn] that I felt myself to be basically a simple individual who has by accident had a complex personality thrown on his rather weak body. And this is exactly my feeling. The simplicity and sometimes naivitee [sic] of my desires, thoughts and pleasures are a violent contrast to the complexity of my psychic structure. It is as if my psychic existence and my true nature were two separate entities joined by a foolish or blind will. Where I asked to choose between discarding my simplicity and my personality, there would not really be a choice.

At twenty-three, Felix was slowly coming apart, yet, his silent suffering only magnified his problems. He had never dealt with the psychological trauma he suffered as a young boy in war-torn Europe. There was much secrecy surrounding the horrific crimes of World War II, and there was no counselling available to the tens of thousands of victims. Those lucky enough to have survived received no special treatment.

Everybody was expected to go on. And outwardly, most did.

In September of 1955, the navy transferred Felix back to a base in Brooklyn, New York, for shore duty. He was unhappy with the assignment and unhappy to be back home. His only consolation was that he could resume therapy with Dr. Goldstein. According to the doctor's records later obtained by the US Navy, Felix attended ten sessions with the psychiatrist. The psychiatrist recorded that he was 'agitated', 'depressed', and 'concerned over sexual problems', 'lacked an interest in a career', and 'was preoccupied with philosophical and cosmic concepts'.

A sexual history compiled by Dr. Goldstein during his sessions with Felix disclosed that Felix began masturbating at the age of twelve, but 'masturbated with guilt' and 'felt confused regarding sexual facts until fifteen years of age'. He began dating at sixteen, and by the age of twenty, was involved in a relationship with a well-to-do aspiring actress. We'll call her Fannie.

Felix's guilt over masturbation and confusion over sexual gender were not remarkable since about 50 per cent of American males reportedly experience those same feelings, according to experts. What was unusual was that, since puberty, Felix had been obsessed with his sister, Evelyn.

'Incestuous fantasies involving his older sister have preoccupied him since adolescence,' Dr. Goldstein noted in his official report.

It is interesting that Evelyn was fifteen when Felix began to fantasise about her – the same age that Susan was when she first went to see him in 1972.

On Friday, 14 October 1955, Felix met with Dr. Goldstein but his session did not appear to lift his spirits, and the following day, he felt no better. While torrential rainfall and high winds only added to his gloom, he had a date that night in Manhattan, so he forced himself to get dressed, pack a bag, and make the forty-mile drive to the city.

It was 5.30pm when Felix met Fannie for their date. Although he wasn't in love with her, he enjoyed her company. She put him at ease and allowed him to be himself. He had gotten tickets to *La Ronde*, a performance based on the 1897 play *Der Reigen* (Hands Around) by Austrian writer Arthur Schnitzler. The story begins with the seduction of a soldier by a prostitute, who transmits syphilis during their encounter. The disease is then passed on to each subsequent and interconnected character in subsequent acts until it finally reaches the Count who, in the end, makes love to the prostitute from the first scene, thus closing the circle. The play was still considered somewhat risqué and had sparked outrage when it was first performed in Germany in the early part of the twentieth century. It had been labelled 'obscene', and for a time, was banned from the theatre.

As the performance progressed, Felix confided to Fannie that he was seeing a psychiatrist and had an appointment the previous day. Fannie noticed that he seemed more glib than his usual sombre self. During his previous visit to New York, he had confided his unhappiness at home – due, primarily, to his relationship with his mother. Now, he seemed more displeased with his naval assignment to Brooklyn and expressed his desire to be stationed somewhere in Europe.

Smiling, Felix turned to Fannie and announced that he had contemplated suicide.

Staring back, Fannie giggled. He couldn't be serious, she thought, he was grinning when he made the pronouncement.

'I've already tried it once,' he announced. Felix said he had actually turned on the gas burners in his house, but while waiting for death, 'had grown bored with the whole thing.'

Unsure how to respond, Fannie grabbed his hand to comfort him and recounted the story of her brother's suicide several months earlier while he was on active duty in the army. As Fannie told the sad tale, she found Felix's response worrisome. Suddenly, he was listening very intently, enquiring about every detail, particularly regarding the method her brother had employed.

After the theatre, Felix and Fannie returned to her place where they spent the night together. The following afternoon, they attended a matinee featuring Marcel Marceau, but once the film ended, Felix became frighteningly sullen and announced that he wanted to go home.

'Call me the minute you get to Harrison,' Fannie begged when he dropped her off around 5.30 that Sunday evening. She knew that his parents, Eric and Johanna Polk, had travelled to Rochester for the weekend to visit their daughter, Evelyn. With Felix's brother, John, stationed overseas, there would be no one at home to look after him.

Felix sounded increasingly dejected when he telephoned from Harrison just after 7pm. Worried, Fannie phoned him again later that evening. She was relieved when he picked up the line just after 10pm, but became distraught as she listened.

'It's too late for the world,' Felix repeated over and over into the receiver. 'Too late, too late.'

Fannie tried to console Felix, but he soon admonished 'don't call back anymore' and hung up the phone.

Frantic, and convinced that Felix was in trouble, Fannie begged her mother to phone the police.

It was nearing 10.30pm when Felix sat down at the typewriter. He felt compelled to release his emotions on paper:

I have done what for a long time, I know I must do. When a rock is thrown into water it sinks. It must sink, as now must I. My minds (sic) is so heavy with wretchedness, with utter loneliness, with an unknown past, a frightening future and an intolerable past present that no choice remains. I don't fear death at all. What it is, but non-life. And what is life but a continuous torture? This final act is not sudden or impetuous. I have known that someday it would take place. The question has only been, where, when, and how. Until a few weeks ago, there has always been some spark, some hope, which prevented me from the obvious. This night there is no hope. There is nothing; and tomorrow and tomorrow.

Of regrets, I have few. It would be folly for anyone to assume the blame for something of which I myself and no one else is responsible. I say goodbye to a hateful world with a smile. In life, I hated pity and in death I want none. Had I not come this far in life my loss would perhaps have been easier. I have forgotten the world and now the world much [sic] forget me.

Rising from the desk, Felix grabbed the keys to the family car. Feeling stronger than he had in a long time, he took one last look around and headed for the garage. Sliding into the passenger seat, he put the key into the ignition and started the engine. The hum of the motor was comforting, and he felt great relief that he had the courage to do what he wanted to do so many times before.

Police records show that an anonymous call came into the Harrison Police Department sometime after 11pm that Sunday night, 16 October. The female caller did not give her name; she was just a concerned citizen who wanted to report a 'possible suicide' at 308 Harrison Avenue, the home of Eric and Johanna Polk.

Officer Pat Pizarello responded to the 'mysterious phone call' and 'lights on' dispatch to the Polk residence. Armed with a torch, he began to examine the grounds. Hearing a noise coming from inside the garage, he flung open the door to find the space filled with carbon monoxide gas. There was a car parked inside with its motor running and Felix was on the floor adjacent to the car's front right wheel. At one point, he had been in the passenger seat but had apparently slipped to the garage floor when he became unconscious.

'I had suicidal thoughts before but never thought I'd have nerve enough to try it,' Felix later told psychiatrists at the US Naval Hospital at St. Albans, New York.

Ironically, Felix Polk would be murdered 46 years later, almost to the day.

CHAPTER EIGHT

A TRAGIC MIX

Three years after his suicide attempt, Felix met and married Sharon Mann, an attractive music student at the Julliard School in New York City, who was just eighteen when the couple was first introduced in 1956. At the time, Felix was on temporary leave from the US Naval Reserve, and he was employed as a social worker at the Cedar Knolls School in Hawthorne, New York County, while studying for a master's in social work at Manhattan's Albert Einstein College. On weekends, he worked as a recreation therapist at the Linden Hill School for Disturbed Adolescents in Westchester to supplement the monthly disability payments of $231 he had begun receiving from the navy. He was also seeing a private psychiatrist three times a week, paying $15 a session.

Two years after his marriage, on 26 September 1960, Felix received an honourable discharge from the US Naval Reserve for a 'physical disability'. That same year, he and Sharon relocated to northern California. There, Felix enrolled at the University of California, Berkeley, where he did additional undergraduate coursework. Deciding he wanted to help people like himself to get well, he applied and was admitted to the university's PhD programme.

While Felix earned his doctorate, Sharon supported the couple, and later, their small family. On 2 October 1962, she gave birth to a son, Andrew D. Polk, and three years later, on 23 March 23 1965, a daughter, Jennifer, was born. That same year, Felix was awarded both a PhD in clinical psychology and a second bachelor's degree – a B.S. with honours – from Berkeley University.

The following summer, he travelled to England on a National Institute of Mental Health fellowship, where he remained for two years treating adolescents and families as a staff clinician at London's Travistock Clinic and Institution. Though records are sketchy, it appears that Felix saw little of his wife and children during that time.

Returning to California in 1967, he landed a plum post as chief psychologist at the Alameda County Mental Health Services in Oakland where he was responsible for overseeing the psychological services for all the clinics and hospitals in the county. In addition, he was an instructor at both Hayward State University in Hayward and at Holy Names College in Oakland. While Felix was beginning to experience success, Sharon, was also excelling in her career, quickly gaining acclaim as a pianist and piano teacher.

By all accounts, the couple seemed happy. Felix and Sharon shared a love of classical music, and for one birthday, Sharon gave her husband a cello. Nancy Lemmon, a teenage babysitter who lived across Cragmont Street from the family in Berkeley, recalled in a telephone interview Sharon's excitement the evening she presented the expensive instrument to her husband, saying that Felix was overjoyed by the gift and was anxious to learn to play. He had long dreamed of owning a cello and was overwhelmed by his wife's thoughtfulness.

Nancy was a young teen when she began caring for the Polk children and recalled the couple vividly, stating that they were respectful of each other's interests and seemed a good match. Felix was always welcoming when Nancy came over, making her feel at ease in his lovely home. While Nancy admitted that she never really knew what type of work Felix did, she assumed he was a college professor because of his intelligence and attire – often a tweed jacket and slacks. Sharon, too, was smart and always attractive in feminine outfits and little makeup.

Nancy was not the only one who believed that the marriage was solid. While their friends agreed that Sharon was the more outgoing of the two, the resounding sentiment was that the two seemed compatible. With Felix's advanced degrees and Sharon's blooming career, the couple seemed destined for success.

Things continued to improve for the young couple when at the age of thirty-six, Felix opened his private practice in the yellow clapboard house on Ashby Avenue in downtown Berkeley, several blocks from the house the couple purchased on Los Angeles Avenue. Their new residence was larger than the one on Cragmont and was located just below Arlington Circle in the centre of the city. By 1969, Felix's private practice was flourishing, and he decided to leave his post with Alameda County to devote more time to his patients. His specialty was the treatment of families and adolescents who were 'acting out'.

In late 1971, he attended a weekend workshop on Erhard Seminar Training (EST), a new-age movement founded on the Zen-based approach of master and disciple. The session, led by the movement's founder, Werner Erhard, had a powerful effect on Polk. Friends reported that the thirty-nine-year-old therapist left the workshop believing he had gained more knowledge in that one weekend than during his four years of graduate school. EST, which literally means 'it is' in Latin, promoted the idea that through the application of 'programming and reprogramming', people can rewrite their lives, allowing them to be 'set free and born again'. Erhard's theory was that all problems and limitations were in the mind, and people had been 'hypnotized during normal consciousness' to develop debilitating habits and beliefs that could be changed through 'conscious rewiring'.

For Felix, this new-age theory made perfect sense, and he embraced it wholeheartedly. Perhaps Susan Bolling was his first disciple, since it was not long after his EST session that the fifteen-year-old walked into his Berkeley office for an evaluation.

There is no written record of exactly when the sexual relationship between Felix Polk and Susan Bolling began. According to Susan, she was fifteen the first time Dr. Polk 'molested' her. She claimed he invited her to sit on his lap during one appointment, and by their fourth session he had raped her after placing her in a 'drug induced' hypnotic trance. When pressed, Susan could not recall details of the alleged assault or explain why it had taken her more than twenty years to recall the abuse. She insisted, however, that it reached a point in her teenage life when the only time she left the house was to attend her sessions with Dr. Polk.

Before long, Susan grew to dread the appointments, but she claims she never really understood why. There is little question that Susan and Felix engaged in a sexual relationship during their time as patient and therapist. What remains unclear is how that relationship began. According to Susan, all she knew was that the panic – the pounding in her chest, the struggle to catch her breath – never subsided. In fact, it grew worse.

Often, therapists who transgress and have a relationship with a patient are depressed. Rather than predators, they are more often broken in some way. Such was the case with Felix Polk. Susan Bolling was fifteen and needed him. The idea of being needed made Felix feel powerful and sexually charged. In his mind, he and Susan were spiritual comrades, connected by their shared abandonment by their fathers. Susan's father had left the family when she was six, just like Felix's father had done – although his action was not by choice, but at the behest of the Nazis.

By falling in love with Susan, he was becoming her father, and Susan hated her father. Susan felt that Theodore Bolling had abandoned the family, and had hurt her mom. Susan recalled a memory in which she walked in on her parents one afternoon at the age of six to find them engaged in a heated argument. Helen Bolling was petite, nearly a foot smaller than her husband, and the impression of her mother dwarfed by her father's six-foot framed stayed with her.

Unbeknownst to little Susan, Theodore Bolling was angry that his wife was refusing to sign the divorce papers. Helen later recalled how she had known for some time that her husband was having an affair. The 'other' woman had been at a New Year's Eve party that Helen and her husband attended, and Helen immediately knew who she was by the way the woman stared at Theodore. Despite his transgression, Helen was deeply in love with the intelligent, dark-haired man and was unwilling to let him go.

Her refusal infuriated Theodore. Helen recalled it was a horrifying exchange, one that persuaded her to release him from the marriage. Unfortunately for Susan, she was never able to let go of that image.

For some time after that, her allegiance remained with Helen, as evidenced in a letter she wrote to her mother in the summer of 1967. Susan and her brother, David, had been sent to stay with her father and his new family for a time. By then, Theodore Bolling was on his third wife. After leaving Helen, he was briefly married to Rita, the woman who had been the cause of his divorce from Helen. Theodore would remarry once again before settling down and practicing law in Sacramento.

While Susan was enjoying her time with her father, her letter indicates a desperate need to be in contact with her mother:

Dear Momma,

I miss you so much already. Tears are streaming down my cheeks already at night. I don't want to leave yet, but I sure do miss you. Oh please write me. Oh please. I love you so much. . . .

By fifteen, Susan was on the brink of an emotional collapse. Even under Felix's care, she continued to feel as if everything was closing in on her. She wanted the claustrophobic sensation to stop. If she could only go to sleep, maybe it would go away.

One evening, Susan's mother returned home to find her daughter sprawled on the bed. Music was blaring from the stereo, and an open bottle of pills lay by her side. Helen Bolling immediately called for help and alerted Dr. Polk to her daughter's near-fatal suicide attempt. The psychologist briefly considered placing Susan in a facility for disturbed children at the University of California Medical Centre in San Francisco. After careful consideration, he decided instead to put her under the care of a colleague and friend who worked at the Kaiser Mental Facility for Adults in Oakland.

At fifteen, Susan awoke to find herself the only minor in the institution. Much worse than juvenile hall, now she was among truly crazy people. In addition, her psychiatrist was Dr. Polk's friend. Again, Felix Polk had overstepped his bounds by having the teen admitted to an adult facility and placing her in the care of a friend. If she had been admitted through the hospital emergency room, those doctors would have found a place suitable for a girl her age.

Administrators at Kaiser insisted Susan leave the facility after only one week of treatment; they didn't want to be liable for a minor. Yet, instead of having the young woman transferred to an age-appropriate facility, Felix Polk took responsibility for her care and allowed Susan to return home to live with her mother in the house she had recently purchased in Orinda.

There was one stipulation – she had to continue to see him for therapy.

In a letter to Alameda County youth officials in 1973, Polk described Susan as a 'severely disturbed girl with strong depressive features', but he failed to mention that his therapy was doing little to help her mental state. Susan was now sixteen. She still refused to go to class, making it clear she had no intention of attending continuation school with a bunch of 'uneducated' and 'unsophisticated' teens. She was unwilling to be among people of 'marginal' intelligence. Remarkably, her probation officer allowed her to remain at home – as long as she continued her therapy with Dr. Polk. The officer had observed a marked improvement in Susan since she started with Felix and believed that the lost teen might actually find her way.

Meanwhile, Helen thought that her daughter was thriving under Dr. Polk's care.

In reality, Susan was deeply troubled and would later report that her therapy was adding to her anxiety. She later claimed that the sessions included hypnosis – and sex with her therapist while she was in a trance.

For her, the choice was clear: either she would surrender to Dr. Polk or risk being locked up in a mental institution. Whether Polk actually threatened the teen will never be known; however, Susan claimed that if she didn't comply with his wishes, he would have committed her to U. C. Medical Centre. She said that, at times, he would employ the plural 'we' when speaking of decisions about her future. Susan was afraid to inquire about the 'other' authorities who were also deciding her fate, choosing instead to go along with whatever Felix proposed.

While other teens her age were preparing for graduation and the prom, Susan claimed to be romantically involved with her forty-two-year-old married therapist. She alleged that her twice-weekly sessions consisted of 'sex on the floor' of Dr. Polk's Berkeley office.

Over time, though, the sex became consensual. Susan had grown comfortable with Felix who, despite his protectiveness, seemed to know how to make problems in her life go away. He had rescued her from school, even helping her to enroll in a course at Diablo Valley College in spite of the fact that she never completed more than the eighth grade.

Finally, someone in her life had taken charge, given her direction, and was really listening to her. Felix was the caring father – and mother – she never had. Even better, he wanted her. She loved that she seemed to be the most important person in his life.

But Susan Bolling was not well, and Felix Polk couldn't see it.

Susan waited all day to tell her mother her secret. It was late 1974. She was seventeen now, and it was time to let Helen know that she was a woman. She had rehearsed the conversation in her mind countless times, how she would tell her mother that she was having an affair with Dr. Polk. She even tried to anticipate her mother's reaction to the news that she was sleeping with a much older, married man.

What Susan failed to anticipate was her mother's anger. Helen threatened to have Felix's licence revoked. Though she had never tried to intervene before, Helen Bolling would later say that she had always suspected that something was going on between the psychologist and her daughter – ever since Susan told her about sitting on Felix's lap during some of their sessions.

Ultimately, Helen opted not to alert the authorities, going directly to Felix instead. It was the 1970s, a time when the victim of rape was often treated like the perpetrator, an outcome that Helen did not want for her daughter. As a minor, Helen had had her own experiences with the courts. She described an incident involving inappropriate contact with her father. The experience had been devastating, and she was determined to spare Susan.

Following Helen's incident with her father, a subsequent investigation determined that the Avanzato home was not a suitable environment for young Helen. At first, she was placed in the care of her older half siblings, but ultimately she was sent to live in an orphanage. Life there was unbearable, and at the age of fourteen, with $100 in her pocket, Helen ran away to Chicago, Illinois.

A friend's mother suggested she go there and loaned Helen money to get on her feet. Fearful that the authorities were on her trail, Helen changed her name to Lois Stokes and set off for the windy city, where she found work as a packer in a warehouse and a room to rent in a good neighborhood. Her first disappointment came at Christmas time when she lost her job at the warehouse. Though she quickly found a new job as a file clerk for an insurance company, she soon grew to dislike it. With little keeping her in Chicago, she agreed to follow a friend to Hollywood, California, shortly after she turned sixteen. The idea of living amid movie stars was appealing, and Helen readily travelled to the West Coast, where she continued to work odd jobs, mostly receptionist positions, to pay the bills.

But this was not the life that she wanted for her daughter. After learning of Susan's affair, Helen telephoned Felix's office, and the two had a discussion. She insisted the therapist 'be kind' to her daughter when he ended their relationship. While Felix did not directly admit to a romance with Susan, neither did he deny that one was taking place, Helen later recalled. He simply promised to do as she asked.

On 25 November 1975, three years after her therapy sessions with Dr. Polk began, Susan celebrated her eighteenth birthday. Turning eighteen was emancipating. Susan was finally 'of age.' In her mind, she was now an adult and no longer needed to hide her affair. She believed she was in love with the well-respected therapist who was old enough to be her father. It was cool to be his girlfriend, and she wanted everyone to know about the relationship.

One afternoon while participating in a group therapy session led by Felix, Susan stood up and playfully placed her arms around Felix's shoulders.

'Felix and I are lovers,' she smiled.

Members of the group sat in stunned disbelief before quietly dispersing.

Susan recalled that Felix was mortified and then furious. His secret was out.

Yet, as Felix worried about how to handle the group, he learned that Susan had also confided their affair to a female therapist, who also worked in Berkeley. When Susan disclosed her romance to that therapist, she never imagined that the woman would promptly report the affair – not to authorities, but to Felix's wife. Sharon Mann Polk was incensed, and according to Susan, both she and the therapist lashed out at *her* for 'spilling the beans'. Susan was surprised that the two women were angry with her – and not at Felix. After all, he was the adult and the one clearly out of line for being romantically involved with a patient, not to mention a girl half his age. Sharon Mann has repeatedly denied requests for an interview.

'They were mad at me!' Susan later recalled. 'Yes, tell the wife, but don't tell the medical board.'

Susan later claimed that she made the pronouncement hoping that it would anger Felix to the point of breaking off the romance with her, but that did not happen. Felix claimed that even though Sharon wanted to stay in the marriage, he wanted to be with Susan. Susan found his proclamation unbelievable. Sharon was beautiful, articulate, intelligent, and successful. For Susan, it was flattering to hear that Felix would choose her over his more accomplished wife.

Maybe Felix just wasn't attracted to his wife anymore. Or perhaps he wanted to mold Susan into his dream girlfriend, she thought. According to Susan, Felix had gone to see a lawyer and was advised to leave Sharon and 'marry her'. Marriage, the lawyer reportedly said, was the best legal solution for Felix, but that may or may not have been the case. According to experts, there may have been other factors at play.

Regardless of his marriage, the reality was that Felix had fallen in love with a woman who at fifteen was already very sick. Then the two began a very complicated social dance. It was not like the failed relationships with his older sister and his mother, women who were always in control. This time, it was Felix who was in control, and Susan was the patient he could help.

However, in this attempt to save Susan, he unwittingly became the focus of her many internal conflicts, a process called transference. In psychological terms, transference occurs when a patient shifts feelings of anger, rage, disappointment, or love onto their therapist. In Susan's case, Felix became her father. Complicating matters was the fact that the transference was not limited to Susan. Felix, too, struggled to reconcile his vision of Susan to reality, as Susan may have became Felix's fifteen-year-old sister whom he had fantasised about as a teen.

It was a deadly mix of transference and countertransference, one that would have explosive consequences.

Felix and Sharon Polk legally separated on 10 October 1978 – one month after the couple celebrated their twentieth wedding anniversary. Ironically, Felix had marked the occasion with a $600 gift of silver purchased at Gump's, the famous San Francisco retail store. Then, he asked for a divorce.

That fall, his teenage girlfriend sat for the Standardized Achievement Tests (SATs). Susan scored a 740 out of 800 in English and a 530 in Maths, without taking any substantive maths courses in high school. She was ranked in the 98th percentile in English and the 80th in Maths. Soon after, she was awarded her GED.

The following year, Susan moved out of her mother's house and in with Felix. By this time, Felix was no longer her therapist; now he was simply her boyfriend. When she demonstrated an interest in college, he chose Mills College, an all-girls school in the foothills of Oakland, and there is evidence that he was footing the bill for her education.

Compliant, and anxious to please Felix, Susan attended Mills for two years. But then she decided to take a semester off, and soon it became clear that her days at Mills were over.

Not long afterwards, she began to feel suffocated by her relationship with Felix. It was okay when she still had all of her high school issues, and Felix was there to save her, but now that they were living together, she was feeling more like a nineteen-year-old hostage than a girlfriend. She couldn't make one decision without his approval. He was exacting and became edgy when things didn't go his way. Finally it reached a point where Susan was afraid to say anything that might upset him.

To avoid confrontation, she often listened and agreed, rather than stir controversy. She began to think back to other points in the past where she had been afraid to disagree with him. During their sessions as therapist and patient, he would set out a number of provocative theories. For instance, he told Susan that all girls had fantasies about having sex with their fathers and that their fathers wanted to sleep with them as well. He also implied that most girls had fantasies of rape. When he asked a teenage Susan if she shared those fantasies, she grew embarrassed and told him 'no'. Felix insisted that these thoughts were natural, and Susan had no reason to question him. Now as she looked back, she began to see the larger impact of those statements, statements that affected her ability to have relationships of any kind.

By 1979, however, she was no longer a naive teenager. For the first time, she felt capable of making decisions on her own. At times, she didn't want to be with Felix anymore but didn't know how to untangle herself from his web. That fall, she enrolled at San Francisco State University and moved on campus. Having a roommate and living on her own in the centre of the city made her realise that being around other people was different than being around Felix. She was less anxious and no longer afraid to speak or have an opinion. It felt good.

At one point, she even mustered up the courage to tell Felix that she wanted to 'break it off'.

Her pronouncement was met by a terrifying threat: Felix warned that he would take his own life if she left him. He had left his family for her and now he was going to kill himself. Worse, he began to cry and accuse her of violating his trust, saying that he had a problem with abandonment and deceitfully claiming that he tried to commit suicide after a girlfriend left him.

Felix's psychological dysfunction seemed to pour from him as he told Susan of his secret troubles. He spoke of his difficult childhood as a survivor of the Holocaust and of his stay in a mental hospital after a suicide attempt. He alluded to a problem with anxiety and panic attacks. He admitted to being jealous and confided that he had issues with 'potency' in his first marriage.

Susan somehow felt responsible. As much as she wanted to be free of Felix, her guilt would not permit it. Besides, he was paying her college tuition and expenses. With this in mind, she resolved to stay in the relationship, despite her reservations.

In May of 1981, Susan graduated magna cum laude from San Francisco State with a B.A. in English. That November, she celebrated her twenty-fourth birthday. One month later, she married her forty-nine-year-old therapist. The wedding took place just two weeks after Felix's divorce from Sharon Mann was finalised. 'Irreconcilable differences' were cited in the couple's uncontested divorce, which was filed with the Superior Court of California, County of Alameda, on 8 December 1981.

After three years of heated negotiations with his wife of twenty years, Felix finally agreed to the terms of the marital settlement agreement, which provided Sharon with $2,500 a month and ownership of the couple's Berkeley home. Felix also agreed to pay the college tuition for his son, Andrew, who was a sophomore at Tufts University in Massachusetts, and to share custody of the couple's then sixteen-year-old daughter, Jennifer.

Susan and Felix exchanged vows at the Berkeley City Club on Channing Street on 26 December 1981. The elegant, buttercup-yellow mansion had vaulted ceilings, ornate mouldings, and sweeping views of the university. It had recently been granted landmark status. While architect Julia Morgan, designer of the Hearst Castle in San Simeon, had built the elegant structure in 1929 for the Berkeley City Women's Club, in recent years it was used as a catering hall.

Family members from both sides waited in the expansive dining room, with its limestone walls and palladium windows. Though several of Felix's colleagues were in attendance, Susan had invited just one guest, Brenda, her roommate from San Francisco State. Brenda had never frowned upon the relationship with Felix, not even when Susan felt embarrassed by his age.

Susan liked that Brenda never passed judgment on her, but as she pulled on her wedding dress, a simple, short-sleeved gown, a terrifying thought came to her. She didn't want to get married – at least not to Felix.

Suddenly, she felt lightheaded.

Susan had given her word to the waiting groom, who was downstairs dressed in a cocoa-coloured suit and tie and surrounded by guests. She couldn't go back on it now. That is not how she was raised; honouring a promise was the proper thing to do. As much as she wanted to disappear, Susan didn't have the courage to become a runaway bride.

That evening, as she stood compliantly next to Felix, delicate and waif-like in a lacey, white dress, a wreath of baby's breath in her hair, Susan consoled herself.

I'm young enough, she thought. I've got plenty of years left.

CHAPTER NINE

THE HONEYMOON ENDS

From the start, trouble was brewing in the Polk household. Soon after their three-week honeymoon in Europe, Felix promptly laid down the law about 'his' household.

They were home only a few days when he stormed into the room and began berating his new bride, calling her a 'pig' and a 'slob'.

'Let me tell you how I expect my house to be kept,' he yelled until he was red-faced, before firing off a list of things he wanted done.

Susan was stunned at how her new husband was 'so transformed and abrupt.' Horrified by how he was treating her, her first reaction was to leave. But as Susan went for the door, Felix stopped her, grabbing her roughly and throwing her to the floor.

According to Susan, he raped her that day.

As she sat on the floor trembling, she thought again about leaving him, but the harsh reality of her situation hit home: she could never try to leave again. With a single act, he had crushed her spirit, which had just begun to blossom. After years of wrestling with her father's abandonment and mother's criticism, now Susan had an entirely new trauma to contend with – her husband. The rape that day set the tone for their marriage. The power and control that Felix wielded would only increase, and his role as the dominant force in her life would shape her character for many years.

In the weeks and months that followed, Susan recalled waking in the middle of the night, petrified with fear. Her terror was palpable, yet she couldn't put her finger on what exactly made her so scared. It wasn't until her husband started to lecture out of town and travel unaccompanied to the East Coast to visit family that she noticed how her feelings changed in his absence. During these times, the weight she felt in her chest abruptly disappeared, only to return quickly when Felix came home. He was completely controlling about everything, from how she did the dishes to what time the meals would be served. Every time Susan endeavoured to do anything as an individual, Felix would squash her efforts.

Part of the problem was that when he wasn't travelling, Felix was always around. While he worked most days from seven in the morning until ten in the evening, he would come out between patients to see what his new wife was doing or where she was going. To conserve money, he moved his office into the couple's home shortly after their wedding. Although he worked seventy hours a week for $50 an hour, Felix was $40,000 in debt. According to court documents, he and Susan borrowed $60,000 from Susan's mother, Helen, for a down payment on their new Berkeley residence, but used some of the loan to fund their lengthy European trip.

News of the extended honeymoon infuriated Felix's first wife, Sharon Mann. That Felix would embark on such an extravagant vacation, and then return home and claim he had no money to pay her, was stunning. Barely four months had passed since he signed the divorce agreement, but he was already incapable of maintaining his parental duties. Sharon's outrage continued to fester when she received a handwritten letter from Felix in April of 1982 outlining his financial burden and insisting they renegotiate the terms of the divorce signed in December of 1981.

The never-before published letter, dated 20 April 1982, became part of their official divorce record:

Dear Sharon,
It is hard for me to write this letter to you but there is no choice left for me ... I can no longer afford to send you the monthly

amounts that I have given you . . . our divorce agreement needs to be altered . . .

The divorce degree [sic] was held up so long and was issued so close to my wedding date that I signed it with great relief and without really reading all the fine print . . .

The reasons . . . are as follows:

1) Each month I borrow at least $1500 in order to meet obligations here and to you. Now, I am borrowed out. I have no savings, no credit left to borrow, nothing to sell other than the cellow [sic] which, if sold, will provide money for the kids education. I bounce cheques not only to you but to the man from whom I bought this house and to others.

2) I work to the point of exhaustion and fear that at the present rate I will in short order become useless to all; patients, children and you . . .

3) Susan worked for me half time so that I can see more patients. The money she earns constitutes our upkeep. She will, in addition, now have to take a half time job.

4) Our life style is lean. The trip to Europe was taken on borrowed money and saved my ass from collapse.

5) As we can no longer afford to support the house in Piedmont, it has been put on the market for sale as soon as possible.

6) As I can no longer afford the payments on my office we are looking for a house which will not only be more modest but will also serve as my office.

7) As I cannot continue (survive) at my present work pace, I have to cut down my work hours to human proportions.

I am aware that I have kept these things from you for a long time . . . I did want you to be able to complete your training at Northwestern without feeling under stress . . . I need to take care of myself first so that I can take care of all those, including you, who depend on me . . .

Felix

It is possible Felix was passively retaliating for what he later termed Sharon's 'manipulative' behaviour throughout their relationship. 'I promised myself many years ago that I would never allow myself to be 'had' by her as was true in the past, and I intend to keep that promise,' he once wrote of Sharon Mann in a letter to his daughter, Jennifer. Quite possibly, it was Sharon's controlling behaviour that had first attracted Felix to the pretty brunette. Perhaps he needed someone to take control, or perhaps, her strong personality was familiar to him. After all, his mother had ruled the household and protected her children during wartime.

Despite Felix's disdain for his ex-wife, Sharon was not about to agree to a reduction in her support payments – not after she'd spent three long years fighting over the terms of the divorce. She had enjoyed a certain financial status during their marriage; she had worked to put Felix through graduate school and had raised their two children. As far as Sharon was concerned, there was no reason to agree to his demands.

On 25 May 1982, Sharon filed a complaint with the Superior Court of the State of California, detailing Felix's failure to fulfill their financial agreement and disclosing the contents of his letter in which he insisted the settlement needed to be altered. The complaint would be the first of many that Sharon would file. Nevertheless Sharon's repeated requests to the court for assistance were ignored. In a personal statement to the court, written in April of 1983, she detailed how Felix's pleas of poverty, and the court's indulgence, had drastically affected her lifestyle.

'When my 23-year-marriage ended, I sought legal counsel and came away with certain assumptions: after a lengthy marriage in a comfortable financial bracket, it was assumed I would retain my station; I would be awarded the family home and have adequate support and protection into my old age; I would have enough financial peace of mind to pursue a doctorate and reconstruct an interrupted professional life,' Sharon wrote. 'Within 16 months, support would be reduced three times, I would be living at an income level 18% of my former life, forced to sell my settlement property and a court of law would rule that a portion of the proceeds of that house sale be consigned to generate income.

'In the first of four court appearances, I was awarded the family home as settlement in the division of assets and a monthly income of $2500. Support was reduced within 6 months to $2150 and I was unable to keep up the house payments of $1425.

'I was forced to sell the family home . . .

'I considered buying another house, a small one, and paying for it in full. But my situation seemed too perilous to put all my assets into the comfort of walls. I began to consider it of utmost importance to provide for myself after age 65,' she concluded.

For nearly two decades, Sharon Mann had enjoyed a comfortable lifestyle. Now, in her mid-forties, Sharon was almost destitute and worrying about a future she once believed was secure.

Meanwhile, her fifty-year-old ex-husband was starting a whole new life with a woman half his age.

Susan and Felix had been married for two years when their first child, Adam Eric Polk, was born on 3 January 1983. The delivery was difficult for Susan.

In a letter to Adam in June of 2002, Susan explained that she had planned to experience natural childbirth, going so far as to read books, attend classes, and hire a midwife in preparation for his arrival. Everything was moving along smoothly until the last month of the pregnancy when she was told the baby was in the breach position. Things worsened when her water broke three weeks before her due date. She was having no contractions, and doctors were facing the prospect of a risky, dry breach birth.

According to Susan, the doctors decided to proceed with the delivery. All they needed was her signature on a consent form. 'I asked a few questions, creating complications,' Susan wrote in the letter:

> They were eager to try out this natural delivery. I was being a problem. Then something welled up inside of me, it was a colossal no. I said, 'Why am I not having a C-section? Why am I not having it now? The longer we wait, the greater the danger of infection to my baby, right? Didn't you just tell me that? What are we waiting for? I want a C-section, and I want it now!' . . . Afterwards the doctors were angry at me. They were annoyed by my willfulness. I was there for a few days. The

nurses were running off with you against my instructions to the incubators where they stuck enormous needles, IVs, in your little hand. I hobbled after you with my cart containing my IVs, ticking off the nurses. You developed asthma in the incubators, possibly a drug reaction.

The doctors blamed it on your premature birth.

It is clear from Susan's writing that she felt a need to control her world – a symptom often seen in people whose lives are out of control. This was her child, and she wanted to make sure that he was okay.

More than two years later on 2 June 1985, Susan gave birth to Eli, while Gabriel arrived on 10 January 1987. Though Susan was a stay-at-home mom who felt comfortable with her boys, she and Felix enrolled Adam in day care shortly after Gabriel was born. It seemed the right time for Adam to get out and enjoy the company of children his age, so the couple placed him in a private day care programme in the home of an upper-middle-class family. There was only one other child in the programme, the caretaker's own child, who was anxious for a companion.

After a diligent check of references, Adam attended the programme about eighteen hours per week, in six-hour intervals. One morning, while standing in the kitchen getting ready for breakfast, Adam told his mother he didn't want to go to 'school' that day.

'Why don't you want to go to school today?' Susan reportedly asked him.

'I don't know, I'm tired,' Adam told her, playfully pulling open a drawer in the kitchen.

Adam said that his mother asked if anybody at the preschool had 'touched' him.

He simply said, 'Yeah, that's it.'

Then only four and still in diapers, he later claimed he was not even aware of what it was she was asking him. But his response set off a chain reaction that landed Adam in therapy. According to Adam's sworn testimony, his desire to stay home from day care that morning led to his mother's belief that he had been sexually abused there. The Polks took Adam to see a therapist who reportedly confirmed that the youngster had been the victim of ritualistic sexual abuse during his four months at the day care programme.

The unfortunate reality was that the fears that the Polks were experiencing were nothing new. At that time, allegations of ritualistic sexual abuse of children were making headlines. Newspapers in California were reporting charges of sexual abuse at a preschool in Manhattan Beach. The mother of a male student there had complained to police that a part-time aide at the McMartin Preschool had molested her son. Police found no physical evidence to support the claim, and the district attorney declined to prosecute. However, the allegations sparked a panic in the community when the chief of the Manhattan Beach Police Department circulated a confidential letter to parents whose children had attended the preschool. The letter speculated that the part-time aide, the son of the school's owner, might have forced students 'to engage in oral sex, fondling of genitals, buttocks or chest area and sodomy'. and it urged parents to question their children. The letter included no proper way to do this, and interviewing techniques employed by parents and local therapists led to hundreds of false complaints.

A local TV station took the story one step further, proposing that the preschool might be linked to child porn rings in nearby Los Angeles. Only later did it surface that the mother of the alleged victim was an alleged alcoholic and had been diagnosed as a paranoid schizophrenic.

During that same period, allegations of ritualistic abuse were lodged against employees of the Presidio Child Development Center, a day care centre run by the US Army in San Francisco. Parents charged that a satanic cult was operating out of the centre and systematically victimising the young student body. Reports that children had been transported to private homes, where they were forced to engage in satanic and sadistic sexual acts, led to a police investigation.

With these allegations rampant, Susan and Felix began to subscribe to the hysteria, believing the worst about the people who cared for Adam. Felix, perhaps because of his personal and professional backgrounds, was acutely vulnerable to the spreading paranoia. Taking matters into his own hands, Felix authored a report entitled *Reflections on Psychology*, describing these cults as 'very sophisticated' and claiming that 'some were set up by the CIA as a way to learn/teach mind control.' In Adam's case, Felix alleged that the perpetrators were 'homosexual cultists' who had 'sodomised and filmed' the boy during his hours in day care.

Using the paper as a catalyst, he took his views to the Fourth Annual Two-Day Conference of the California Consortium of Child Abuse Counsels in Berkeley in 1988, where he outlined the alleged abuse. Felix was one of two speakers to address the audience that day. The first was a woman who claimed to have been a survivor of ritualistic child abuse at the hands of cultists, some of whom she described as family members. Interestingly, she was also a patient of Dr. Polk's who was treating her for the trauma.

Felix asked that he be introduced not as a therapist but as a 'parent of a ritualistically abused child'. although he provided the audience with an overview of his credentials during the twenty-five minute address. Displaying a piece of paper he held in his hand, Felix explained that he was going to read aloud a letter that his not-quite five-year-old son had written to the governor of California.

'I want you to get the bad people because I hate them,' Felix began in a deliberate monotone. 'I want to punch them and my daddy wants to punch them . . . And my mommy can bite them, and that's all she can do . . . And my brother Eli can throw a truck at them.'

To shock the audience, he detailed the abuse his son had allegedly suffered during his time at the day care centre. 'He was taken from the house in what he called a school bus,' he recited. 'Other children were picked up along the way.' They were taken to what 'sounds like a warehouse, with a cement floor . . . It had cages, and a stage, people dressed in red triangular masks, professional cameras like on TV sets. There were performers. He and other children were raped on stage in every form. Children were killed.'

Felix said that Adam's most troubling recollection was that of a 'baby put in a plastic bag and hammered to death.'

According to Felix, the youngster also claimed to have witnessed 'other ceremonies' in which adults and children drank blood and urine and ate faeces and a 'bloody substance' that he believed was flesh from bowls. Some of the children were black, and others might have been mentally retarded, he contended.

He next insisted that his young son 'is now a multiple personality' with three clear identities: 'a girl because he was professionally made up and raped on stage; a killer because he has the eyes of a killer because he was looked at by people who were killers and he has their glance; and he's himself . . . a wonderful little boy.'

The statements were remarkable – and outrageously unbelievable. Perhaps Felix was trying to 'right' his own childhood trauma when he took up Adam's alleged cause. It is possible that Susan had made up the elaborate tales of abuse or that she simply borrowed them from the headlines and 'transferred' them onto her young son. As a Holocaust survivor with his own mental issues, it may be that Felix indulged in a 'shared delusion' with his wife. Perhaps his crusade to 'get the bad people' was a way to right what had been so wrong when he was a small boy. It is not impossible that Felix Polk truly believed that something bad had happened to his son. After all, he purportedly witnessed men in black helmets wearing swastikas systematically round up men, women, and children for extermination. In Felix's mind, the two incidents may have been fused; his own childhood trauma and the one he believed happened to his son. Indeed, he spoke of his family's ordeal at the hands of the Nazis during his presentation in Berkeley.

'I am an older father,' he told those attending the workshop that day. 'I am a survivor of the Holocaust. My family and I were in hiding in Europe unable to talk for one year. I have a built-in sense of survival. I have a commitment to not let anything happen to my children. It was a horror what happened to us.'

It was after this recollection that Felix vowed to keep up the fight on his son's behalf. 'I've alienated some people, some police and FBI. But I don't care . . . My rage is omnipresent. I wake up with it every morning. My fantasy, of course, is to kill them,' he said of his son's alleged abusers. 'I am a rather moral person. But I won't stop, not now. People are not in a place to protect our children,' Felix asserted. 'My son cannot be protected.'

The supposed inability of authorities to prosecute those allegedly responsible for harming his son prompted Felix and Susan to establish a new organization, 'ENOUGH!' to help victims of ritualistic and other forms of child abuse. Its main goal was to change legislation so that children could testify against their alleged attackers in a public court of law.

While Felix denied charges from some in the psychological community that he was using his son as a way to gain publicity for his practice, his behaviour with Adam was certainly not that of a trained therapist. He clearly exhibited poor judgment when he paraded the youngster before an audience during one presentation and detailed the abuse he supposedly suffered while in day care. Even Felix's daughter from his first marriage had raised questions about her father's conduct and motives in a letter to him in early 1988. Though the twenty-six-year-old Jennifer Polk had recently joined her father and his new family on a vacation in Hawaii, in the letter she made it clear that she was now estranged from her dad, expressing her frustration that during the trip she was unable to live up to either her father's expectations or Susan's. She expressed distaste for Felix's crusade in Adam's name and accused her father of always needing a cause to cling onto.

Her accusation evoked a response from Felix, who responded venomously in a return letter: 'It is a lie that I need to hang onto a cause, that I need something to be upset about,' Felix replied in a four-page typewritten response on 4 March 1988. 'However, I note that is true of you . . . Your latest cause to refer to Adam enrages me,' he continued. 'I want to shove those words down your throat. My son Adam was brutalised, and I, his father, have not been able to protect him or see that something happens to the people that raped him.'

Felix's response was ironic and telling. Was he really disappointed in Jennifer's comments or in himself for what he perceived as another 'failure' to protect a loved one from harm? Now he was facing the prospect that he delivered his son to a cult, proving once again that he was unable to protect his charge from evildoers. Worse yet, his own daughter was condemning him for trumping up false accusations in order to satisfy a need to be needed.

In the letter, Felix denied being judgmental of his daughter, yet went on to voice disapproval of Jennifer's recent weight gain and assertive behaviour, which he described as 'lacking femininity'.

'It is a lie that I have not recognised your changes or that I haven't liked them,' he wrote. 'It is true that I haven't liked some of them such as your putting on tons of weight, your increased rigidity and pseudo-feminism.'

Was he now projecting his negative feelings about his own mother, whom he once described as the 'power' in the family, onto his daughter? Or did Jennifer represent someone else? Jennifer Polk had just turned sixteen when Felix and Sharon legally separated in October of 1978. Perhaps Felix was not leaving Sharon when he left the couple's comfortable Berkeley home that year, but the temptation of his pretty teenage daughter.

Notably, it was around the time that Jennifer was maturing that Felix began his affair with young Susan.

'I have examined by looking inside myself and by talking with others what the basis may be for my reaction to your irresponsible and hurtful behaviour,' Felix wrote in a second letter to Jennifer in March of 1988:

> What I will take responsibility for is that I have a particularly strong sensitivity to loss, to having somebody I love dearly taken away from me . . .
>
> You have ripped yourself away from me, and to me that feels like a deep and familiar loss . . . I tried to meet your needs in growing up . . . while I well may have been overly protective of you at times (to balance out your attacking and critical mother) . . . You need to work on the tendency to project and to have good and bad people in your life.
>
> Mom [Sharon Mann] is in now, and I am out.

Interestingly, the theme of 'good parent', 'bad parent' would reemerge in Felix's second marriage to Susan Bolling.

CHAPTER TEN

THE MIDDLE CHILD

In the days following the discovery of Felix's bloodied body, it became clear to investigators that the victim's sons were divided. While Gabriel and Adam believed that their mother was 'delusional' and capable of committing the murder, the Polk's middle son, Eli, described Susan as a woman who tried to hold her family together while living with an 'abusive' husband.

On 15 October 2002, the day after Gabriel Polk found his father's body in the guesthouse, detectives from the Contra Costa Sheriff's department interviewed Eli at the Byron Boys' Ranch. At over six feet tall, Eli towered over the officers as he followed the men to a small, private office to talk. It was unclear to the detectives whether family members had contacted Eli about his father, and Detective Steve Warne thought that he might be the first to deliver the sad news.

Taking a seat across from the strapping teen, Detective Warne motioned his colleague, Roxanne Gruenheid, to join him behind the desk. He observed that Eli's physical stature and crew cut made him appear older than he really was. Warne was anxious to see the teen's reaction to news of his father's murder.

It was soon apparent that Eli had no idea what had transpired at the Miner Road compound that past weekend. He was 'appropriately shocked' and 'upset' as he struggled to come to grips with the news, Detective Warne wrote in his official report.

'It's definitely not my mom,' Eli insisted. 'She would just never do it. That's not even a remote possibility. My mom did not do it. That's a fact.'

Though Eli tried to answer the detectives' questions, it was clear he was in shock.

His troubled world suddenly collapsed around him. Away from home for just two weeks, now his father was dead and his mother was in jail charged with Felix's murder. It seemed his parents had gone berserk without him there to keep the peace.

After several minutes of conversation, Eli suddenly halted the interview. 'I don't want to talk to you anymore,' he announced. Rising to his feet, he left the room. The officers made no effort to stop him, giving the teen a chance to pull himself together. Five minutes later, he reappeared in the doorway and slid back into his seat across the table. He was visibly upset but agreed to cooperate as best he could.

In response to questions, Eli told the officers he had been at the Boys' Ranch for only twelve days, since 3 October 2002, when a judge sentenced him to juvenile hall. He was allowed limited contact with his family – weekend visits and five-minute phone calls. His father had visited him on Sunday, 6 October and Susan had been to see him on 13 October, while his father and brothers were driving to Los Angeles.

During her visit, Susan told Eli that his father was staying at a hotel while she was in town visiting from Montana for a few days. He didn't know which hotel, only that his father was there because his parents were in the process of getting a divorce. Eli believed that Susan was in Montana looking at homes to buy and that she returned to deal with her financial affairs, mostly a 'debate' with his father over 'cheques' and a court date that she missed. His parents had begun having problems the previous September, causing Felix to move to Berkeley. At the time, Susan said the marriage 'was not working out'. She had given the house back to Felix then set out for Montana to find a place to relocate.

When asked if he could provide any information as to who might be responsible for his father's death, Eli pointed to one of his father's longtime patients, a man named Tom Pyne. 'My dad had people, patients, who hated him,' Eli added, claiming some were 'disturbed' and 'wielded razor blades and hammers' when they came for therapy. Detective Gruenheid jotted the name 'Tom Pyne' on a notepad, noting that she would check it out later.

When asked about a court proceeding the previous month in which his mother had been arrested for contempt, Eli said the hearing revolved around a violation of a 'time out' while he was on electronic home detention for a probation violation. He was charged with 'felony assault with a deadly weapon' in February of 2002 for striking a teenage boy in the face with a mini-torch in the parking lot of a fast-food restaurant. At the hearing in California Superior Court, he told Judge William Kolin that he had gone to the Jack in the Box that night to 'get a look' at the boys who had jumped his friend and stolen the boy's marijuana. Things got out of hand when the alleged victim and about twenty of his friends came after him. Eli unsuccessfully argued that he was only defending himself when he struck the teen in the face, breaking his nose and causing facial lacerations that required stitches.

Susan was uncooperative when officers came to the Miner Road house and presented her with a search warrant they had obtained after the assault. She refused to put the family dogs away and then blocked the officers from going upstairs to search for evidence that might tie Eli to the assault. Her difficult behaviour continued when she would not tell them where the laundry room was located, since it was there that investigators believed they would find the garments Eli was wearing at the time of the assault.

Susan's repeated attempts to prevent the officers from carrying out their search landed her in handcuffs, and Eli was temporarily placed in the custody of Felix, who at the time was living in the apartment at the couple's Berkeley property on Arch Street.

In April 2002, Eli was ordered to meet with officers from the county probation department to determine an appropriate punishment. A confidential report to the court noted that Eli had adjusted well to juvenile hall. Yet when placed in his father's custody on Juvenile Electronic Monitoring, he had violations for being 'out of range' and 'not complying with reporting on time to home supervision.'

Shortly after he was released into his father's custody, Eli violated the court order by removing the ankle monitor at Susan's urging. He subsequently disappeared, and Susan assumed full blame for her son's actions. In a letter to Superior Court Judge William Kolin, she begged for leniency, but she refused to apologise for convincing her son to break the rules.

'I have nothing to put forth in my defence other than I felt Judge Kolin's order served to provide my husband with custody and to divide our family, I mean me and my children,' Susan wrote in the four-page handwritten note to the Superior Court judge. 'I do not consider Felix to be a member of my family, nor myself a member of his.

'I do feel responsible for Eli's violation of probation,' she continued. 'I worked hard to persuade him to do so. He was obeying his mother.'

Susan alleged that she had convinced her son to 'hide' with her in Orinda for the summer. Her letter did little to change the judge's opinion. To the contrary, Susan infuriated Judge Kolin with her defiant behaviour at the disposition hearing, where the judge sentenced Eli for two counts of felony assault. Her outburst, and her refusal to remain in the courtroom until the hearing was over, promptly landed her in jail, but not before she was handcuffed and dragged away.

Judge Kolin called a break. When the family returned for the afternoon session, Felix Polk asked to address the court.

'Thank you,' Felix said, rising from his chair. 'My son Eli will have a problem with some of this. My perspective is the truth, over the four years we lived in an environment of paranoia at home.'

'With mother?' the judge asked.

'Yes, and she in so many ways is wonderful, and that's also true. It's just the way it is. The kids have all been affected by that. The kids, Eli maybe especially, is loyal and protective of his mother, which is one of the things that you just saw represented. My youngest son, Gabriel, is also like that. They both protect her, and they love her and protect her. So there's been a lot of stress in the family,' Felix continued.

'My son Eli has great values. He's a good kid and has, like the rest of us, been affected by that. Each of the three boys have [sic] been affected in that way. Eli is. And so that's just a background to the kind of behaviour I think, from my perspective, in terms of what Eli needs.

'Ideally, he would get counselling. He is in counselling right now. He needs more of that. And ideally, his mother and I both should be involved in that as well,' Felix said. 'And he acts out when he just has had it. It's too much stress for him. It's been going on for four years.

That's a long time. All of this has been a long time. So I respectfully request that that be a consideration in his disposition.'

Susan was certain that Felix pulled strings to get Eli sentenced to the Boys' Ranch. She felt he was hard on their middle son; however, a review of the official court record indicated that Judge Kolin simply followed the recommendations of the probation report when he sentenced Eli to time at Byron.

'Will I be able to attend my father's funeral?' Eli asked Detective Gruenheid.

'You'll have to work that out with the staff at Byron,' one of the officers replied. The detectives pressed on with the interview. 'What about previous domestic violence in the house?' Gruenheid asked.

'There have been a couple of physical altercations,' Eli replied. He described them as 'mutual combat',' claiming that both parents had been responsible for instigating the fights and recalling one argument in which his mother was actually arrested. Eli told the detectives that he hadn't seen what transpired during that fight. A subsequent check of the police report indicated that, in fact, he was witness to the incident, labeling his mother as 'the aggressor' at the time of the arrest.

'My mom did not murder my dad,' Eli told the officers. 'It's very important that you know that my mom is a very mellow person. She wouldn't do it. She would just never do it, that's a fact.'

Eli's willingness to cooperate ended when the female detective pushed him to respond to a question that might portray his mother in a bad light.

'I don't feel right answering any more of these questions,' he asserted. 'I would never do anything to put my mom in jail and that is where this is leading.'

Springing from his chair, Eli terminated the interview for the second, and final, time. 'I think it's rude and extremely stressful,' he mumbled under his breath as he exited the room and returned to his dorm at the Boys' Ranch.

Later, officials at the juvenile hall told Detectives Warne and Gruenheid that Eli had asked to call his mother in Montana on 10 October. Eli's probation officer at the facility said he was nearby when Eli placed the call. After ten minutes, the officer asked Eli if he could speak with Susan.

Taking the receiver, he introduced himself as Eli's probation officer and asked if she had any questions regarding her son's program at the ranch.

'No,' Susan replied, and hung up on him.

PART 11

THE INVESTIGATION BEGINS

CHAPTER ELEVEN
THE CHILDREN UNRAVEL

Susan's hands-off parenting style had long been a point of contention with Felix. Whenever there was a problem with one of the boys, Felix was quick to blame Susan, charging either that she was too lenient or that the children were taking after her side of the family. After all, he said, she was the one who dropped out of school in the ninth grade, and it was her household that had been dysfunctional, a comparison that Susan deeply resented. She was upset that Felix would dredge up things she had confided during their therapy sessions at his Berkeley office.

In truth, Susan prided herself on giving the boys space and allowing them their independence. While other mothers were congratulating themselves on how 'obedient' their children were, Susan was chuckling at her sons' displays of strong will. She believed in free will and self-determination and hoped that by giving her children room, they would find that on their own. She wanted her boys to think things over for themselves, and unlike other mothers, she didn't want to tell them what to do. To Susan, so much control could only lead to 'a society of storm troopers or Spartans.' She was about self-expression. The idea of controlling her children went against all that she believed and all that she experienced under the tyrannical Felix Polk.

There was another reason, too. She didn't want to be like Felix's mother – completely controlling about everything. According to Susan, Johanna 'Joan' Polk was a micromanager, and Susan resented her intrusiveness. Johanna's approach was quite different from the hands-off style Susan had known with her mother. During her visits to Susan and Felix's house, Johanna was compelled to comment on things big and small, even on the way Susan washed the dishes. Although he resented his mother's overbearing nature as a child, now Felix saw no problem with her behaviour, hoping that her presence would influence Susan's parenting. He made no secret of his disapproval of Susan's skills, constantly insisting that she needed 'to train the kids'.

Susan never liked the sound of it. Training was something people did with animals, not people. Nevertheless, the lack of structure and rules in the household continued to be an issue for the family, and Felix was not the only family member to take issue with Susan's parenting. Adam had problems with her child-rearing abilities as well, going so far as to accuse his mother of fostering a pattern of antisocial behaviour by allowing his younger siblings to blame their troubles on others instead of demanding they take responsibility for their part. In a letter to the court dated 10 September 2004, Adam noted that, when called up to school to deal with misconduct on the part of Gabe or Eli, Susan defended her sons – pointing a finger at administrators for their failure to carry out their duties properly. When the boys were arrested for various infractions, she accused the other party or police of 'inappropriate' treatment of her and her sons.

The letter went on to point out that, as far as Susan was concerned, it was not her children's fault when things went awry. When Eli was caught with marijuana, it was only because he was 'holding it' for someone else. When he struck a schoolmate with a torch, breaking his nose and causing a great deal of bleeding and facial cuts, Susan claimed Eli didn't even have a torch in his possession that night.

The information in the letter was tough medicine, but it contained a number of legitimate complaints. Yet it failed to address other crucial problems, such as Susan's distaste for authority. Indeed, her openly hostile treatment of authority complicated matters for her and her sons during difficult situations with the police or probation officers.

Though she would later deny it, Felix claimed Susan cursed out the principal of Gabriel's middle school, telling him to 'go fuck himself'. She also penned an angry letter to the chief of the Moraga Police Department, complaining about officers who executed a search warrant in February 2002 to collect potential evidence in an assault case against Eli.

In that instance, Susan was furious that officers accused her of interfering. 'Officer Harbison announced that I was obstructing the search, twisted my arm painfully behind my back, placed handcuffs on me,' she wrote. 'Sergeant Price then led me downstairs and told me to sit down. I was not violent, threatening or getting in the way of the search.'

While Felix and Adam viewed Susan's parenting and problems with authority as having a negative impact on the family, Susan had her own issues with Felix's fatherly skills. She detested Felix's need to single out one son as the 'golden' boy, much like his own father had done with his twin brother, John. She observed that in his first marriage, Felix had lavished praise on his firstborn son, Andrew, while his daughter Jennifer received the criticism. Now in his second marriage, the pattern was repeating itself as Felix tended to favour their eldest son, Adam, while being outwardly critical of Eli and simply forgetting Gabriel. In many ways, Adam was more akin to Felix's twin brother, John. He was smart and athletic, and things came naturally to him – qualities that Felix envied.

In a letter to Eli, Susan confided that Felix's need to pick one of his children to be an example for the rest of the family members

is a way of maintaining control over the family members. When Dad went to graduate school in England, he studied under a psychiatrist, R. D. Laing, who wrote a book about how 'crazy making' families do this: they pick one of their children to be an example for the rest of the family members, to express for the family what they are afraid of, what could happen to them. . . . The 'example nigger' also expresses for the leader of the family . . . characteristics in his own nature that are not tolerable: for example violence, suicide, impulsivity, feelings of failure, craziness, homosexuality, whatever it is the leader is anxious about or driven by. In a sense, this child is selected as a sacrifice.

Of the three Polk boys, Susan viewed Eli as the most sensitive and emotional. In his teens, Eli displayed anxiety and separation issues similar to those Felix battled as a young man. In a diary, Susan noted that her middle son found it difficult to be apart from his dad. During grammar school, Eli had come home early from a hockey camp in Canada, and on a trip to Paris with Susan in 2001, he became so anxious he boarded a plane for home after just three days abroad. To Susan, it was clear that Eli's issues were directly connected to his father's poor treatment of him.

'You have systematically treated Eli as if he had something wrong with him, just as you did Jennifer in your first family,' Susan wrote of Felix in her computer diary. 'You seem to have a need to scapegoat somebody.

'According to you, Sharon was to blame for Jennifer's poor self-esteem. You forget that while Jennifer lived with us, I had time to observe how you treated her. Consistently, you behaved as if her intelligence was subnormal, when in fact it appeared to me there was nothing at all the matter with her except for her poor self-esteem . . . I can't pretend to understand this family dynamic: how a family selects a child for success (in your first family, it was Andy, in ours, Adam), and a sibling or siblings for failure . . . It has broken my heart, and I can no longer live with your sadistic parenting.'

In addition to his favouritism toward Adam, Felix, like Susan, suffered from an inability to properly discipline and control the boys. Such was the case on the night of 25 May 2001, when police were called to investigate a 'rowdy' party at the Miner Road compound where underage drinking was supposedly occurring. Responding officers found more than twenty-five underage partygoers around the pool, and Felix was the adult in charge. 'Throughout the area, I saw empty cans of Budweiser and Coors Light, cans of Budweiser beer full or partially full and still cold, unopened cans of beer still cold, a glass filled with an alcoholic beverage resembling red wine, and a half-full bottle of Smirnoff Vodka,' Officer K. Mooney of the Orinda Police Department documented in the official report.

Officer Mooney was familiar with the location, having been summoned to the residence numerous times for loud, juvenile parties. 'All of the alcoholic beverage containers were located in and around groups of persons who I separately identified as being in age from 16 to 18.'

Mooney noted that Frank [Felix] Polk, was in the kitchen, which overlooked the pool and the pool house, when he and his partner arrived at 10.20 that night. 'Both the alcoholic beverages and the large group of juveniles were in plain view,' Mooney wrote. 'Shortly after my arrival, Frank came outside, and asked what I was doing on his property. I told him that we had a complaint of a loud party. Frank said that it was just a graduation party and that it wasn't loud.

'I told Frank that there were minors on his property while alcoholic beverages were being consumed and reminded him of my previous warning on 5/5/01. Frank replied that it was a graduation party.

'Frank's son, Adam, approached as I was speaking with Frank. Adam told me that he was 18 years old and that it was his party and that he was responsible for the party.'

It was then that the officers placed Felix and his son under arrest and charged them with 'contributing to the delinquency of a minor' and 'unlawful juvenile gathering on private property'. Though both men were later released at the scene and got off with mere citations, the episode was a disturbing example of Felix's double standards. This hypocrisy would only worsen over the course of the next year; the Orinda police were regularly summoned to the Polk house in response to complaints of loud parties with underage drinking and fistfights. During one such call, in May of 2002, police arrived to find nearly one hundred teens, the majority of them minors, holding red plastic cups filled with beer. While there, a fight erupted in the crowd near the guesthouse and officers worked to break it up. Police found Felix Polk at home and admonished him for allowing alcohol to be served to minors.

Despite his claims of Susan's negligence when it came to disciplining the boys, it became increasingly clear that Felix suffered from a similar inability to set boundaries for their teenage sons. While he would routinely belittle Susan's ability to parent her children, his own attitudes proved just as dangerously nonchalant. Furthermore by allowing these unsupervised parties, he risked not just the well-being of his sons but of other teens as well.

In the days after Susan's arrest, the questionable parenting of both Felix and Susan was examined as police reviewed their files and learned a lot more about this dysfunctional family. Officers were summoned to the Polk house frequently to deal with situations involving Adam, Eli, or Gabriel. Indeed, problems of one sort or another with the Polk family went way back – particularly with regard to Eli who had been in and out of trouble since 1998, when he and several friends allegedly entered another schoolmate's house without permission and stole one hundred fifty dollars worth of alcohol. He was twelve at the time.

The following January, Eli was stopped for driving without a licence. The officer who flashed him over intended to cite him for a broken headlight until he discovered the driver was just thirteen years old – far too young for even a learner's permit.

Even worse, he had three female passengers in the car with him.

Susan and Felix took custody of Eli and his three young passengers, and Eli was fined one hundred twenty-five dollars for the violation.

In addition to his recklessness, Eli also displayed severe problems with aggression and harassment. It was no secret that he loved to fight, but he ran into problems when he brought this inclination to school with him. In April of 2000, he was expelled from Piedmont High School for harassing a classmate, calling the teen a 'fucking fag', and speaking derogatorily about homosexuals. He further inflamed the situation by yelling back 'I say we kill all homosexuals' as he was ordered from his fourth-period classroom and directed to the principal's office. Eli was ultimately suspended for his comments and for passing a note that read 'u r gay' to the classmate. In addition, his teenage victim filed a police report alleging that Eli was so threatening, he 'feared for his life'.

Unfortunately, Eli was not the only son with a tendency towards violence. In April of 1998, Adam was accused of battery for allegedly punching a classmate of Eli's in the face at a middle-school dance. At the time, he was attending De La Salle High School, a Catholic all-boys school in Concord. Adam told officers who came to the family's Piedmont home to investigate that he was simply 'preventing Eli from getting a beating'. Adam claimed he went to the school that night to make sure Eli was 'protected', after hearing rumours that the kid had threatened to 'jump' his brother and carried a knife. According to Adam, he approached the teen, who was standing with friends in the schoolyard, and asked if he was 'talking' about Eli. Words were exchanged and, at one point, Adam hauled off and punched the kid in the nose, fleeing the school grounds in the aftermath.

Not surprisingly, the victim's recollection of the night's events differed significantly from Adam's. In the ensuing police report, the boy said Adam punched him twice, once in the nose and once on the cheek, while he was outside on the street in front of the school waiting for his father to pick him up that night. He didn't even know who Adam was when he walked up and announced that Eli said the kid had been 'talking about him [Adam]'.

'If I were to punch you, would you block it?' Adam reportedly asked the teen.

'No, I don't want to start nothing,' the boy replied.

The victim claimed that Adam hit him in the face two times without provocation, and then walked away. When it was all over, Adam was issued a ticket and released to the custody of his mother. He was also ordered to receive counselling from a member of the Contra Costa Sheriff's Office on the dangers of taking situations into his own hands, agreeing that in the future he would call police for help.

In the summer of 2002, people attending a party at a nearby home in Alamo charged that Adam stole silver dishes and a Sony Play Station, worth in excess of five hundred dollars. Officers were dispatched to the Miner Road house to interview Adam but learned that he had already left for UCLA. Gabriel answered the door that day and insisted the accusations were false. He said Adam told him that the girl who hosted the party 'wanted to sleep with Adam' but Adam 'didn't want to sleep with her'. It was for this reason that she named him as the culprit, he said.

When police reached Adam by phone, he denied any involvement in the theft and pointed a finger at another area teen.

Despite being the youngest, Gabriel was not immune to the problems that his brothers faced. On 24 March 2000, Gabriel and five of his friends burgled a neighbour's home, stealing six speakers, DVDs, and one hundred dollars from the homeowner's wallet, which they took from a pocketbook in the kitchen. Police found all six boys in the backyard of the Polk's house in Piedmont. The homeowner declined to press charges, asking that the boys be counselled and released to the custody of their parents. A police report indicated that the stolen property was returned.

Also in 2000, Gabriel got into a fight with a fellow student in the hallway of Miramonte Middle School. He claimed the boy was a 'snitch' and accused the kid of 'acting gay'. Gabe claimed the boy got in his face, provoking a fight. There were indications that friction had existed between the two boys dating back to the sixth grade. At first, Gabriel sought to avoid a fight with the boy. But when the boy struck him in the back of the head with a set of keys, Gabriel turned to confront the youth. Gabe was later taken to the hospital, where he was treated for a gash that required staples to close it up. A subsequent investigation revealed that Gabe had been struck with a T-shaped weapon, a two-inch steel rod with a flat metal base, however this did little to quell the ongoing feud. School authorities accused Gabe of bringing 'manufactured' weapons such as a roll of taped quarters, a brass card holder made into brass knuckles, and an eight-inch weighted blackjack to school to seek revenge. Police confiscated the materials and later learned the homemade weapons were brought to school by several of Gabe's friends. The boys were arrested on charges of 'possession of a deadly weapon' and ordered to attend an anger management course.

While the dangerous behaviour of the three boys had been going on for years, in the summer of 2002 the situation went from bad to worse. On July 29 2002, Adam was arrested for drunk driving. He was ordered to participate in a two-day, county-sponsored Alcohol Offence Programme in Contra Costa County. The first session was set for 12 October – the weekend of his father's murder, which could explain why Adam was home in Orinda for the weekend.

Adam was already facing dismissal at UCLA. Authorities were poised to expel the teen because he hadn't completed enough coursework in his freshman year. He had dropped several classes without authorisation, intending to make up the work in his sophomore year. School officials advised him that they could only reverse their decision under 'extraordinary' circumstances. In August, Felix wrote a letter of explanation to the vice provost of undergraduate education at UCLA on Adam's behalf, blaming 'problems at home' for his son's decision to reduce his course load without first obtaining permission. Adam thought lightening his load would make the spring term 'manageable for him because of the stress he was experiencing in relation to his family situation.'

'During this past year, Adam's family, as he has known it, has fallen apart,' Felix wrote in the letter dated 17 August. 'In the fall of 2001, my wife and I separated under extremely tense and difficult circumstances. The stable family and security he had known for most of his life was dramatically altered. It was under these difficult circumstances that Adam began his freshman year at UCLA.

'Adam has always been a winner academically, socially, and athletically,' Felix wrote. 'At De La Salle High School in Northern California, he was class president for three years and graduated near the top of his class in grades. He was a starting footballer for two years for the highest ranked football team in the country. He received public recognition and honors for his athleticism. He has known only success and achievement. And at UCLA, he was the only freshman on the Varsity Rugby Team and became a starter. He is also now an enthusiastic member of a fraternity.'

Ultimately, Felix's efforts on behalf of Adam proved successful, as UCLA officials agreed to allow Adam to return for his sophomore year, but just as soon as he'd extinguished one fire, another one spread, only this time Felix proved unable to help. The son in question this time was Eli, who violated the terms of his probation and was now trying to avoid juvenile hall.

In a letter to the court, Felix defended his middle son, pointing to his varied accomplishments in the sporting arena as proof of his potential.

'At De La Salle, he was the only freshman on the junior varsity team,' Felix wrote in the three-page letter. 'At Miramonte High School, Eli was the only sophomore on the varsity football team. At the University of California basketball camp, [the coach] selected Eli out publicly as the kid who was "most likely to make it" because of his skills and discipline. Currently, Eli is the youngest starting player on the Lamorinda rugby team.

'For many reasons, Eli has tremendous potential,' Felix stated. 'I am deeply concerned that if Eli now becomes more involved in the correctional system that it will permanently deflect him away from leading the constructive and successful life which he is capable of doing . . . In my view, my son Eli is very much a salvageable young man who can make it in the world. In my view, steering him away from the correctional, institutional system is imperative. In light of this, I respectfully and urgently request that the court consider . . . that he be placed in my custody in Berkeley, where I have secured a spacious two bedroom apartment . . . that he continue to receive psychological counselling in which I will participate with him, if he prefers that . . . and that he be involved immediately in a drug programme.'

While Felix's plea appeared heartfelt, it failed to convince the judge to ignore the recommendations of the confidential probation report to the Juvenile Court of Contra Costa County.

'It seems like the minor [Eli] could use a respite from his parents' bitter dispute and conflicts so that he can separate himself and work on his own individual issues and make rehabilitation a true priority,' the confidential report cited.

Indeed, the 22 May 2002 report painted a disturbing picture of the Polk family dynamic. 'The minor [Eli] is currently caught in the middle of a bitter custody dispute between the mother and the father, both who have heaved a barrage of insults and allegations against each other, even in an open court setting,' it stated. 'The mother has been problematic with authority figures, including the arresting police officers, the probation department, home supervision staff, and was arrested in court for contempt and failure to follow court orders. When the judge ordered that the mother receive a psychological assessment, the mother flat-out refused and said she would remove herself from the case rather than to comply with those orders.

'The father who has housed this minor in the last few months has also had problems due to the fact that the minor has accused the father of child abuse resulting in a report to CPS [Child Protective Services] and the minor being put back in custody. It is unclear whether the minor really felt threatened by the father or was fabricating the abuse in hopes that he would get moved back with the mother, the minor was eventually released back to the father and has continued to attend Berkeley High.'

Included in the lengthy report was an evaluation from a deputy of the probation department who met with both parents regarding Eli's situation. 'The father denies all the allegations of abuse saying when the minor was younger and had hyperactivity from hypoglycaemia, the father would "swat him" but that was approximately eight years ago,' the deputy wrote. 'The father says he's a nonviolent person and believes the minor lives in a paranoid environment due to the intensive conflict between the mother and father and their impending divorce. The father said under the current conditions, he wasn't sure if he wants to live with Eli because of his present hostility, paranoia, and aggressiveness . . .

'Mother felt Eli did something very wrong, but felt there was mitigating circumstances to cause him to do it,' the deputy continued, referring to an interview he had with Susan Polk. 'The mother says the minor hadn't been in a fight since reaching physical maturity and felt he wasn't sure of his own strength. The mother's concerns are that the minor grew up in a violent household and that he needs anger management. The mother felt Eli was the target of the father's anger, and so is expressing his anger that he has kept inside. The mother felt the minor could benefit from drug and alcohol counselling, as well as family counselling.'

The deputy noted that during the interview with Susan, she contradicted Felix's assertion that Eli had suffered from hypoglycaemia as a youth, claiming her son had never been diagnosed with the illness. Also in the report were claims by members of the probation department that Eli had been self-medicating with drugs and alcohol in an attempt to deal with the turmoil at home. Eli told officers that he smoked marijuana on a daily basis and drank alcohol three to four times a month, occasionally experimenting with drugs such as Ecstasy and mushrooms. Denying suggestions that he might be 'depressed', Eli did admit that he suffered from chronic 'stomach problems', which officials attributed to stress.

During his visit to the probation department on 22 May, Eli charged in private that his father was physically and emotionally abusive. Felix had accompanied his middle son to the evaluation that day, but when they arrived, Eli announced that he wanted to speak with a deputy alone. Only then did Eli present the officer with a four-page handwritten letter about 'physical and mental abuse' he claimed Felix was inflicting upon him.

'The minor was periodically shaken and emotional as he talked about wanting to move back with his mother and how he felt he couldn't live in such close confined space with his father,' the deputy wrote in his report to the court. 'The minor described the father as having in the past "beaten the crap" out of him and his brothers and been mentally abusive with continual putdowns, mental mind games, and intimidation.'

Attached to the report was a psychological evaluation of Eli conducted on 13 May 'one where the parents present in a compelling, provocative manner,' the psychologist wrote in a three-page letter to the Court, also dated 22 May 2002. The father is a mental health professional who appears depressed, ineffective, and passive. [The] mother is aggressive, emotionally labile, and often contradictory in her behaviours and statements,' the psychologist continued.

Both parents care for Eli but have not been able to address his psychological needs. The greatest 'risk' for Eli lies not with each individual parent but within the dynamics of the family.

The family system is marked by conflict and turmoil. Role reversal is common with Eli, often given more power and recognition than is warranted for any child of his age. Authority issues are flagrant and pervasive for both parents. When one adult tries to be in charge, even in a healthy manner, the other sabotages the process by name calling and undermining. While his mother's participation in this sabotage is obvious, the father also undermines the mother with his passivity and reluctance to be in charge.

Eli is very identified with his mother who is viewed by Eli as a victim in the dynamic. Part of this identification is based on the natural fact that his mother has been his primary caregiver with his father, by his admission, over involved at work. Part of this identification is also a defence against maternal anger and feared abandonment. It is not surprising that according to Eli and police records, his involvement in the crime was as a protector – looking out for his friend, the underdog in this case.

Susan and her brother, David Bolling.

Susan at age 15. Around the time this photo was taken, she began seeing Felix Polk for therapy.

Above: Susan and Felix on their wedding day. Though she had reservations about the wedding, she went through with the ceremony. Not long after, tensions between them began to grow.

Below: Felix and Susan in a happy moment with their children.

Above: Felix enjoying the company of his son. Although he and Susan disagreed over parenting techniques, Adam and Gabe felt that he was a good father.

Below: Susan in a calm moment with her son. Though situations with Felix were tense during the boys' youth, it was not until they were older that the tempers began to escalate.

Felix takes over the feeding duties.

Above: Susan and Eli during their ill-fated trip to Paris. Eli's decision to leave Paris early and return home would later be used against him at the trial when the prosecutor attempted to portray his parental loyalties as fickle.

Below: Susan and Adam before their relationship soured. Until his father's death, Adam was close to his mother, but all that changed on 13 October, 2002.

Together the boys of the Polk family would prove difficult for their parents to handle, as each one struggled with authority in his own way.

Above: The main house of the Polk's Miner Road estate. The sprawling property would be the site of numerous police visits, as the Polk sons and their parents found themselves in trouble with the law.

Below: The Miner Road pool house where Felix was living when Susan killed him. Due to his fear of Susan, Felix claimed to have 'barricaded' himself inside the pool house in the days before his death.

CHAPTER TWELVE

CHASING DOWN LEADS

As local news channels were airing details of the gruesome Orinda murder, Detective Costa and his team were chasing down leads. Their first stop was Felix's Berkeley office. It was late morning on 16 October when Costa and his colleague, Jeff Moule, climbed the steps to 3001 Dana Avenue. The two men looked almost like father and son as they strode into the office building. Costa was in his fifties, with jet-black hair parted to one side. His moustache was short and neatly trimmed, just like Moule's.

Moule was fair-haired, twenty years younger and forty pounds thinner than his superior officer. But still, the two men were of similar height and possessed the authoritative demeanour of law enforcement officers. Once inside, they found the office door locked and an 'out' sign posted on it. There was no receptionist; it wasn't that kind of complex.

Costa knocked on the door of an adjacent office. A psychiatrist named Justin Simon poked his head out the door. He told the detectives he was the building's owner and that he leased space to Felix Polk, but theirs was strictly a tenant/landlord relationship. Still, Dr. Simon indicated that he was aware of marital difficulties between Felix and his wife. Detective Costa elected not to inform Simon of

Felix's murder given the vague nature of his relationship with Felix. He was certain Susan had mentioned Dr. Simon during their interview at headquarters as the psychiatrist who supposedly prescribed medications for her husband. Costa would check into it.

Before leaving Berkeley, he and Moule conducted a sweep of area streets in search of Felix's missing vehicle. The Saab was not there. Grabbing the radio, Costa contacted the Bay Area Rapid Transit (BART) police to request that they check their stations for the black Saab. A short time later, an officer radioed back to report that he had located the sedan at the Orinda station in the upper west lot, in space number 1268. Orinda police were directed to secure the vehicle and have it towed to an impound yard to be examined. The officer assigned to move the car told Costa there were no visible signs of blood, weapons, or other evidence that might link the vehicle to the crime. He noted there was a coat in the back seat, along with a collar and dog bed.

Their next lead took them back to Orinda not far from the BART station. Costa and Moule had heard that Susan's mother, Helen Bolling, had once lived in the town. They wanted to check out the address. A call to headquarters yielded a listing for a Bolling at 52 Barbara Road.

The modest residence was across the train tracks from the ritzy country club section, where Susan and Felix lived. While the landscape was mainly farmland and orchards when Helen first purchased the house on Barbara Road in the 1970s, the city of Orinda had grown substantially over the years. The north end, where Susan and Felix bought their home two years earlier, was now sprinkled with million-dollar residences.

A dark-haired man in his late-forties answered the door. He was not very tall, about eye level with the detectives.

'Do you know a Susan Polk?' Detective Moule asked.

'She's my sister,' the man answered, identifying himself as David Bolling. He told police that his mother still owned the property, and another in San Diego, where she was currently residing and that he and his mother had had little contact with Susan over the years.

It soon became clear to the officers that in spite of the strained relationship with his sister, David Bolling was aware of the 'incident' and that she had been arrested on suspicion of killing her husband.

'I have a hard time believing that Susan could kill someone,' David told the officers. 'But she does have an attitude towards authority.'

Detective Costa took notes. He told David about his interview with Susan at headquarters the day before. She claimed their father had abused her when she was a young girl. 'Do you know anything about that?' Costa asked.

'I know she's been telling people that,' David replied. 'It's just bullshit.'

David said that as far as he knew, his father had never done anything like that. He said he last spoke with his sister about two or three months earlier.

She had been avoiding family members lately, David told the detectives.

It was late in the afternoon of 16 October when Detective Moule went to the detention centre in Martinez to interview Susan again. Detective Jeffrey Hebel would participate in the interrogation. The two had been paired up on Monday night when they questioned Susan's son Gabe about the murder.

This would be the third time in thirty-six hours that Susan was interrogated by police. She was being held at the Contra Costa detention facility on suspicion of murder in lieu of one million dollars bail. Two days had passed since her incarceration and she continued to maintain her innocence. Hebel and Moule decided to take a forceful approach, in an attempt to scare her into admitting her role in the crime.

But the detectives' efforts failed. Susan remained detached and composed during the lengthy interrogation. Even as the detectives worked to trip her up, she didn't break a sweat. It was as if she was disconnected from the entire incident. In response to questions, she again recounted her movements during the past week. While some details differed slightly from her original version, her basic story remained the same. Susan claimed she didn't see Felix's Saab at the house that Monday morning when she returned from dropping Gabe at school. She spent much of the morning watering the small garden she tended in the terraced area near the home's front entrance.

'I am clear about that time line,' Hebel said. 'I want to go back and talk about some other stuff about your background. I understand several years ago you kind of had some recollection about some abuse from your childhood and that caused some tough times for you. Is that correct or am I getting bad info on you?'

'Well, you are hearing it from my children.'

'If you tell me something, I am not going to them and say this is what your mom said,' Hebel assured Susan.

'Partly, it's a story that my husband cooked up for the kids as to what was happening,' Susan said. From there, she went on to recount how the story of uncovering past trauma was how Felix manipulated the truth in order to avoid informing the boys of Felix and Susan's marital difficulties. As the detectives hung on her words, Susan once again offered her version of the last twenty years, explaining that she threatened a divorce several times over the course of their marriage. Sitting in the room, Susan coolly told the detectives how her threats to leave him were often met with death threats from Felix, who had even gone so far as telling Gabriel that he would kill Susan if she left. On another occasion, one that Susan later documented in their divorce papers, Felix made another threat on her life, this time in front of Adam and Eli. Coming in 2000, during a time when Eli's allegiance was to his father, the threat was in response to an ongoing quarrel Susan and Felix were having over his office. Like so many of their fights, this one ended with Susan telling Felix that she wanted a divorce. His response was quick.

'He [Felix] backed me up all the way across my room,' Susan explained to the detectives, 'and he said, "You make me so mad, I could kill you. I feel like punching you in the face or punching you."'

But unlike past occasions where Felix had hit Susan, this time he did not get the chance. As he raised his fist to strike her, Eli stepped in first, punching his mother hard on her lip. The reaction was instantaneous as blood began to pour from Susan's nose and mouth, dripping off of her face and onto the floor. Later, in addition to her eyes severely swelling and the side of her face bruising, Susan received several stitches on her lip that would leave a scar.

Having witnessed the entire drama unfold, Adam excitedly told his father and brother that this constituted abuse and called 911, a move that made Eli fearful of going to jail. Susan was also worried that Eli's punch would land him in police custody, so in order to avoid seeing Eli in jail again, the family concocted a story in which Susan had hit her face on the bed. Like so many of their lies, this one covered up the painful realities of the family's life, but still it worked. Eli was never reprimanded for the attack on his mother.

According to Susan, while her repeated attempts to exit the marriage were rebuffed, at one point, she even went so far as to try and obtain a restraining order against Felix. But her efforts stalled in March 2001 after Felix allegedly incited a physical altercation with her and later claimed, with Eli as a witness, that she kicked him in the back. Once again the police were summoned to the house on Miner Road and while there, Susan apparently attacked Felix again, this time in front of the officers. The incident landed her in handcuffs and promptly ended her attempts at getting a restraining order. Though Felix didn't press charges, the damage had been done.

As Susan told her side of events, the detectives continued to remind her of the evidence that was rapidly mounting against her and the fact that she was their number one suspect.

'We were at your house all day today and the scientists, they're still there,' Moule said. 'They call themselves CSI, crime scene investigators . . . We collected all of your shoes . . . and there's a shoe present. It's not the same shoe, I'm not going to say it's the same shoe . . . but it's the same size shoe, it's your size in the blood, okay?'

'There is no way that I went in there,' Susan said, referring to the guest cottage where Felix's body was found.

'I'm not saying you had some big grand plan and you thought about it for a year. Things happen for different reasons . . . you had a struggle with him. There's DNA in his hand. You have injuries on your face consistent with injuries on his body. You were in a struggle with him.'

'No, I was not.'

Hebel jumped in. 'Your DNA is in that room.'

'You're done,' Moule announced. 'Your footprint, your DNA. It's not about an interest, it's about what happened and about your future right now . . . Be honest.'

'I was not in there,' Susan maintained.

'Susan, this isn't going away, you're not getting out of jail. You need to give your side of this so that we can tell the court. Our job is just fact finders.'

'Well, then find the facts. Find out who did it.'

'We found the facts,' Moule said.

'We're done,' Hebel added.

'We have to know why,' Moule said.

The detectives kept after her, but even under the intense questioning, Susan maintained her innocence. When they brought up the possibility of using a polygraph test, Susan adamantly refused, claiming that if it's not reliable in a courtroom, then it's simply not reliable.

As Susan sat there denying any involvement, it was unclear what, if anything, was her strategy. Susan was a very intelligent woman, and as such, her continued profession of innocence in the face of the evidence against her was baffling. While Moule and Hebel were trying to elicit a confession, the other investigators were in the process of building a substantial case against her. Still, she maintained her innocence, almost as if, in her mind, she really had not been involved. As Susan had on so many occasions, she seemed to be shaping her own version of reality, a version that had removed her involvement in Felix's death. It was a harmful proposition in any situation, but in Susan's case it had a profoundly negative impact. Eventually investigators and prosecutors would use these denials and lies to demonstrate the cold-blooded nature of her killing, arguing that her attempt to cover up denoted premeditation, making this a case of first-degree murder.

Now apparent to Detective Hebel that his current strategy was ineffective, he changed tactics, insinuating that the scratches on her eyes were a result of the deadly fight she had with Felix in the guesthouse that night. Susan said she'd been roughhousing with the family dog when he bit her.

'I've been doing this a long time,' the detective smirked. 'That's not a dog bite.'

Detective Moule jumped in. 'Susan, how did you sustain this mark right here on your right eye?' he asked, pulling at his moustache. 'Do you want me to get a mirror and you can look at it yourself, and maybe it will jar your memory?'

Susan didn't crack a smile. 'I fool around with the dog all the time,' she insisted. 'The dog jumped in my face.'

'Okay,' Moule grinned. 'You have a little bit of darkness under your left eye, your left eye right here, a little bit of darkness. Did you also sustain that from the dog?'

'I don't know.'

'Do you mind putting your hands out again?' Detective Hebel instructed. 'Can you stretch them all the way out.'

Susan complied.

'On your left hand there's some scratches right in here and some redness right here,' Hebel noted, pointing a finger at Susan's hand. 'And on your right hand near your right index knuckle, there's . . . it almost looks like bruising or redness. It's light bruising.'

'Uh-huh,' Susan acknowledged.

'Can you roll them over,' Hebel directed. 'You have some cuts on your left hand near the pad under your small finger.'

'Under the left thumb,' Moule added. 'And then right here. Has that redness been there for a while?'

'There's also, it looks like a scratch right there under her left arm, a little red mark,' Detective Hebel added.

'I was gardening barehanded and I played rough with the dog,' Susan persisted.

'Okay. Will you look at me and close your eyes, please,' Detective Moule commanded. 'That's quite a mark,' he said, referring to the scratch on her eyelid.

'He hit you,' Hebel announced, referring to Felix. 'That's why you got into this altercation with him.'

Moule jumped in, lunging forward at Susan's face. 'He was violent with you. He abused you and he had been doing it for a long time. Detective Hebel and I have been involved for years in domestic violence.'

'You know what . . . it didn't happen,' Susan declared.

Later, looking back on the transcripts, it was hard to believe that a smart woman, who was so blatantly associated with a crime, would profess her innocence with so much passion. Most suspects, when faced with such insurmountable evidence would, at the very least, have come clean that they played a *role* in the crime. However, this was not the case with Susan, who continued to steadfastly maintain her innocence for more than a year after Felix's body was discovered.

Back at headquarters, Detective Costa was juggling calls. Adam Polk phoned that morning. The eldest of the Polk boys wanted Costa to contact a man named Barry Morris, an attorney who represented the family in the past.

It was midafternoon when Costa got the lawyer on the line. During the call, Morris said he had known Felix and the Polk family for twelve years. Felix counselled his son in the past, and Barry, in turn, represented Adam, Eli, and Gabriel in different criminal cases. Morris was aware of the ongoing tension between Susan and Felix. After Susan's March 2001 arrest ended her entreaties to get a restraining order, Morris had encouraged Felix to file charges against Susan. Despite Morris's efforts, Felix declined.

Morris told Detective Costa there had been other instances in which Felix declined to involve the authorities. Just over a week earlier on Sunday, 6 October, he received a call from Felix, alerting him that Susan had just phoned from Montana. During the conversation with Morris, Felix claimed that Susan had purchased a gun and intended to kill him with it. The information got Morris's attention and he encouraged his friend to call police immediately to report the threat. But Felix didn't want to, afraid that the move would further infuriate Susan.

A few days later, Felix called Morris back, informing his friend that he spoke to an Orinda police officer about Susan. Costa learned it was Chief Dan Lawrence who took the call. Lawrence confirmed that Felix phoned headquarters on 10 October – just three days before his murder – seeking advice concerning Susan's impending return from Montana. Felix was concerned because she told their son 'she was going to blow his head off' with a gun she'd purchased in Montana, while threatening Felix that she would kill him if he went to the police.

Despite Felix's terrified voice on the other end of the line, the call was nothing that Lawrence hadn't heard before. He advised Felix to obtain a temporary restraining order, leave the house immediately, and avoid any contact with his wife. Costa noted that Felix did not heed the chief's advice. It was as if he wanted people to know that he was in danger but was unwilling to protect himself.

It was almost noon when Costa received a call from Gabe Polk, who said he had just remembered something about the night he discovered his father in the guest cottage. After he found the guesthouse door locked, he returned to the house and asked Susan if she had seen his dad. She said she hadn't – and then asked if Gabe wasn't happy that his father was gone, to which Gabe responded that he wasn't happy about the situation. But Susan then said that she was. Looking back, Gabe said he now believed that his mother was implying that she had done something to Felix.

Susan then said something else that struck Gabe as odd.

'I guess I didn't have a shotgun, did I?' she told her son.

It would have been an odd statement at any time, but under the circumstances it was downright worrisome.

'Did you ever actually see her with one?' the detective asked.

'No,' Gabe said, although he felt that she had definitely researched some firearms. She was using terminology that indicated she had been shopping around for the right weapon. A subsequent check of the records revealed that Susan did, indeed, own a gun. She was the registered owner of a Smith and Wesson .38-caliber revolver. She told Costa about that gun during their interview at headquarters on Monday night and said that Felix had removed it from the house at her request. There was no indication that a shotgun had ever been purchased, and a search of the Miner Road residence yielded no firearms.

In addition to Gabriel and Morris, several more calls came in to Costa that afternoon. One was from Andrew Polk, Felix's forty-year-old son from his first marriage, who was currently living in lower Manhattan and working as an actor. It was the first time that Andrew had spoken to Costa, and he reported a call he received from Felix that past weekend after Susan had threatened to shoot him with a shotgun. It was a call similar to the one Felix had placed to Morris and Chief Lawrence around the same time, with Felix expressing concern that Susan 'was going to do something to him' upon her return from Montana.

That same afternoon, Felix's daughter from his first marriage also contacted Costa. Jennifer Polk was also residing on the East Coast in a quiet suburb of Boston. Her father had left a voice mail on her cell phone that past Friday, stating that 'things were getting critical' and 'Susan had threatened to kill him'. He also stated that Gabe told him 'Susan had a gun.' Jennifer said she never got back to her father, that was the last she ever heard from him.

In subsequent interviews, additional friends and patients of Felix reiterated Felix's fears of Susan, adding that he had begun barricading himself into the bedroom at night. Upon closer inspection of the

Miner Road guesthouse, investigators found no evidence of such barricades. It did not appear that new locks or safety latches had been installed on the three exterior doors, and there was no lumber or heavy furniture strategically placed as a makeshift obstacle.

To Costa, it seemed clear that Felix Polk had contacted a number of people to alert them to his wife's threats, yet he did nothing to protect himself, ignoring everyone's advice – including suggestions from the Orinda police. While his inability to take the precautions necessary to protect himself seemed strange to the investigating officers, it was quickly becoming clear that this inability was part of a larger, systemic problem that Felix had when it came to stemming Susan's threat of physical violence. All he had to do was press charges against her on one of the numerous occasions that he dialed 911, or use past events to obtain a restraining order against her, and then avoid the house.

Instead he opted to stay in the guest cottage, just yards away from the main house, even as Susan allegedly issued her threats. It was a costly decision – one that Felix paid for with his life.

CHAPTER THIRTEEN

DISSECTING THE TRUTH

On the morning of 16 October, Detective Roxanne Gruenheid was dispatched to the Central County Morgue to attend the autopsy of Felix Polk. Criminalist John Nelson, who photographed the body and collected physical evidence, was already at the Martinez facility when the young officer arrived that Tuesday morning.

The county had retained Brian Peterson, a private forensic pathologist to perform the autopsy. At the time, he had performed close to five thousand autopsies and testified as a forensic expert in hundreds of criminal cases. His resume spanned more than twenty years and included a forensic fellowship at the Armed Forces Institute of Pathology in Washington, D.C., and work as a general medical officer with the US Marines.

In the months following Felix's death, Dr. Peterson would gain notoriety for his role in the case of missing Modesto housewife, Laci Peterson, who disappeared on Christmas Eve of 2002. Dr. Peterson conducted the autopsies on Laci and her unborn son, Connor, after their bodies washed up in San Francisco Bay. A California jury later found Scott guilty of the double homicide and sentenced him to death for the murders.

At 8am, Felix's autopsy got underway. The body of the seventy-year-old was laying in an opened body bag on a gurney, clad only in the pair of black men's briefs that Polk had been wearing when he was killed. Peterson began by washing off the dried blood that covered most of his torso and the bottoms of both feet. Once the corpse was clean, it was easier to locate the multiple red stab wounds and countless scratches on his arms, hands, and feet. Dr. Peterson observed that five of the wounds had pierced the victim's lung, stomach, and kidney, while the remaining twenty-two slashes were determined to be 'superficial' cut-type wounds or defensive wounds. One cut that actually penetrated the muscle and tendon of one finger indicated that Felix had tried to grab the blade of the knife.

From these details, the pathologist concluded that Felix's death had been violent, with the stab wounds occurring in rapid succession. He determined the cause of death to be 'a combination of the blunt force trauma injuries and the numerous knife wound injuries' Polk had sustained during the assault. 'Probably the easiest way to think about them [the injuries] is that the victim is trying to protect himself, so he's either trying to block the knife with his hands, with his forearms, [or] maybe he's trying to grab the knife to prevent from being stabbed again,' Dr. Peterson later told a Grand Jury.

Dr. Peterson described five of the injuries as 'significant stab wounds' that had penetrated deep, entering the body cavity. The first was five and half inches deep, located just beneath the collarbone. According to Peterson, the knife entered the chest wall and punctured the right upper lung lobe, causing it to collapse. There were several scratches around the wound, indicating the tip of the knife had slashed the skin. Beneath the first wound was a second major stab wound that measured one and half inches deep. Here the knife had penetrated the pericardial sac, the soft tissue sac surrounding the heart, and had stopped just short of puncturing the heart. A third stab wound was identified in the lower left abdomen, just below the rib cage, where the knife penetrated the abdominal wall and pierced the front of the stomach. Dr. Peterson was unable to determine how deep the injury was because of the partially digested food in Felix's stomach, which Dr. Peterson hypothesised had prevented the knife from doing further damage to the stomach.

On the upper left side of Felix's back, there was a fourth stab wound measuring three inches in depth that penetrated the chest wall into the diaphragm. The fifth injury had an odd pattern that Peterson identified as a 'combination cut and stab'. The actual stab wound was five inches deep and surrounded by a jagged surface laceration. There was a bruise just above the stab wound that indicated the victim suffered a blunt force injury in that same location. Dr. Peterson concluded that the knife entered the fatty tissue but did not reach the kidney. 'Either the knife was being moved vigorously up and down, or else the victim was moving so there was stabbing and cutting and a scratch of the tip where the tip came out,' he later explained.

Based on this evidence, Dr. Peterson surmised that the blade used in the attack was a single-edged knife, measuring at least five and a half inches long, but he was unable to determine in what order the injuries had occurred or a precise time of death.

After he analysed each of the individual stab wounds, Dr. Peterson determined that the wound where the knife penetrated the right lung lobe and the one just below it where the knife entered the sac around the heart had caused the most internal bleeding and 'could have been lethal'. He classified the remaining twenty-two stab wounds as 'relatively superficial', noting that they varied in severity.

In addition to the wounds from the knife, there were also three different 'blunt force injuries' on Felix's body. There was an abrasion on one knee and a bruise in the middle of his back, just below one of the five deep stab wounds. Peterson ruled that neither of those was particularly significant in terms of death. A third injury, however, located three inches above the right ear canal and measuring one and a half inches long by one-eighth inch wide, indicated a 'relatively good impact' to the head. There was no associated brain injury, but it appeared the bruise was consistent with 'being hit with something', the pathologist said. Dr. Peterson theorised that the injury to the head might have incapacitated Polk and limited his ability to fight back.

'If the injury had occurred at the onset of the fight, it's possible his struggles were less effective,' he theorised. 'In other words, Felix could have been stunned, or partially stunned, by getting hit in the head and less able to defend himself in any effective way.' While Dr. Peterson could not determine what caused the three blunt force injuries, he believed it was 'from a blow' rather than a fall.

Nevertheless, he could not find any pattern on the skin, such as a shoe tread or hammer impression that could help police identify the instrument that was used.

Interestingly, the forensic examination revealed that Felix Polk had high blood pressure and suffered from coronary heart disease. The left main coronary artery and the left anterior descending artery that provides blood to the left chamber were both blocked; a condition that 'causes a lot of problems, including sudden death', Dr. Peterson noted in his testimony to the Grand Jury in August 2003. Meanwhile, Felix's heart weighed twice that of a normal heart for someone of his size and age. 'It was a significantly sick heart,' Dr. Peterson said. 'It didn't cause his death, but it's likely a factor . . . He had heart disease going into the attack, and as emotions ran high as [he was] being killed, it wouldn't have been unusual for him to have heart symptoms,' he observed.

Later, when asked by a member of the Grand Jury why Felix Polk did not scream for help, Dr. Peterson pointed to three factors: Felix's heart disease, the blunt force trauma to the head, and the two quick and deep chest wounds. 'Faced with that kind of attack, I think, I personally would have spent more time trying to defend myself as opposed to calling out,' Dr. Peterson said. 'Again, he was relatively stunned from the blow to the head . . . confused, and simply not able to.'

In the days following the Orinda murder, journalists reported that Felix Polk was brutally stabbed – conjuring up images of Anthony Perkins in the movie *Psycho*. At a press conference at Orinda police headquarters, Police Chief Dan Lawrence allayed fears that a killer was on the loose in the community. He assured residents of the quiet East Bay community that the homicide at the Polk residence was 'not a random murder', but a 'domestic-violence issue'. In the weeks prior to the murder, officers were summoned to the Polk home in response to domestic disputes, he said. In addition, evidence found during a search of the residence indicated the victim's wife played a role in the crime, he said.

'These things can happen time and time again anywhere,' Lawrence said.

Though there was an everyday nature to the situation, the public's response to the savage death and bizarre history between Felix and Susan was far from average. Within days, Felix Polk's death quickly became fodder for TV news shows such as *Dateline*, MSNBC's *Rita Cosby Live and Direct*, *Inside Edition*, and *Geraldo*. Not long after the autopsy was complete, there were even reports that one of the newsstand tabloids offered as much as fifty thousand dollars to a source close to the case for autopsy photos.

While the Polk case was quickly turning into a media frenzy, it was by no means the first time Orinda had been privy to a high-profile murder investigation. At the press conference, Orinda's chief of police was quick to point out that the last murder to occur in the sleepy hamlet was in June 1999. Ironically, that homicide also happened on Miner Road, about one-quarter mile from the Polk residence. In that case, the body of a fifty-six-year-old woman was discovered decomposing inside her ramshackle brown ranch house on seven wooded acres at 616 Miner Road. Police later identified the victim as Margaret Bodfish, a wealthy recluse who had reportedly undergone a sex change operation. Diary entries revealed that Bodfish led a double life and had been living for the past sixteen years as a man. Orinda residents knew her as a woman, while residents in Mill Valley, where she owned a second home, knew her as a man.

Bodfish wrote that she 'hated her body' and wished to be 'beaten to death'.

Investigators suspected that her only son was involved in her murder. Like his mother, Max Wills also kept a diary that contained a list of people he wanted dead; his mother was at the top of the list. But police never got a chance to interview Wills. The thirty-three-year-old took his life in the bathroom of a motel in Santa Monica the day after his mother's body was found. A maid discovered Wills' body in a bathtub; he had slit his throat and wrists with a razor blade. A suicide note indicated that he had long suffered from depression, but was reluctant to kill himself while his mother was still alive.

'It would devastate her,' Wills wrote in his diary.

The discovery of a floor safe in the closet of Bodfish's home six months after the murder temporarily took the spotlight off of the victim's son and suggested robbery as a possible motive for the murder. Inside the safe, police found sixty thousand dollars in gold and coins. A drill had been found in that same closet during an earlier search of the house, but there was no indication anyone had tried to remove the safe from the floor. With no fingerprints on the drill and the victim's only relative dead, the case went cold.

While Bodfish's murder remains a mystery, her memory lives on in Orinda. In her will, she bequeathed her sprawling oak-lined property to the City of Orinda to be used as a public park and recreation area. In July of 2003, the seven-acre parcel was transferred to the Muir Heritage Land Trust and is now an official wildlife sanctuary. Bodfish also left three hundred thousand dollars to the National Organization for Women (NOW), the largest organisation of feminist activists in the United States.

Another celebrated murder in Orinda's criminal history occurred eleven years earlier, in 1984, when Bernadette Protti stabbed fifteen-year old Miramonte High cheerleader and classmate Kirsten Costa to death with a kitchen knife.

Prosecutors argued that Protti was jealous of Kirsten's popularity and angry that the cheerleader and her friends excluded her from their clique. Priotti denied involvement, but later confessed to the crime. She served less than eight of the nine years she received under the jurisdiction of the California Youth Authority for the murder and was released in 1993 over strong objections from Costa's family.

The story later became a TV movie of the week that aired in 1994.

And yet despite the attention that both of those cases received, there seemed to be something different about the Polk case. There was no good explanation for the media free-for-all that captivated millions around the country, except that people seemed drawn to the bizarre details unfolding about Felix and Susan. From the relationship's unhealthy origins to its dramatic conclusion, their story embodied psychological dysfunction in the truest sense. In their own way, each of these characters was haunted by their inescapable pasts – pasts that came to define their entire lives.

While the essential facts had been reported, the case was far from solved. Slowly, contradictory stories were hitting the airways as the Polk sons staked out opposing positions on their family history and their mother's culpability. Friends began to describe the chaotic household in the press, but despite the reputation that the family was quickly earning, there was still one key player who had to be interviewed: Susan's mother, Helen.

CHAPTER FOURTEEN

HISTORY REPEATS

Helen Bolling was at home in San Diego when her son, David, telephoned on Wednesday, 16 October, with the stunning news that Felix was dead and Susan was in jail, suspected of his murder. Though Susan had been incarcerated late Monday evening, no one had contacted remaining family members to alert them to the arrest. Even after police came knocking on David's door on Tuesday afternoon, he waited to inform his mother of Susan's arrest. During the phone call, David told Helen that he attended a press conference at police headquarters in Orinda where detectives shared limited details of Susan's detention. News outlets were reporting that the autopsy revealed a very violent death.

Felix had been stabbed twenty-seven times, the headlines screamed.

Helen could barely comprehend what her son was telling her. 'It's just not possible,' she told him. Susan was a petite woman, she thought. How could her daughter overpower someone of Felix's size? Besides, if Susan wanted to murder him, would she have planned such a violent and risky encounter? She would never have undertaken such an assault on her own, Helen thought.

Reeling from the news, Helen dialed the Contra Costa Sheriff's headquarters. She wanted to speak with someone in charge. Detective Mike Costa took her call.

He told Helen that her daughter was refusing to speak with authorities.

'Well, it's no wonder,' Helen replied. 'To experience that kind of event, sometimes you almost can't talk.'

The detective was silent.

Helen next inquired about the family car. David told her that transit officers had found Felix's black Saab in the parking lot of the Orinda BART station.

'She just drove it there,' Costa replied flatly.

To Costa's dismay, transit officers who interviewed taxi and bus drivers servicing the Orinda station failed to discern any evidence or witnesses tying Susan to the Saab. A search of the vehicle showed no signs of forced entry, and investigators had been unable to locate the car keys.

'That doesn't sound reasonable. How did she get back?' Helen asked the detective. 'You can't walk back. Those roads are too dark and narrow.' The Polk's home was quite a ways from both the train station and the downtown area. It would have taken at least three hours for Susan to walk from the BART station to her home, Helen told the detective. That just didn't make sense, she said.

Costa was aware of the distance. His officers had mapped the roughly three-mile route from the Polk house to the station using both city streets and cross-country shortcuts. They determined the time needed to travel that distance on foot to be well under three hours. While he had no evidence to back up his assertion, Costa maintained that Susan had driven the Saab to the BART station immediately after dropping Gabriel at school that Monday morning, and then walked home to retrieve her Volvo wagon for the 12.30pm pickup at Del Oro High.

Helen found Costa's theory preposterous. She believed that if Susan had left Felix's car at the BART station, she had to have had an accomplice – maybe Gabriel – to drive her home. Gabe had been home at the time and recently he had been extremely angry with his father. The teen was so angry that he had taken a sledgehammer to Felix's Saab that past June, damaging the sporty sedan. Gabe later explained that his mother had provoked the incident, after angrily describing Felix as the 'great and powerful destroyer'.

David Bolling was at the house the day a tow truck arrived to transport the Saab to an auto body shop for repair. He asked Gabe about the damage and was surprised by his nephew's response.

'I never liked the guy,' the teen reportedly said, referring to his father.

While Helen was not one to start accusing her grandchildren, she was hard-pressed to believe that her daughter had masterminded and carried out such a brutal attack alone. The whole murder scenario seemed so out of character for Susan, who had never displayed such violent tendencies. If what police were saying was true, something must have triggered an uncontrollable rage. Or maybe, Helen thought, her daughter had no choice; Susan had to kill Felix or be killed herself.

As Helen spoke to Costa, she began to reveal the complicated relationship between Susan and Felix. She recounted the tumultuous years that followed her divorce from Theodore Bolling and the traumatic impact that the breakup had on Susan. The young girl had watched her once happy, loving mother slowly come apart when her husband left the family. To compound matters, Susan suffered again when her father divorced his second wife, Rita, for a third woman. People close to Theodore recalled a significant change in the youngster, who seemed to view the breakup with Rita as yet another betrayal by her father. Susan had accepted that perhaps Theodore and Helen were simply a mismatch and that Rita was a better fit for him. She even befriended Rita and, according to witness accounts, the two were close.

But news that her father was walking out on his second wife for yet another woman truly upset Susan. She could no longer excuse his inability to honour a commitment. He had rejected both Helen and Susan when he left the marriage in 1964. Now, he was rejecting Rita, as well. From a psychological perspective, all daughters want to believe they are second in line for their father's affection, but suddenly, it seemed, there were lots of women who came before her.

Around this time Susan began suffering from the paralysing anxiety that landed her in Felix's office. Anxiety is often a symptom of buried emotion, and for Susan her father's second divorce seemed to spark a rage within her. This volatile emotional state and her young age made her extremely susceptible to Felix's advances. Felix was charismatic and magnetic – compelling to a girl who had long been seeking the approval of an older man. He had mastered the art of concealing his underlying objective: to control everything and everyone around him.

Helen believed this was how Felix lured Susan into his world. It pained her to think that she was partly responsible for failing to report the therapist to the authorities. If only she had gone to police when she first learned of Susan's inappropriate relationship with Felix, her daughter might not be in jail on charges of murdering him. Instead Helen confronted Felix on her own, in the hope that he would do the right thing.

But Felix never let Susan go, and instead, things only got worse. Helen tried to intervene and take her daughter on a trip to Santa Barbara to meet boys her own age; Susan was not interested. She was completely entranced by Felix, or 'glued in', as Helen put it. The therapist had become a father figure, and this unhealthy relationship distorted Susan's teenage years. She made few friends in high school and at college. Eventually, Felix was all she had.

Since Susan's world was so narrow, Helen was not surprised to learn of the impending marriage. She never approved of the union and even called Felix's first wife to apologise for her daughter's involvement in the breakup of that relationship. Despite her sixty thousand dollar loan to the newlyweds, Helen soon found herself all but banned from their home.

When Helen finished telling Detective Costa her version of the Polk saga, she fell silent. She had provided a myriad of details that clarified some of the history behind Susan and Felix's marriage, but her role in the case was only beginning. After hanging up the phone, she headed for her beat-up blue sedan as she prepared to make the drive to Orinda.

CHAPTER FIFTEEN

INCITING EVENTS

On Thursday, 17 October, a day after Helen spoke to Detective Costa, Susan sat quietly in the holding cell of the Martinez jail, waiting for officers to escort her to the Walnut Creek Courthouse where she would be formally charged with Felix's murder. She barely looked up when a uniformed guard unlocked the cell door and admitted a conservatively dressed man.

'I am Dr. Paul Berg,' the man smiled, extending a hand to Susan.

Dr. Berg had been sent to the jail by Contra Costa County prosecutors to form an opinion of Susan's mental state before the scheduled 2pm arraignment. At first Susan was compliant, listening intently as the Oakland psychologist explained the psychological evaluation. Even when he informed her that their conversation would not be confidential and his findings would be used in court, Susan agreed to cooperate. 'However, she very quickly changed her mind, asking a number of relevant questions, before declining to speak further,' Dr. Berg reported without revealing her concerns.

Obviously, Susan had a firm grasp on the magnitude of her situation. Emerging from the room, the psychologist advised Detective Costa that Susan halted the interview. Still, Dr. Berg said he was able to form an opinion on the suspect. He believed Susan was

'sane' and asked 'appropriate questions' for a 'person in her position' –
a person under arrest for murder.

In a confidential letter to Assistant District Attorney (ADA) Tom
O'Connor four days later, Dr. Berg reiterated his findings, writing 'my
observations . . . were that she was calm, composed, mildly
withdrawn, and quite serious-minded. She did not show any obvious
signs of mental disturbance, particularly none of any loss of contact
with reality or other signs of a Thought Disorder.'

That afternoon, Susan was brought before a judge as scheduled.
Handcuffs encircled her thin wrists as she was led to the defendant's
table flanked by armed court officers. She possessed an air of
elegance, even when wearing the prison-issue gray sweatshirt and
baggy blue slacks. Her short hair was neatly combed and a touch of
lipstick defined her lips.

Susan's voice was barely audible as she stood before Contra Costa
County Superior Court Judge Bruce Mills and announced her need for
a public defender. There was a sudden interruption from a well-
dressed man standing in the gallery.

'Your honour,' the man addressed the judge.

Recognising the voice immediately, Susan broke into sobs. It was
her father, Theodore Bolling. He had come to court to request an
adjournment. He had retained a prominent San Francisco attorney,
William Osterhoudt, to defend his daughter and wanted the case
postponed until the new lawyer could be present in court. Susan
stood speechless, tears rolling down her cheeks, as her father
addressed the court. Judge Mills agreed to adjourn the case until 1.30
the following afternoon.

Rising to his feet, the prosecutor in the case, ADA Tom O'Connor
asked the judge to raise Susan's bail from the standard $1,050,000 for
murder defendants to upwards of $5 million.

'This was an extremely violent murder,' O'Connor said. 'The
defendant owns substantial property in Orinda as well as in Berkeley.
We also know that prior to the homicide, Mrs. Polk had been living
out of state.'

O'Connor argued that Susan had substantial financial assets at her
disposal and was a flight risk, as well as a danger to the community
– especially to her son, Gabriel, who discovered his father's body in
the guesthouse.

Turning to Theodore Bolling, Judge Mills enquired as to whether his daughter would be able to post bail in the next twenty-four hours.

'There is no chance, your honour,' Susan's tall, dark-haired father replied.

Mills ordered that a bail hearing be scheduled along with the Friday afternoon arraignment.

The following afternoon, Susan was back in court with defence attorney William Osterhoudt by her side. Helen and David Bolling listened from the gallery as another judge, Merle Eaton, explained his decision to hold Susan without bail. He cited the letter Susan had written to juvenile judge, William Kolin, on behalf of her son Eli, noting that it contained threats to 'sell her home' and 'leave the state'.

Osterhoudt tried to argue that Felix's death would make it difficult for his client to borrow money against their real estate holdings, but Judge Eaton was unmoved. He maintained that the letter introduced to the court by ADA O'Connor was convincing and set a hearing for 1.30pm the following Wednesday to revisit the bail issue.

Ultimately, Susan chose not to keep Osterhoudt as her attorney, reportedly because of his association with her father. Though a public defender, Elizabeth Grossman, was later assigned to Susan's case, she too would be dismissed by Susan. While Susan claimed that Grossman was not doing enough on her behalf, those close to the case suggested her dismissal occurred after Grossman pushed Susan to present an insanity defence at trial.

Regardless of who represented her, Susan faced twenty-five years to life in prison if convicted of Felix's murder. Prosecutors would not seek the death penalty, but that decision did not make the defence any easier.

That afternoon, as Susan was being led from court in handcuffs, Detective Costa and his team were in Berkeley executing a search warrant at 3001 Dana Street, Felix Polk's office. The building's owner, Justin Simon, used a passkey to gain entry to the tastefully furnished space, complete with a working fireplace on one wall.

Mindful to avoid any patient mental health records, the investigators began their examination. They believed a review of Felix's private records, documents, writings, and files pertaining to his treatment of his wife might reveal evidence of their marital problems, past abuse by either party, and any prior threats that might offer a motive in the case. Investigators noted a computer connection and computer mouse on the desk indicating that Dr. Polk used a laptop, but there was no machine in the office.

Leafing through a pile of papers on the desk, investigators came upon a fax copy of the court order granting Felix sole occupancy of the Miner Road residence and custody of Gabriel. There was also a copy of the minutes of the telephone conference that occurred on 27 September 2002 that resulted in the court order. Susan mentioned that call to Detective Costa at headquarters, claiming that during the conversation Felix informed her that he intended to hold a custody hearing in her absence.

Costa collected the documents, as well as other legal papers scattered on the desk. Among them was an unsigned contract granting a lien on the Miner Road residence in the sum of thirty thousand dollars from Felix's portion of the proceeds to Felix's divorce attorney, Steve Landes. There was also a letter from Landes asking that Felix bring his legal account current. Felix had not made a payment to his attorney in over eighteen months, and Landes was getting anxious. Costa, who had spoken to Landes on the phone earlier in the day, was familiar with the payment problems. According to Landes, Felix first retained him in April of 2001, but payments were always late for one reason or another. The Polks had just sold an apartment building in Piedmont and each had received $226,000 from the sale. While Dr. Polk had immediately invested his share in another property, the lawyer believed Susan still had her portion. Landes wasn't aware of any physical violence between Felix and Susan. As far as he knew, Felix and Susan had been staying away from each other, although Felix had mentioned one incident that occurred before Landes came on board as counsel in which Susan kicked Felix in the back.

Landes last spoke to Felix by phone on 11 October, the Friday before he was murdered. At the time, Felix was upset that Susan was refusing to vacate the Miner Road house. He claimed that police were unwilling to enforce the court order granting him sole occupancy of the residence and full custody of his teenage son. As with the other calls that Felix made in the days before his death, he expressed to Landes his fear that Susan might harm him. Landes advised Felix to 'simply get away from there' because he was 'so afraid of his wife', Costa learned.

During the phone call with Costa, Landes made no mention of Felix's grossly overdue legal bill or the lien he was proposing on the Miner Road residence. Police found two outstanding bills from Landes on Felix's desk, along with a four-page letter dated 23 September 2002 outlining Landes' work on the case and demanding payment:

> In our last several conversations you have pointedly avoided the question I raised with you of fees. Last week you said something about a line of credit . . . and then nothing else. I simply can not run an account of this magnitude which, because of Susan's unwillingness to settle on any issue, even the time of day, will probably become larger . . .
>
> I will reiterate. You need to refresh your retainer immediately, within the week, by at least $10,000. This is a very reasonable request. You have not made a payment on your account for a year and a half. You have been billed. I know of no professional, whether therapist, attorney, dentist or doctor, who would run such a tab . . . You made arrangements to refinance Miner Road without any consultation with me, paying off credit card bills for Susan without including my fees. I don't feel that this is being unreasonable.

At Felix's office, there were other indications that the Polks were in financial straits. Credit card statements found on the desk showed balances in excess of thirty-five thousand dollars. Landes' letter to Felix indicated that Polk had used a portion of the money from a refinance of the Miner Road property to pay off those debts. However, there were no documents to substantiate that claim.

There was also a property assessment for the Arch Street apartment complex that the Polks co-owned with Susan's mother, Helen Bolling, showing a value of $675,000 as of 17 May 1999. A typewritten letter found on the fireplace mantel from Susan to her mother, dated 21 May 2002, indicated that Helen had recently requested that Susan and Felix sign the property over to her:

> Dear Mother,
> . . . You seem to be claiming that your share has increased from 50% to 100% because you did not receive your share of the

income for the last few years and proceeds from the refinance.

In addition, you have written me out of your will.

It is not worth my while to waste any more time on this property when it does not benefit me. . . .

Please have your attorney contact me . . . with a proposal for buying me out if you think that I am entitled to any share of the equity.

Sincerely,

Susan

Inside a yellow folder, marked 'Divorce – Landes,' was a typewritten letter from Susan to Felix dated 21 May 2002. In the four-page, single-spaced document, Susan coherently made recommendations on what the divorcing couple should do with various properties, pets, and tax returns, as well as accounting and spousal support issues. Susan also used the letter to alert Felix that Gabriel's 'excessive absences' from Miramonte High School had resulted in his being 'dropped from classes'.

'Miramonte has a unique policy of dropping students when their absences exceed fifteen . . . In Gabe's case, all of his absences were related to illness and were excused,' Susan wrote, claiming that the teen 'appears to have mononucleosis.'

'As you well know, Gabe does not cut school or get into trouble . . . so all of Gabe's excellent and hard work this semester has been uncredited [sic].'

As to Gabe's custody, Susan wrote, 'Judge Berkow, at your request, ordered me to undergo a psychological evaluation as a precondition.

'In your declaration filed in February, you described me as "healthy". Now, you are taking the position that I need to be evaluated. You are a psychologist. You have known me for some twenty-five years. Surely, no one would know better than you whether I am fit or not to parent my children . . . It is clear that you are determined to punish me by taking the kids away from me. You have said repeatedly . . . that you will not let them go. It's time to move on.'

Pulling open the desk drawer, Costa discovered more letters that were written and signed by Felix Polk. One was his appeal to the vice provost at UCLA to keep Adam from being dismissed. Another, dated Saturday, 15 June, was addressed to Gabriel, and detailed Felix's belief that his teenage son had vandalised his Saab several months earlier:

'I know that you are very, very mad at me and won't talk on the phone,' the one-page single-spaced letter began. 'I do want you to know that I think about you all the time and miss you terribly and have some deep concerns about what the future holds for us . . . in spite of the way you have rejected me and turned on me, I am not angry at you. Frustrated yes!

'Both you and Eli seem to have bought into mom's horror stories about me. They are for the most part not true stories, but I don't really have a chance to speak up for myself. I am faced with a closed system in which mom says what she says so hatefully about me, and I have no chance to point out what is true and what is not . . . I have some real flaws and yet I am not the monster she portrays me to be.

'What you did to my car was uncalled for, destructive and senseless. You must really have been worked up into a lather to have done that. I am holding you responsible for the damage.'

There were also typewritten letters from Felix to Peter Weiss, an attorney, asking for a five thousand dollar disbursement from the 'children's trust' to cover legal fees in connection with Eli's assault and subsequent probation violation, as well as several requests for monies for Adam's UCLA tuition. During the course of the investigation, Costa learned that Weiss was Felix's cousin and was serving as executor of a trust fund the Polks had set up for their children.

Detective Costa perched himself on the desktop and listened to the thirty voice mails on Felix Polk's answering machine as investigators marked the mounds of paper into evidence. Most of the calls were from patients wanting to schedule appointments. Two were from a 'Tom Pyne' also requesting an appointment.

'I recognise that name!' Detective Roxanne Gruenheid announced. Gruenheid was among those executing the search warrant that day. She explained that Eli Polk had offered his father's patient, Tom Pyne, as a possible suspect during the interview that she and Detective Steve Warne had conducted at Byron Boys' Ranch several days after Felix's murder.

In another drawer, investigators found an envelope with Pyne's return address in El Sobrante, a small East Bay city north of the Richmond Bridge. They would pay him a visit later that week.

Moving their search to the office closet, police discovered a manila envelope containing the blue .38-caliber revolver that Susan had mentioned in her first interview and a red plastic ammo container, along with the keys for the trigger lock. The gun was loaded with the trigger lock in place, and a quick check of the weapon confirmed that it was registered to Susan Polk. The detective noted it hadn't been fired in some time. Unloading the weapon, Costa booked it into evidence for safekeeping.

Also in the closet was a rambling six-page letter Susan had faxed from the T-4 Bucks Motel on Highway 191 in Big Sky, Montana, on 3 October 2002. The letter appeared to be a portion of Susan's personal diary. In it, she wrote about Felix being a member of the Israeli 'Mossad' and knowing about the September 11 terrorist attacks, Costa noted.

'Susan mentions the recent divorce court rulings in which she claims that Felix got his spousal support reduced,' the detective wrote in his report. 'Susan writes about being a medium and how Felix used to put her into trances. Most of the letter is talking about the Israeli army and the Mossad and how Susan believes they were involved in the 9/11 attacks.'

Several days after searching Felix's office, Detective Costa received an interoffice envelope from a deputy sheriff employed at the county's Court Services Division. It was addressed to a Judge Rivera at 725 Court Street in Martinez and had a return address of Jackson, Wyoming. The postmark indicated it had been mailed in 2002.

Costa immediately recognised the envelope's contents as a duplicate of the six-page letter Susan had faxed to Felix from the T-4 Bucks Motel in Montana on 3 October – only this copy was one paragraph longer than the faxed copy. It began, 'thought you might be interested in the journal excerpt about a Mossad agent's failure to provide a warning to US Intel. Re. Terrorist attacks on US.' Looking over the letter, Costa speculated that Susan had mailed a portion of her private diary to Contra Costa Superior Court Judge Maria Rivera in hopes of proving that her husband was a double agent working for the Israeli government and that he had used his influence as a spy to derail her custody efforts. It is not clear why Susan chose to send the correspondence to Judge Rivera. Although she hoped the letter would strengthen her argument, after reading it, it was clear that this wouldn't help at all. The letter was a shocking window into Susan's confused world, one in which her paranoia and delusions were abundantly clear:

I called F last night and found out this piece of information straight from the horses [sic] mouth as it were. 'Brace yourself, Susan,' he said. 'You're in for a shock.' Yes, I was shocked. I shocked him too, accusing him of misusing his position as a Mossad agent to influence the court. It doesn't help that the judge is Jewish. At first he tried the 'poor Susan you really do need help' routine. But when I persisted, objecting that I had no idea that I was marrying into a Mossad cell when I married him, that I never would have wanted to do that, that all of his friends and family members are Mossad like M who is stationed in Germany and B the lawyer who trots off to Pakistan on field trips and that I would tell my story on the Internet, F responded 'No one will ever believe you Susan.' I said, 'The Arabs will.' And he said, 'Are you going to go to the Arabs then, Susan?' And I said, 'No, I don't like them any better than the Jews.' I asked him, 'How could he betray his own country?' Doesn't he think of Americans as his countrymen? Or does he think of himself as part of the Greater Jewish Nations that exists without borders?

'You'd better think about your children,' he insinuated. 'You better think about the consequences for your children.'

'What are you going to do that you haven't already done?' I asked. Eli is in juvenile hall, and Gabe, well Gabe is in a continuation school. 'Eli will get six months,' F said. 'How'd you arrange that?' I asked. 'Did you pay off the judge or did you just have something on him?' And F just grunted.

I don't know how to get out of the dilemma I am in. Joining is impossible. I will not become an actress like the members of F's disgusting family, pretending all the time, shaming kindness and humanity when underneath there is nothing but betrayal, sadism, and in the best of them, a kind of robotic obedience. F is evil and he is a traitor.

The letter then spoke about the September 11 attacks on the World Trade Center. Susan claimed to be a medium and that she had advised Felix on world events related to Israel through visions she experienced while in a trance:

> I am not happy about being a medium,

the letter concluded:

> First of all, I am only partly conscious of what is happening when I do what I do, and sometimes, I am not conscious at all until later when I get flashbacks. I don't know whether this is because F hypnotised me so frequently when I saw him as a patient. (It was under hypnosis that this ability was discovered by F and instructed me not to remember, or whether it is a function of being a medium.)

Later that evening, a canine search and rescue unit was dispatched to the Miner Road crime scene. Investigators were hopeful that dog handler Eloise Andersen and her scent dog Trimble could sniff out some clues. It was after dark when Anderson and Trimble set off from the driveway at 728 Miner Road as investigators recorded the dog's movements. But it was soon obvious that the direction the dog tracked 'was consistent with the way any occupants of Miner Road would go if proceeding to the Lafayette area' and the search was called off.

Interviews with the Polks' neighbours yielded no witnesses to the murder. Indeed, the neighbours knew very little about the Polk family. One Miner Road resident told police she had met Susan Polk twice since moving onto the block that past June. In response to questions, she said that both she and her husband were at home on 14 October, but didn't see or hear anything suspicious. In fact, she hadn't seen Dr. Polk in months. Because of the age difference between Felix and Susan, she assumed that he was Susan's father.

Another woman on the block recalled that the Polks moved onto the street about two years ago, but she thought that Felix Polk had moved out of the residence. Eli Polk had once backed his car into their retaining wall; Felix had paid for the repair.

The woman assured officers she never saw or heard any domestic abuse occurring at the Polk house, although on Monday, the 14th, at about 8.30pm, she did hear 'some yelling'. She described the yelling, 'as not being out of anger but just in the background' and attributed it to the Giants baseball game on TV.

CHAPTER SIXTEEN

PIECING IT ALL TOGETHER

In the days after the murder, Susan steadfastly maintained her innocence, even as police accumulated evidence of her complicity. Detective Costa had no doubt about Susan's guilt. All the elements were there: strands of her hair in Felix's death grip, a bloody footprint on the floor of the guest cottage that matched Susan's shoe size and panicked calls to 911 from Felix in the days before the murder.

Susan had the means, the opportunity – and the motive. Her alimony had just been reduced by nearly five thousand dollars a month, and Felix was awarded custody of their minor son and the Orinda residence. Costa had the right suspect in jail, and he was determined to build a solid case. This was not the first homicide he had handled in which a battle over family finances had spurred a spouse to murder.

As part of his investigation, the detective reached out to Janna Kuntz, the realtor that Susan hired to assist in her relocation to Montana. He found a business card for Kuntz during his search of the Miner Road house, and in a telephone interview, Kuntz confirmed that she had shown Susan a number of properties during her two visits to Montana.

According to Kuntz, she met Susan in the late summer of 2001, when Susan came to Bozeman to look at homes. Kuntz took an instant liking to the fortyish woman from San Francisco who was soft-spoken, intelligent, and interesting. The estate agent was intrigued by this woman who was tired of city living and wanted to slow down. Susan loved nature and the idea of residing in the country where she could hike and spend lazy afternoons honing her skills as a writer. When they first met, Susan was living with her two sons in a small cabin she rented in Gallatin Gateway, a small farming community about twenty minutes outside Bozeman. Susan liked the country setting, but Eli and Gabe complained bitterly about being so far from town. For them, the location was too remote.

Kuntz had few details about Susan's first stay in Montana. She and Susan got to know each other better when she returned the following September accompanied by her yellow Labrador puppy, Dusty. After years of abuse, Susan and her husband were splitting up, and she was eager to settle in Montana and 'enjoy a quiet life', the realtor told Detective Costa. Susan had just sold some apartments in California and had $225,000 to put down on a home in the Big Sky area. She wanted to stay in that price range.

While out viewing properties, Susan received a number of calls on her cell phone, mostly from her children. She was proud of her three sons and spoke of them often. In fact, she told Kuntz that she wanted to buy a condo near the ski slopes of Big Sky for them to enjoy. Susan envisioned taking the boys on lengthy treks and spending quiet days reading and discussing literature.

When Costa asked about Susan's emotional state, Kuntz said she seemed to be taking the bad news in her divorce with a mix of disappointment and frustration. 'Can you believe this?' Susan would say, as she related each new development about the couple's finances and custody battles. Susan appeared calm, seeming more bewildered than angry, Kuntz recounted.

'Did she ever make any statements about wanting to hurt her husband?' Costa asked.

'No. Never, not even after the phone call from her lawyer informing her that she was "losing" the divorce case,' she said. 'Susan was upset, but not enraged by the news.'

Kuntz was referring to an in-chambers conference that took place in Contra Costa Superior Court on 1 October. Neither party was present at the closed-door meeting that resulted in the temporary reduction of Susan's support payments, pending a review of the couple's finances by a court-appointed accountant. Attorneys for the couple appeared on their behalf.

As Costa spoke to Kuntz, it became clear that the timing of that decision couldn't have been worse. Susan had just plunked down a one thousand dollar deposit on a small two-bedroom condo near Big Sky. Now, she was being forced to make a trip back to California to deal with the fallout. Had Felix left things alone, Susan might have signed the deal and quietly moved out of state, but faced with a reduction in spousal support, Susan would no longer be able to afford such a move. The estate agent told Costa that she begged Susan not to return to the West Coast. While Susan never mentioned her husband by name, she had related enough horrific details of alleged abuse that Kuntz feared for her client's safety. Susan was stoic, assuring the estate agent that she intended to pack her belongings and return as soon as she could.

Once en route to Orinda, however, her plans seemed to have changed. Susan called Kuntz from the road. 'She phoned to cancel the purchase of the property, a problem had arisen and she needed to take care of some business before she would be ready to buy something in Montana,' the realtor recalled.

Susan promised to call again when she was ready to return.

'Did Susan look at any sporting goods stores while she was there, specifically to purchase a shotgun?' Costa asked.

'I have no knowledge of that. Susan never mentioned wanting to buy a gun of any sort,' Kuntz said.

After speaking with Kuntz, Costa again contacted Justin Simon, Felix's office landlord, and asked if he was treating Dr. Polk, as Susan alleged. 'That is not true,' the psychiatrist replied. 'Sometime ago I prescribed some medicine for him so he could sleep better. But as far as I know, Dr. Polk was not receiving any psychotherapy from anyone.'

Dr. Simon said that Felix had been a tenant in the building for about two years. 'I would not even describe our relationship as friends, just colleagues,' he said.

Neil Kobrin, president of Argosy University's Point Richmond campus, claimed to be one of Felix's closest friends. He had known Felix and Susan for more than twenty years, first as Felix's student and later as a colleague. A longtime member of the faculty at Argosy, Felix taught classes two days a week and was well regarded by students and faculty members, alike. A number of Polk's students had acknowledged him in thesis papers and during graduation speeches.

After learning of Dr. Kobrin's close relationship with Felix, Costa set out to interview him. The conversation provided several interesting bits of information. Dr. Kobrin, who was well into his seventies and still holding a full-time post at the university, told Costa that over the years Felix claimed that Susan 'was becoming more and more erratic, paranoid and delusional,' Kobrin related. Kobrin said he knew about Susan's belief that Felix had poisoned one of the family dogs.

Costa heard that allegation from Susan. Apparently, Susan believed that Felix fed their German Shepherd, Tucky, a lethal dose of Ex-Lax. She claimed to have saved the animal by administering the antidote, Pepto Bismol. The incident did not seem likely, but Costa noted it for the record.

In response to questions, Kobrin said he last spoke to Felix on Thursday, 10 October. Felix phoned his office to say he wouldn't be able to make the afternoon faculty meeting or his teaching session later that day. Things with Susan were so bad that he was 'barricading' himself in the bedroom at night to prevent her from gaining entry. He would be staying at a local hotel in Lafayette.

'Susan has a gun and is going to kill me,' Felix said during the call.

Korbrin acknowledged there were marital problems, but he had not seen or heard of any abuse, physical or emotional, during his decades-long friendship with the couple. In his opinion, Felix really didn't want the divorce.

'He was trying to keep the marriage together, if for anything, for the boys,' he said.

As they spoke about the complicated relationship, Costa was surprised to discover that Korbrin, Felix's close friend, had no idea how the couple met. He was unaware that Susan had been under Felix's care as a teenager, and that their romance had stemmed from that unethical relationship. Apparently, there was truth to Susan's claim that Felix hadn't wanted people to know those details, Costa noted.

On Friday, 25 October, detectives knocked on the door of Felix's longtime patient, Thomas Pyne. Pyne was the name Eli Polk had thrown out as a possible suspect in his father's murder.

It was just past noon when Detectives Costa and Moule pulled up to the sprawling house in the hills of El Sobrante. Over the past four decades, the small town had undergone a transformation similar to that of Orinda, evolving from a farming village to a busy suburban centre. Pyne lived on a rambling property several miles from the commercial district. He was at home and quickly answered the detectives' knock.

From behind dark sunglasses, Costa introduced himself to the sixty-something male who appeared in the doorway. Soft-spoken and friendly, the man introduced himself as Thomas Pyne.

Pyne was 'devastated' by news of Dr. Polk's death. He had been a patient for thirty-five years and was still seeing the psychologist on a regular basis, at least two times a week. His voice cracking, he affirmed that Felix was having marital problems, but he had no idea they were so serious. He first met Susan and the boys while a patient at Polk's home/office in Piedmont. Susan was friendly and usually greeted him with a wave, Pyne recalled. Costa learned that Pyne had never been to the couple's home in Orinda. As a patient, Pyne saw Felix at his office in Berkeley.

'Did you have an appointment with Dr. Polk on Monday the 14th?' Costa asked. 'Because I'm trying to determine if he missed appointments that day.'

'No. But during the past couple of weeks he's missed some appointments. Not shown up, you know.'

Pyne said he phoned the office on Tuesday, 15 October, and left a message on Felix's machine. When he received no response, he enquired about Felix at the office and the landlord, Justin Simon, informed him of the murder. Polk's patient was surprised when told his name had been mentioned in connection with Felix's death. 'Did the person say that I was the one who killed Dr. Polk?' he asked.

'That was never said,' Costa replied. 'It was more inferred. I have no reason to believe that you are involved, but anytime we have a name given to us under any circumstances, it is our job to talk to that person.'

Pyne was silent. 'I'm at a loss,' he blurted out. 'I will greatly miss having Dr. Polk as a therapist.'

A warm breeze blew through the house as the men discussed Pyne's decades-long relationship with the slain psychologist. While Costa already had his primary suspect in custody, protocol required that he pursue all avenues of investigation. Pyne did not strike Costa as a threat, but he still needed to rule him out as a suspect.

'Did you ever have an argument with Dr. Polk or give the doctor a reason to be concerned about you hurting him?' he asked.

'No. Felix and I got along fine.' There was a long pause, as if Pyne was silently reliving his sessions with the doctor. His responses were slow and deliberate, his tone measured. 'There were times over the years that during our sessions he might say something that angered me and I would simply tell him that and we would move on. And I guess there were times I would say something that would anger him and we would talk about it for a few minutes and move on with the session.'

In a subsequent interview, Pyne related that Felix was not himself during their last session together on Friday, 11 October. While Felix never wore suits to work, he was always neatly put together in tennis shorts and a pullover or slacks and a sport jacket. That Friday, Felix looked a wreck, Pyne recalled. Polk was not only physically unkempt, he was also distant and remote. Felix had always been an active participant in the therapy sessions. In fact, the two often practiced role-playing to help Pyne work through his relationship with his stern, detached father.

Felix agreed to treat Pyne even though he often had no money to pay his fees. Tom was grateful, promising to make good on his debt when he inherited his parents' estate. Pyne recalled that over the years Felix kept a running tab that he presented to him upon his father's death. It was a sum that Tom happily paid.

The detectives questioned the man until they were satisfied with the responses. Listening to Pyne discuss the positive impact that Felix had on his life, it was obvious that this man had no motive or desire to see Felix dead. If anything, his death would have an adverse effect on the patient. As their conversation wrapped up, Costa had to wonder why Eli had mentioned Pyne's name as a possible suspect. It seemed odd that the boy would suspect someone, who as far as Costa could tell, had no desire to see Felix dead.

CHAPTER SEVENTEEN

IN HER OWN
WORDS

When Detective Costa initially found Susan's diary, he did not know its value. While many who had been working on the case were hoping that the document would provide enough information to convict her, others remained skeptical. Police believed the file might reveal Susan's motive, personal thoughts – maybe even the planning of Felix's murder. Meanwhile Susan had told Detective Costa that the diary contained both 'real and imaginary events', as she tried to downplay the significance of the text.

Despite her attempt to discredit the writings, all of the entries in the document were dated and easy to follow, and they depicted Susan's thoughts, desires, and frustrations in startling detail during the seventeen months prior to Felix's murder. Her notations portrayed two very different sides to this bright and complicated woman. On the one hand, some of Susan's writings were articulate and thoughtful. She had a firm grasp on the couple's financial picture as she managed the household budget and myriad investment properties they owned. She was well-read and spent a good deal of time perusing a mixed bag of literary works.

Yet sprinkled amid the coherent writings were the ramblings of a woman who regularly suffered from delusions. Susan was convinced that she was a medium, that Felix was a Mossad agent, and that he had been putting 40 per cent of his money into an account in the Cayman Islands for the past twenty years.

Susan's journal began in May 2001, just four months after she attempted suicide at Yellowstone National Park. At the time, she was residing in a rental cottage in Stinson Beach, just over the Golden Gate Bridge via a winding road from San Francisco. According to her writings, she had moved out of the Orinda house the previous month after yet another violent encounter with Felix.

Interestingly, Susan's inspiration for the diary came from the book *Bridget Jones' Diary*. She loved how the book's protagonist used a journal to poke fun at her trials and tribulations and decided to adopt a similar sense of humour about her own situation. However, after reading a few pages, it quickly became clear that Susan's diary was not funny. Instead, it represented a series of disjointed ramblings by a woman who clearly harboured deep-seated anger and perhaps hatred for her husband. At one point she even referred to Felix as Dr. Josef Mengele, the ruthless Nazi concentration camp doctor.

In addition to the diary, Costa and his team had also turned up several of Susan's personal papers during their search of the office in the main house, including a number of letters written by her to various people involved with her divorce. One of the first letters went to Felix's divorce attorney, Steve Landes, in which she offered to sign over custody of Eli and Gabe in exchange for a speedy resolution to the divorce. Her return address was listed as a post office in Stinson Beach.

'This is to confirm that I will not be pursuing physical custody of my children, Eli and Gabriel,' Susan wrote to Landes on 12 May 2001. 'They wish to remain in Orinda, and I intend to relocate out of state . . . I am not requesting regular visitation . . . If you draw up the custody documents, I will sign them.'

Susan had requested the legal papers be drawn up prior to the couple's court hearing on 6 June. Yet Detective Costa found no such agreement among the written materials he confiscated.

In a second letter written that same month, Susan informed Felix of her intent to leave the Bay Area following the sale of the Orinda residence. She cited 'cost of living' and 'the damage' he had done to her reputation by 'maligning me publicly as "psychotic" and "delusional",' as reasons for moving out of state. She also related her displeasure with Felix's decision to use monies from their rental income to pay his personal expenses and suggested he refinance the Orinda property to cover real estate taxes until the residence was sold.

Susan also blasted Felix's request that she undergo a psychological evaluation before gaining custody of their minor children. In her recent letter to Steve Landes, she stated that she was not interested in custody of her children, apparently giving up on the idea of custody because of the court's continued reliance on his psychological opinion.

'As the court already has demonstrated that it has been and, in all liklihood [sic], will continue to be influenced or swayed by your opinions or recommendations, it seems likely that any professional you hire to do the evaluation will also be swayed. It is clear that you are determined to punish me by taking the kids away from me. You have said repeatedly to me, and them, that you will not let them go. It's time to move on.'

Susan closed by reiterating her willingness to forgo physical custody of them, but demanded prompt payment of her monthly support cheques – $6,500 in spousal support and $2,853 for her share of Social Security. She suggested Felix set up automatic payments directly from his account.

While she was writing letters, Susan continued to fill her diary with entries that shed light on events and her mental state in the days leading up to her suicide attempt on 16 January 2001. 'Felix had thrown all of my clothes on the floor and gone on one of his tirades, and I got very upset and left and went to Yosemite. It just seemed hopeless. I love my children so much and it felt like he was changing the character of my children and that he was turning them into people like himself. I had this moment of despair and I took a bottle of aspirin and Scotch. And then I realised I had made a mistake. I didn't want to die.'

Susan wrote that she phoned Felix for help and was admitted to a local hospital where a doctor found her to be depressed but sane. When the psychiatrist asked her what was going on, Susan was momentarily silent. Oddly enough, she was concerned about Felix's reputation and wanted to protect him. What she didn't know was that Felix was in an adjoining room insisting that she be committed for treatment.

'Here he is saying these stupid things about me, and I've got his power of attorney,' Susan noted. 'It was bizarre. Here I am managing all of our assets and Felix was trying to insinuate that I was crazy.'

In late May 2001, Susan and Eli boarded a plane for Paris. Her diary entries made it clear that Susan had high hopes for the European jaunt. She planned to use the vacation as an opportunity to 'bond with her middle son' and to show Eli the proper way to treat a woman. She felt her teenage sons were becoming abusive just like their father and wanted to intervene before it was too late. It did not take long for reality to hit home, and it was on the plane to Paris that her fragile psychological state became apparent.

'Half way through [the flight], I started feeling sick to my stomach . . . and go to the bathroom . . . One of the stewardesses was coming down the aisle . . . and told me that I was going to get "trapped in the bathroom by the carts" . . . Went ahead to the bathroom and was inside . . . for at least twenty minutes. Came out, and was jumped on by her partner for not wearing shoes on the plane . . .

'Ordered by rude fellow to put shoes on immediately and go back to my seat. Told him he was very rude. Started up aisle only to run into (rude attendant with cart) . . . Told me to get out of her way . . . I couldn't because other attendant was blocking me . . .

'She ordered me to go back to my seat, raising her voice, and grabbing my arm several times. I told her not to touch me and to stop shouting.'

Upon arrival, her hopes for the trip quickly receded as Eli quickly lost interest in the European holiday. On the second day after their arrival, Eli slept a lot, and Susan speculated he was getting sick. The following day proved no better as Eli informed her that he missed his friends and wanted to go home. The conflict climaxed while Eli and Susan were on their way to eat dinner.

'Taxi driver does not seem to know where restaurant is. Drops us off on street corner in Montparnasse . . . Eli launches into diatribe about how stupid I am. Don't know where I'm going. Don't do anything right. Certainly not knowledgeable like Dad . . . Meanwhile, I am trying to consult map but having considerable difficulty as am being bombarded by Eli in an all too familiar way about my numerous inadequacies.'

Susan described in some detail the foods she and Eli enjoyed during their two-hour meal, and the 'delicious bottle of wine' the two 'polished off'. Despite these indulgences, the meal did little to quell the rising fury between them.

'We stagger into a cab, stagger home, and Eli promptly gets on the phone and dutifully tells dad he's coming home', Susan recorded. 'I don't get it ... Asks dad to get him on flight ASAP ... Have uncomfortable feeling that Felix is somehow behind all this ... It is strange to hear Eli say now that the thought of my returning home is intolerable because nothing has changed. "Be nice to Dad," he says, "you have to be nice to Dad." He says that I have spent Dad's money today and now I must be nice to him. He doesn't seem to understand that it is also my money. "Dad's worked for that money, you don't work," Eli says. "Dad works every day of his life." Whatever I've done is completely unacknowledged ... Now, feel like failure.'

On 27 May, Susan dropped Eli at the airport and stayed in Paris to complete her holiday. The goodbye was hard on both mother and son, as the expectations for the trip crumbled before their eyes. 'Hugged him goodbye, and hurried away to hide my tears ... Eli in obvious guilt conflict ... Seems to feel he is betraying dad with me ... What has Felix done to him? ... If it's like what he did with me, Eli has a tremendous amount of suffering ahead of him ... Felix has all of the children brainwashed into believing that they have to stay with him.

'Eli has always had panic attacks when away from home ... Reminds me of me when I was too anxious to leave my room as a teenager. Couldn't imagine living without Felix ... Felix has a way of instilling these feelings – it's part of his controlling persona ... None of us will have any peace of mind as long as Felix is living with us.'

Once Eli left, things improved for Susan, who wrote enthusiastically about her Parisian museum romp on 28 May. Susan's entries remained upbeat and positive for the remainder of the vacation. 'Tomorrow, leave for home, which am not looking forward to at all,' she wrote on her final night in Paris. 'Must still find resolution. Cannot live with crazy, immoral, morally sick man. Also, destructive, sadistic, cruel, twisted, profligate, disturbed, criminal. Need I continue?'

Susan arrived back at the house in Orinda on 3 June. By 7 June, she had had enough. 'How can I describe how horrible it is? No, Felix

doesn't hit me anymore. Nor does Eli. So far, no more violent scenes.
But I detest every minute in his presence. All day long, all I do is clean
up after Felix, the children, the dogs, and the bird . . .

'I hate being in this country. I hate the smug, indifferent faces of
Americans. They have turned something off inside. Maybe it is their
humanity. They pretend to care about the poor, about children, about
the environment, about violence, when inside they are indifferent.
They are obedient. They are good Germans . . .

'I don't see how I can stay here until Gabe graduates. Friday, he is
having a Toga Party to celebrate his graduation from eighth grade.
Gabriel is flunking maths. He is not allowed to participate in his
graduation ceremony. He has invited an unknown number of children
to his party . . . It is going to be another mess to handle.'

On 13 June, after detailing an entry about a 'very strange dream'
involving Felix and the boys, Susan wrote the letter she would send to
Felix's first wife, Sharon Mann, if she had the courage:

> I am so sorry for any pain I ever caused you. But really, you
> should be grateful to me for having spared you the last twenty
> years with this monster. I wish he would let me go as readily as
> he let you. I want to thank you for having warned me . . . How I
> wish that I had listened to you . . .
>
> All these years, I have heard from him how terrible you were,
> how crazy, bitchy . . . I know you must have been a very good
> mother to have offset Felix's deadly parenting . . . I hope that
> life has compensated you in some way for what you must have
> suffered living with such a malevolent person.

In mid-June 2001, Susan signed a Power of Attorney granting Felix
permission to refinance the Miner Road house. She was departing in
two days for Thailand with Gabriel and was determined to pursue a
divorce upon her return on 6 July.

Before her departure, Susan penned a letter to Felix: 'I have resolved to
proceed with the divorce despite your objections that you don't want a
divorce. [The children] have reported to me the belief that they cannot
survive without you because you make all of the money . . . Should you
persist in claiming custody of the children, I will not deplete our financial
resources in fruitlessly contesting your claim . . .'

According to the diary, Susan's trip was filled with confusion over accommodations and confrontations with Gabriel. While her trip to Paris was salvaged once Eli flew back home, the Thailand vacation offered no such relief.

Asked Felix to book reservations at Club Med...on Phuket...After hour long drive to Club Med, informed by management no record of reservation. Club Med full of overweight Americans hanging out in packs at the bar and doing calisthenics together in the pool. Finally offered single room with one bed. Declined. Offered two rooms next to each other. Declined. Reservation was for adjoining rooms. Argued with concierge who had adjoining rooms available but refused to give them to me at same price. Departed Club Med in a huff and returned to Bangkok....

24 June 2001...So here we are at the Kiahuna and having a horrible time. Gabe is convinced I am a misanthrope. He makes one remark after another about how I hate everybody. Why is it so difficult to explain that I don't hate everybody? I'm selective.

On 26 June 2001, Eli arrived in Hawaii, where Susan and Gabe eventually ended up after their situation in Thailand continued to sour. Upon Eli's arrival, he claimed that he 'came on a mission to save our vacation.' Much to everyone's surprise, he actually did help quite a bit. Susan recalled that they 'had a lovely day . . . The only thing to mar it was to discover that I was over my limit on my credit card, and to hear from Felix. He said he needed certain documents to obtain the loan, which as far as I knew had already been approved . . . When I objected to his bothering me when I'm on vacation, he sounded amused. Felix has so much fun disturbing others. How disturbed he must be.'

While the trio appeared to avoid major confrontation for the remainder of the journey, returning home proved no easy task. 'Came home to tension and messes left by Felix for me to clean up,' Susan's entry of 9 July began. 'The man seems to thrive on it. Have resolved to go through with divorce. Can't stand lifestyle with him. Too depressing. F. oozes depression out of every pore. Adam's comment: "Dad is depressed. He's always been depressed." Little by little, it eats away at us all.'

On 12 July, Susan recorded the details of her meeting with a divorce attorney, Dan Ryan, whom she described as 'a self styled "tough Irishman"'. She had been without legal representation since 1 May 2001, when she fired her divorce lawyer because she was dissatisfied with his representation. At the meeting, Ryan informed Susan that she would have to go through a custody evaluation if she intended to fight for the kids.

In addition to meeting with Ryan, Susan also met with a therapist named Heidi Leslie on that July day. 'I had lots to talk about by the time I got inside . . . The therapist was kept very busy ahhhing, yessssssing, and mmmmming, by the virtually incessant stream of descriptive prose, which issued from me as if the plug had been pulled. . . . Why is it that at the oddest moments, the phrase "butter wouldn't melt in her mouth", just seems to pop into my head? Well, butter wouldn't melt in her mouth. How is it that human beings become so inhuman?'

Moving on, Susan wrote, 'Last night, Felix was in fine fettle. How did he put it? "Someone should do you a favour and just kill you." And Leslie [the therapist] wanted to know if I was afraid; if I believed I was in danger.'

One week later, on 18 July, Susan informed Felix of her intention to take the children to live out of state. 'F. went crazy. . . . Yelled at G. and E. that if they chose to live with me, they were not his sons. Threatened he wouldn't support me, and then that he wouldn't support them.' Susan explained that she wanted to get away from the congestion in the Bay Area and purchase or rent a ski house in Wyoming or Idaho 'in order to live a more relaxed peaceful lifestyle, ski, hike, and just enjoy the outdoors.'

Later on, she discussed the issue of physical custody of the children. She was sure Felix would insist on joint custody whether the boys wanted to live with him or not. It would be his way of preventing her from moving the boys out of state.

'F. yelled I had brainwashed the boys, and that if we left, we would get no support from him.' She described how Felix tried to divide the boys, first attacking Eli, telling his middle son that he didn't care what he thought, was more interested in Gabriel's feelings, and was not convinced that Gabe was really all that enthused about moving to Montana.

Susan pointed out that Felix had allowed his first wife to take their daughter, Jennifer, to live in Illinois when she was sixteen. 'He said that was different because I'm crazy and Sharon wasn't. The boys then pointed out that F. had told them that Sharon was crazy many times . . .

'F. finally blew his stack and threw things at me and Gabe (a bowl of maccaroni [sic] and cheese, spoons, cups), then walked over and kicked the big screen T.V. which cost $5,000 after overturning an antique mission oak chair valued at over $2,500 . . .

'Adam came home and suggested F. go out for a drink. Said it was time for our marriage to end as some marriages do . . . Asked me if he could visit me in Wyoming or Idaho. I said of course. F. accused Adam of making fun of him and stormed off. Sounded very paranoid himself after having accused Eli of being delusional and paranoid earlier.

'Adam said he was worried about me and Gabe, felt we were not safe with F. while he was so angry.'

The incidents on 18 July set off a chain reaction in Susan as she began researching life in Wyoming and Montana and becoming increasingly serious about leaving the marriage and the state. On 31 July she wrote that it was 'as if I had been hypnotised into seeing in F. my ideal man. Now that I have awakened from the hypnotic state, which lasted most of our twenty eight year relationship, have stripped off the suave, urbane image of a gentleman pasted onto Felix, can see him as the crude, weak, mean spirited little bastard that he is . . . obsessed with power and control and proving his potency.'

As the fall approached, Susan's diary entries reflected a growing debate between Susan and Felix about her plan to take Eli and Gabe out of state. They argued repeatedly over schools for the boys and the practical aspects of Susan raising Eli and Gabe in Montana. During this time, Susan often wrote about Felix's verbal and physical abuse, saying that he 'seems to still have a lot of angry feelings about my moving him out of the bedroom. Said he felt like slugging me in the face. Called me a criminal and a swine for the umpteenth time.

'My criminality, according to F., lies in my having turned him out of my room and brainwashed the children against him . . . He lost control of himself again and struck me in the face with a roll of papers. I suggested he get some help. Chased me out of his room. Then kicked the TV screen, much to Eli's dismay who was watching it.'

On 1 September, Susan informed Felix that she was leaving California on 7 September, and revoked 'any powers of attorney' she had given him. 'If you get a court order, as you have threatened to do, forbidding me from taking Eli and Gabe out of California, I will not take them with me,' she wrote in a letter.

Still she persisted with the idea that they would accompany her, outlining a plan for Eli to enroll in a public school in Bozeman until the spring term. 'The move would benefit Gabriel, as well,' Susan insisted. He failed several of his eighth grade classes at Orinda Intermediate and was beginning to 'hate' school. 'A change of scene will do him good,' Susan noted.

'I don't want the children to lose you . . . ' Susan noted at the end of the letter. 'I do want the children to have a father as a resource: a reasonable, mature, unselfish father who is primarily concerned with his children's best interests rather than with using his children as leverage.

'You have stated that you will obtain a court order restricting me from removing the children from California. You have also threatened to kill me, to stop working to support the family, and to kill yourself. I don't take any one of these threats more seriously than the other, and intend to proceed with planning as if you will come to your senses.'

While Susan made much of Felix's determination to thwart her move with the two boys, it appears he did nothing to stop her when she actually departed. On Friday, 7 September, the three set off for Montana without incident in Susan's Volvo wagon, which was packed with personal belongings and pieces of furniture 'important to the boys'.

Several days later, she sent Felix an update.

'We all miss our home in California,' she wrote in a letter dated 13 September. 'Montana will take some getting used to. It gets very cold here in the winter. Main Street in Bozeman is like stepping back in time . . . The good news: the drug scene is very small here; the kids are focussing [sic] on their home work; both are eligible for their driver's licences . . . Best regards.'

After nearly a month of living in a cabin outside of Bozeman, Susan wrote this entry in her diary: 'I feel incredibly sad about Adam, who is gone in more ways than one. He has started school at UCLA. Just before we left, he threatened to kill me, provoked by Felix to a great extent. But I am still stunned by it. Not even Eli ever threatened to kill me. Adam hates me.'

Though Adam and Susan remained at odds, by late November 2001, it was clear that the change of venue did nothing to help Eli. Once again, he was involved with drugs. By month's end, the teen was on his way back to Orinda. 'After talking to us both, he [Eli] got into his car and drove to California,' Susan wrote in a letter to Felix on 26 November. 'On the way, he received a speeding ticket for going over 90 mph. This is the second speeding ticket he has gotten in the two months since I purchased his car . . .

'His decision to leave was based on the restrictions I placed on his truancy and marijuana usage . . . limiting his access to money: I purchased a safe to keep my wallet in, and refused to provide him with his usual allowance while he was binging on marijuana and until the stolen money was paid back.'

Susan demanded the keys to Eli's car until he got clean. 'Eli decided, against my wishes, to drop out of school and return to California.'

Once home, Eli was continuing with his 'out of control drug binging'. Susan noted that her son had a car accident during the Thanksgiving holiday.

'I suggest that his car not be returned to him until he has completed a drug treatment program and either enrolls in school or gets a job,' she advised Felix in the letter. 'I also do not believe that he should have access to large sums of cash on weekends for the time being.'

Susan, too, would return to the East Bay by month's end, and she alerted Felix of her plan. Pointing to their 'difficulty agreeing on disciplinary measures' Susan instructed Felix to find a home 'elsewhere'. 'Eli . . . is living unsupervised in the cottage in Orinda . . . which he uses as a "party pad" . . . a gathering place for teenagers to drink and drug,' she wrote. 'It seems to me that you attempt to garner sympathy with the children by reversing my decisions. For example, when Adam ran up a $2,000 phone bill in June, and then followed with a $250 phone bill for his cell phone in September, disciplining him was left to me. When he ran up a $540 phone bill for his cell phone for the past month, I finally said enough and confiscated his cell phone OVER YOUR OBJECTIONS.

'You demanded repeatedly that I return it to him. You felt I was being too hard on the boy, which made you very popular with Adam and made me look very bitchy ... When Adam stole $100 out of my wallet ... then lied and said Eli or Gabe took it, adding that I was "paranoid", a term for me he got from you, you supported Adam. You did ask me to tell my side of the story as if I were one of the kids as you have been used to doing ...

'You are going to have to set selfish concerns aside and do what is best for the boys.'

On 27 November, Gabriel was on a flight for San Francisco and Susan followed by car the next day. Susan was returning to Orinda and to Felix, the man she held responsible for her lifelong misery. Diary entries revealed that the fighting between the couple escalated once she returned to California, and by the end of 2001, Felix had moved out of the house and into a one bedroom apartment.

Nevertheless, the two continued to squabble over money and the payments he owed her. 'Meetings with you tend to end badly with threats from you,' she wrote on 18 February 2002. 'Your attorney has my phone number. We can communicate through attorneys ... With respect to financial support: your continued support of this family is not contingent upon my persuading the children to see you, my talking to you, or being "nice" to you, or the children's being "nice" to you.

'You are responsible for supporting the children through college. ... I am reducing expenses as much as possible. I have let my cleaning lady go. The boys and I are taking care of the home together. I cannot afford to give Adam an allowance of $100 per week, which I have been doing while he is at college. Adam has gotten a job, as you know. You are legally and ethically responsible for this payment ... Should you continue to shirk your responsibilities, I intend to take legal action against you.'

The scenario was familiar. Felix's first wife, Sharon Mann, had written similar letters during their divorce, especially in regard to his supposed inability to pay tuition for their son, Andrew, then a freshman at Tufts University. It is interesting that, like his first divorce, Felix's marriage to Susan was ending after exactly twenty years of marriage, the very year his eldest child, Adam, was a freshman at UCLA.

On 26 February, Susan typed what appeared to be a suicide note to her sons that seemed more an introductory lesson in how to invest in real estate – counselling them to consult an attorney before taking any major steps and urging them not to have any rental properties in low-income areas:

> Dear Boys
> I want to leave you with an explanation for my actions so that you do not make the mistake of blaming yourselves for what has happened

In the letter, Susan reiterated the abuse she suffered as a child and the abuse she suffered by their father when she was a girl:

> I married your father believing that I was in love with him. From time to time, it seemed as if I had forgotten something, and I would begin to remember what he had done, as well as the horror of my childhood that I had put away. . . .
>
> After years of being blamed for every mishap in our lives, after threats to take you away from me and have me confined to a mental hospital, I attempted suicide last year believing that perhaps your dad could do what he threatened to do. . . .

Susan reassured her sons that she loved and admired them, noting their many talents and attributes:

> The series of misfortunes that have dogged our lives just leaves me tired . . . It is through no fault of yours that I have decided to give up. I just need to rest.

In wanting to leave her children with some guidance after her death, Susan outlined some advice they could follow:

1. Marry wisely.
2. Don't spend all the money I leave you. Money is freedom to a certain degree although it also brings responsibilities.
3. Never relax your guard.
4. If anyone offers to include you in any get rich quick or quicker schemes, say NO. . . .
5. Do not invest in real estate partnerships . . .

6. but choose carefully. Avoid low-income areas for rental property.
7. Hold onto the rental properties, which you have.
8. Consult an attorney about rent laws. . . .
9. Be extra careful in Berkeley. . . .
10. Forsake violence.
11. Do not follow your father's example, or anyone else's for that matter.
12. Drugs and alcohol cloud your good judgment.
13. So do your emotions. Make your decisions when you have calmed down, but be flexible. . . .
14. DO NOT BE SUGGESTIBLE. . . .
15. You are inheriting enough to last you the rest of your lives if you don't spend it all when you get it . . . Don't touch your investments. . . .

I leave you all of my love. Find good homes for the dogs. You can't take them with you, and they won't want to go where I'm going.

Despite the letter's pessimistic tone, Susan was aggressively pursuing the divorce. She contacted Felix's lawyer with solutions to their divorce settlement. While there is no indication that Felix agreed to her terms, Susan's entries remained upbeat as she wrote of the vast improvements to their lives since they returned from Montana and Felix moved out of the house.

'So much has changed in the last few months . . . we returned to Orinda, booted Felix out, and began having the time of our lives. Eli got off of drugs. Gabe worked hard in school. And we all had fun together. Then Dad happened. He filed for custody.'

Detailing the unfortunate turn of events, Susan discussed Eli's arrest in late February for hitting a boy, an action which landed him in juvenile hall. 'He [Eli] was placed under a programme called "home supervision". He wears an electronic monitoring device on his ankle. He has to get permission from "peace officers" at juvenile hall to leave his dad's cottage.'

Susan noted that Eli was sleeping on the couch of Felix's one-bedroom apartment in downtown Berkeley. But the arrangement was not working out.

Susan acknowledged that she was accused of being in contempt of court with regard to Eli's court case, and, sentenced to five days in jail, 'The judge gave me a few days to think about it. I did, and still I refused. Eli continued to come over, and finally just began to live at home again.'

Her diary continued, 'When Eli was arrested, I made an offer to F's attorney to settle our differences by leaving the country and relinquishing custody of the children . . . I would not return or have any contact with the children until after F's death. In exchange, he would not bother me. I would inherit my share of the property at his death, the kids would inherit their share, F's kids would not inherit from what we had acquired during the course of our marriage. F has salted away millions. They could inherit from that.'

When Felix declined, Susan said she offered to compromise. She would still move away. 'They just ignored my offer. F. expects me to struggle . . . to negotiate over the children . . . F. expects the children to accept his version of reality: mom is sick, mom is crazy . . . He has offered to live in our cottage so that I can see Eli . . .

'At first, I pretended I would trade places with them and live in their cottage. But . . . I can't live there . . . Berkeley is such a cynical community of smug, self-satisfied university people. I would suffocate . . . It was a mecca for people like F. who saw themselves as the cleverest, lightest, fittest in the fifties and the sixties . . .'

Susan noted that in the same week Eli was sentenced, she learned that her mother had cut her out of the will. 'I lost my home, my children. I am looking forward to never setting foot in this country again.'

In addition to her diary, Susan's writings included a number of postcards and letters that she mailed to Eli at Juvenile Hall while en route to Montana in the fall of 2002. These would be her last correspondences until after Felix's death.

'Sun Valley is pristine (undeveloped) and like a Hollywood set – picture perfect,' Susan wrote in a postcard dated 22 September from Salmon, Idaho. 'But there are too many Hollywood people there. Am moving on.'

Another postcard to Eli read: 'I hope to find a place I feel comfortable in. I can see it in my imagination. No crowds. Lots of trees. Animals. Empty roads. Rivers. Clear skys [sic]. Privacy. You will come to see me there when you are free to do so.'

Susan wrote to her divorce attorney, Dan Ryan, as well. In the letter, she reacted to news of the 27 September telephone conference in which the Contra Costa Superior Court judge awarded Felix 'legal and physical custody of Gabriel' and 'exclusive use and occupancy of the family residence located at 728 Minor Road.'

'I object to holding the hearing scheduled for Wednesday in my absence,' Susan said of the judge's decision to schedule a follow-up hearing for 3 October. 'Please request that the hearing be postponed until I can return. The issues to be addressed might reasonably be resolved outside of court, those issues being spousal support, custody, and family support . . . I left Gabe with Felix while I was looking for a home.

'Meanwhile, it is impossible for me to bid on a family residence when I have lost physical custody of Gabe and when my support award is subject to Felix's whimsy. Whether or not I have physical custody of Gabe will determine whether or not I buy a residence. The amount of support I can expect to receive reliably will have bearing on where I choose to settle as well as what kind of home I will buy.'

Susan asked that the attorney make a motion on her behalf to have the physical custody order rendered that Friday vacated.

'I have not abandoned Gabe,' she noted.

Susan went on to explain that she had identified several affordable properties and was arranging to have Gabe fly out to Montana to see them. She noted that it would be impossible for her to proceed with negotiations for the purchase of a home until she learned for certain that she could have her children with her.

In a follow-up letter dated 3 October, Susan fired Dan Ryan and then set off for California. Angry that the scheduled hearing occurred despite her objections, Susan blamed Ryan for his role in the events.

In subsequent entries made upon her return to Orinda, Susan claimed that she and Felix had reached 'some verbal agreements'; they were $170,000 in debt and couldn't afford to have one of them occupying the apartment in Berkeley, as that would be a loss of $2,400 a month in rental income, she wrote. They agreed that one of them should stay in the guesthouse, but the question remained: which one? Susan felt that it should be Felix, while her husband felt he had won the right to reside in the sprawling estate and was unwilling to compromise.

These discussions of their tentative oral agreement proved to be the last of the rambling, often confused entries in Susan Polk's diary. While Susan's writings chronicled events as she viewed them, as well as her growing dislike of her husband, they contained no evidence that she was plotting his murder. The diary merely revealed page after page of motive, providing insight into Susan in the months and years predating Felix's murder. The lengthy memoir failed to provide the 'smoking gun' police had anticipated when they listed it as part of the 15 October search warrant of the Miner Road residence.

Despite the inherent bias in the pages, the reality that they detailed was unsettling. The years of abuse and emotional scarring were apparent on both sides, and regardless of their history, it was clear that both Felix and Susan were growing tired of the status quo. And yet, Susan did not seem like a person on the edge of murder – particularly in her last entries where there is little to suggest that she was a woman who was about to be pushed too far. In the end, the diary created more questions than answers, and chief among them was – why had all this happened now? While Susan was still irate over the actions that took place in her absence, her final entries show a woman whose divorce was on the path to settlement. Her pragmatic, conciliatory tone when discussing Felix's financial situation didn't show a woman who was sharpening her knives; they showed a woman who had finally come to the table.

But in spite of their progress, many sticking points remained, including the role that the cottage would play in their lives. One of them had to give up claim to the main home and move to the guesthouse. It was a dispute that would last until the very end.

CHAPTER EIGHTEEN
THE REAL FELIX?

'Dear Mom, I'm going to Dad's funeral this Saturday,' Eli wrote to Susan from juvenile hall on 5 November, 2002. 'I don't think I am going to say anything. What would I possibly have to say about him? Nothing good.'

Eli made good on his word. He was granted permission from juvenile officials to attend the 9 November memorial service for his father at Christ the King Parish in Pleasant Hill. With his close-cropped hair and broad shoulders, the teen was easily identifiable in the sanctuary's front pew, where he sat shoulder to shoulder with his siblings, Adam and Gabriel.

Although Felix was Jewish, his funeral could not be held immediately after his death as is the Jewish custom; police insisted on an autopsy as part of the murder investigation. Once the autopsy was performed, it would be another three weeks before the memorial service was held. Felix was not a practicing Jew and had even gone so far as to tell Adam that he was an agnostic. Still, Susan had felt it was important for her sons to know about their father's heritage and orchestrated the Jewish holidays at their home in an attempt to honour both her faith and that of her husband's family. Sometimes the

Polks celebrated Christmas and other times they celebrated Hanukah – with no discernible pattern.

After some discussion, it was decided that the funeral would be held at Christ the King Parish, a small Catholic house of worship in San Francisco's East Bay, and funded, at least in part by Argosy University where Felix taught. Mourners arriving at the church on Brandon Road that autumn day were momentarily taken aback by the psychedelic rock and roll music that filled the sanctuary. Adam had chosen the song, 'Wish You Were Here', the 1975 hit from the British rock band, Pink Floyd, to kick off the service, although it was not clear why Adam selected that track to memorialise his father; perhaps it was because Pink Floyd was a group that Felix counted among his favorites.

As the words of the song droned from overhead speakers, old family photos of Felix flashed onto two large screens set up on either side of the altar: a young Felix embracing his infant son from his first marriage, playing cello accompaniment to his first wife, Sharon Mann, and another of Felix trekking outdoors and carrying a child on his back. The pictures elicited smiles and laughter from those who came to pay their final respects to the slain therapist. There was silent anticipation that one of the photos would contain an image of Felix's spouse and alleged killer, but the photomontage had been edited to exclude any photos of Susan Polk.

Like the slide presentation, the tender eulogies that followed also failed to mention Felix's second wife. Instead, friends and colleagues publicly remembered a warm, caring man who loved his work and his children. One of the speakers was Ernst Vaulfer, a fellow Holocaust survivor who had known Felix for more than forty years. Another person who took the pulpit that afternoon was Felix's former patient, Sheila Burns, the psychologist who Susan suspected of having an affair with her husband.

Susan made no request to attend Felix's funeral, and his children from his first marriage, Andrew and Jennifer Polk, decided not to fly in for the ceremony, electing instead to hold their own private memorial on the East Coast some days later. Adam and Gabriel told Court TV's Lisa Sweetingham that Jennifer and Andrew were rarely a presence in their lives. Andrew, who was already in college when Felix left Sharon, did not stay in close contact with his father. Their relationship worsened after Felix declined to pay for his college tuition. Jennifer was in and out of the picture over the years. She had lived with Felix and Susan for a brief time after their marriage but as time passed her visits became infrequent. Nevertheless Adam and Gabriel elected to fly east to share their father's loss with their half siblings. Eli, still in custody in the juvenile facility, was not permitted to make the cross-country trek.

It is not known if Felix's first wife, Sharon Mann, attended that service. She was not among the mourners at the 9 November ceremony in California. Sharon had reacted with a mix of surprise and sadness when she learned of Felix's death from police the day after his body was found in the guest cottage.

'I feel so sorry for him,' she tearfully told a reporter who reached her for a reaction. 'It's such a horrible tragedy.' Though polite, Sharon declined to comment publicly about her relationship with Felix or the circumstances surrounding his death. While many of his friends and colleagues expressed similar remorse over Felix's death, they also refused to discuss Felix's relationship with his second wife openly. In addition to their disapproval of his dual relationship with Susan, there was also quiet talk during the subsequent coffee hour in the church meeting room of Felix's propensity for inappropriate relationships with other patients outside the confines of his office. Felix thought nothing of socialising with them and even soliciting their professional services – be they piano lessons from his music teacher patient or legal advice from an attorney he was counselling.

Several of his colleagues even suggested they knew of his affair with Susan around the time it began and quietly denounced his involvement with the fragile teen. While it is true that in the late 1960s there was no California law against a therapist having intercourse with a patient, most viewed it as an ethical violation of patient/doctor privilege. In Susan's case, the violation was even more serious because she was allegedly underage when the sexual relationship began.

Sexual contact between a patient and therapist is now a crime in California that is punishable by six months in jail. The law, however, permits sexual relations between therapist and patient two years after the termination of therapy. The stipulation stems from the theory that transference will have worn off after two years, however, many in the field assert that transference is everlasting. Experts have even suggested that Felix's inappropriate sexual relationship with his teenage patient might have caused him to misdiagnose Susan. It's possible that he failed to recognise that she might very well have been a borderline personality, a diagnosis that brings with it lifelong symptoms of depression, rage, and hostility.

And while there were no other accusations of inappropriate sexual relationships with patients over the years, Felix had a widespread reputation for regularly violating protocol. One such incident occurred in October 1997, when Felix was accused of providing insufficient care for a child because of his close relationship to the boy and his father.

During the ongoing investigation into Felix's murder, we obtained access to the family court file that involved the custody of this ten-year-old boy who was in therapy with Felix. In a five-page letter to the judge presiding over the case, the family, and the child counsellor asked to render an evaluation, accused Dr. Polk of 'limiting the effectiveness of his therapy because of his dual and inappropriate social relationships with the boy and his father.' The counsellor wrote: 'These dual relationships have resulted in unorthodox treatment protocols (doing treatment at the father's home, picking the boy up from school, and taking him home after the therapy, not attending treatment on his mother's custodial time) that can make it difficult for the child to experience the treatment as emotionally safe and neutral.

'Additionally, Dr. Polk has involved himself in the current litigation between the parents by speaking to the father's attorney about the boy's treatment and relationships with his parents without notice or consent from the mother. These behaviours on the part of Dr. Polk are in contrast to current ethical standards and practices.'

Psychotherapist Karen Saeger, a colleague of Dr. Polk's at the California Graduate School of Professional Psychology in Berkeley from 1979 to 1986, claimed that Felix had a 'widespread reputation' on the campus for his twofold relationship with Susan. Saeger portrayed his actions as 'disturbing and improper'.

'There were two Felixes,' she said of Polk. 'One was tightly coiled like he could spring at you; the other was charming and charismatic.'

Kathy Lucia, a former patient of Polk's, had a similar reaction. Lucia, who, along with Susan, had participated in the group sessions that Felix led during the 1970s, said that she recalled Felix 'was trying to control' Susan during the meetings.

Susan was 'dependent on him [Felix] in a lot of ways,' Lucia said.

It is not uncommon for at-risk patients such as Susan to form attachments to their therapists. Professionals are trained to anticipate these feelings of transference and take steps to avoid vulnerability on the part of patients, as well as themselves. In Felix's case, it seems he threw caution to the wind in acting out his own personal fantasy with his teenage patient.

Despite his professional recklessness, he had to have known the emotional danger that existed when a therapist disappointed or violated his patient in some way. According to the famous 1966 study conducted by William Masters and Virginia Johnson, the damage a woman can suffer as a result of a sexual relationship with her therapist is tantamount to rape. (Not surprisingly, Susan often described her sexual relationship with Felix as rape.)

Nevertheless Felix ignored all of the studies, judgment, and professional common sense when he crossed the line from therapist to lover with Susan, and in the end the realities of her psychological state overwhelmed him. Indeed to become someone's doctor and husband is always too much, but in Felix's case the combination proved deadly. Instead of improving, her problems seemed to worsen over the years and Felix couldn't possibly absorb all of her love, trust, and paranoia.

Long before his murder, Felix had become the ultimate authority figure in Susan's life, the embodiment of her years spent listening to others. While once she obeyed his every word, during the final years of their marriage it was clear that her subservience was a thing of the past, and there was nothing he could do to regain his lost ground. Unlike the police or a judge, he could not hold her in contempt or arrest her; he had no rebuttal for the fear she instilled. He was incapable of taking the steps necessary to protect himself – not because he didn't know what was right – but because the very fact that he needed help was an outward sign of his failure.

It shouldn't have been this way. In his mind, he believed he had 'fixed' her at age sixteen and to think that her persistent problems stemmed from those residual issues was to admit his failings. For Felix to obtain a restraining order against his wife, for him to abandon his home for a hotel, would have been to admit the truth: Dr. Polk had lost his patient long ago. He'd lost her back in his office on Ashby Avenue. He'd lost her when he should have been helping her the most. He'd lost her the moment he laid a hand on her.

It was a reality too intimidating to confront, a failure too grand to realise. And so when all of his friends insisted that he move out, when all of his logic told him to leave the house, he could not, choosing instead to remain in the confines of the guest cottage with the door unlocked, waiting – perhaps even hoping – to find a way that he could heal Susan before it was too late.

CHAPTER NINETEEN

BROKEN BONDS

On 23 October 2002, Contra Costa County Superior Court Judge Merle Eaton honoured the prosecutor's no-bail request and ordered Susan remanded to the West County Detention Facility in Richmond. In court, Judge Eaton agreed with Contra Costa County Assistant District Attorney Tom O'Connor's claim that Susan was a flight risk. He pointed to statements she had made in the letter she wrote to Superior Court Judge William Kolin in September 2002, regarding Eli's probation violation.

'In one part of the letter, the defendant clearly indicates she would sell her home and leave the area,' Judge Eaton stated in his ruling. 'It was those statements that caused Eaton "great concern" and prompted him to make the no-bail ruling,' he wrote.

Susan's no-bail status meant that Gabriel would need to find another place to live. He was released to the custody of his eldest brother, Adam, after spending the night of 14 October speaking with detectives at the Martinez headquarters. While Adam was technically old enough to care for his minor sibling, he wanted to complete his college education. There was brief talk of Gabriel joining Adam at the frat house at UCLA in Los Angeles, but the authorities immediately rejected that plan.

Since leaving police headquarters, Gabriel had been staying at the home of a Lafayette couple, Marjorie and Dan Briner, who were the parents of Adam Polk's close friend, Andy. When the couple learned of Gabriel's situation, they immediately opened their home to the teen. The Briners had never actually met Gabriel or his parents, but they thought highly of Adam and wanted to help. Marjorie was a middle-school teacher and Dan worked in commercial real estate, and the pair lived in nearby Lafayette.

Gabriel's stay was intended to be temporary, but as time passed, the Briners invited him to remain on a permanent basis. He fit in well with the family and was flourishing in their care. When he arrived, Marjorie noted that he was 'the most angry boy I've ever met'. He wanted nothing to do with his mother, tearing up some of her letters and leaving them in shreds in the trash. At first, Marjorie taped them back together. But after Gabe threatened to leave if she continued to repair them, she just left the remaining letters in a pile unopened for him to read when he was ready.

Despite the initial setbacks, Gabriel was soon able to form a bond with the family, and the Briners were among the few family friends invited a few days after the funeral to accompany Gabe and his siblings – Adam, Eli, Andrew, and Jennifer – to their father's cremation and the sombre hike that followed. Felix once told Adam that he wanted to be cremated, like his father. Eric and the other children intended to honour that wish, deciding to pay homage to Felix's love of the outdoors by releasing his ashes at the end of a lengthy trek to the top of Mount Tamalpais. Located just north of San Francisco's Golden Gate Bridge, it was one of Felix's favourite hiking spots with more than fifty miles of trails, towering redwoods and oaks, and a serpentine road to the top of the park's summit. After the long walk, the siblings and the Briners released his ashes into the breeze as the dust of Felix hovered in the air, drifting down on the San Francisco Bay.

Initially, Susan had no objections to her son's placement with the Briners and even seemed to be fairing well in jail. She sent out homemade holiday cards at Christmas time 2002, and in the months after her incarceration, she wrote furiously to her sons, receiving responses from Eli and Adam, but not from Gabriel. Instead, she learned how he was doing through letters from Dan and Marjorie.

In one letter, dated 12 March 2003, Dan praised Gabriel's progress. 'His studies are really quite good,' Dan wrote. 'He is improving on his study skills, reluctantly, like most teenagers that I know and he is beginning to be willing to recognise those areas that he needs to work on.'

Keeping the imprisoned mother apprised of every detail, Dan informed Susan that her son was now a member of the De La Salle rugby team and the junior varsity football team and that he 'was getting along well with our family.'

'We have had no problem with him breaking primary rules such as smoking, drinking, or significant defiance,' Dan noted. 'And we communicate openly and frankly so that he knows he has both commitment and support. He continues to work with his counsellor twice a week . . . He is still not reading your letters. We always tell him when they arrive and we keep them unopened for him for a later time. We recognise that they are very important to him . . . Gabe sees more and more that he has a lot of opportunity and a lot of potential and Marjorie and I think he will excel.'

These letters to Susan continued until July or August of 2003, when Susan and Marjorie Briner had a verbal confrontation over the telephone. The altercation, which came after months of angry letters and phone calls from Susan, prompted Marjorie to cut off all communication with Gabe's mother. At first, the couple obliged Susan's myriad requests, including shopping for Christmas and birthday gifts for her sons for which she promised to reimburse the couple. However, this arrangement soured after Susan raged at Marjorie for refusing to buy Adam a DVD that he insisted he didn't want.

Susan's pattern was to blow up, rant and rave, and then follow up with a kind letter as if the angry incident never took place. It was a difficult routine for a family that was just trying to help a young teenager get back on his feet, and by August of 2003, Marjorie Briner could not bear any more confrontations. In addition to her verbal abuse, Susan was now claiming the Briners were conspiring with others to rob the Polk estate, accusing the family of brainwashing her sons against her in order to get their hands on the family money.

This conspiracy theory was further complicated by the fact that Susan was convinced the Briners were in cahoots with Felix's twin brother, John, and John's attorney, Bud Mackenzie, who was representing John in the Polk estate proceedings. She even went so far as to blame the couple for pocketing Gabriel's monthly social security check of twelve hundred dollars to spend on personal indulgences, a check that Gabe's half sister, Jennifer, had arranged for him to receive after their father's death.

In reality, Gabriel was turning over his cheque each month to help offset the couple's expenses. Although they both held good jobs, the Briners were not rich. Dan Briner was hoping to teach Gabriel how to manage his finances, and in the early days, he was giving the teen a four hundred dollar monthly allowance, which he increased as the boy showed he could handle his own financial affairs.

The success that the family experienced with Gabriel eventually led them to take responsibility for Eli after he was released from Byron Boys' Ranch in the summer of 2003. The arrangement did not last long, and Eli stayed just two weeks, claiming the couple tried to sour him on his mother.

'He was essentially living out of his car, but sleeping at the house,' Dan Briner said of Eli's brief stay. 'He had his girlfriend downstairs. We were trying to help him. The plan was to send him out to a school in Colorado that would take him. He liked rugby and we thought that the estate would cover the tickets.

'His Aunt Evelyn helped with the planning,' Dan said of Felix's older sister, who had gone on to become a concert pianist. She was also one of Eli's biggest supporters, offering to help in any way she could, but there didn't seem to be anything that Evelyn could do.

'It was all set up and then Susan called [Eli] and said "It's a trap, they're manipulating you." Then, just like that, it stopped,' Dan Briner said. 'Then there was this falling out with Marjorie and I asked him [Eli] to leave because he wasn't following directions. Once you put any pressure on Eli, Susan just goes off.'

After the situation at the Briners eroded, Eli moved to Los Angeles to live in the university frat house with Adam, but that arrangement, too, quickly turned unmanageable. Susan grew furious when she learned that Eli was burning through his trust fund, spending in excess of twenty thousand dollars in just a few months on food and entertainment. Eli explained that he had no choice: he had to eat out because the frat house had no kitchen.

Eventually, Eli ended up back at the Orinda house. He was living there only a short time when he was arrested and charged with reckless driving after leading police on a high-speed chase, reaching speeds as high as 130 mph on Interstate 680.

It was around midnight on 14 October 2003 – the one-year anniversary of Felix's death – that a sheriff's deputy from the City of San Ramon Police Department initially spotted Eli's Camaro passing by with expired registration tags. After radioing his dispatcher, Sheriff's Deputy Mark Johnson flicked on his red and blue police lights to make a traffic stop, causing the Camaro to accelerate to speeds of between 40 to 50 mph in the 35 mph zone. Johnson turned on his siren and sped after the Camaro.

As the car approached I-680, Johnson watched it fishtail before entering the highway. Flooring his accelerator, the trooper muttered under his breath as the Camaro pulled away. At one point, he glanced down at his milometer and noted that he was travelling at 130 mph – twice the legal limit – and quickly terminated the pursuit because of the danger to himself and other motorists.

He watched in frustration as the Camaro sped off, weaving through traffic before exiting the Interstate on Bollinger Canyon Road, where a second trooper, Deputy Sheriff Jeffrey Schraeder, picked up the chase. Shraeder observed the Camaro skid sideways with tires screeching across three lanes of traffic before its driver regained control of the vehicle. Seconds later, he saw the car turn off the road into an empty parking lot and come to a stop, its engine smoking and right front tire flat. Shraeder followed the Camaro into the darkened lot, with Trooper Johnson pulling in a short time later to make the arrest.

Striding to the car, Johnson observed that the driver had 'red eyes' and 'smelled strongly of marijuana', He demanded that Eli open his mouth and stick out his tongue. Using a flashlight, Johnson observed that the back of Eli's mouth was 'green', suggesting he had swallowed some marijuana. Eli was arrested and charged with reckless evasion of a police officer and several other traffic infractions. During cross-examination at his trial, he later admitted that he had a bag of marijuana in his possession and had smoked marijuana earlier that day.

In the end, Eli was found guilty of reckless endangerment of a police officer and in February of 2005 was placed on three years probation, conditioned on ninety days in the county jail or electronic home monitoring.

Susan, meanwhile, was behind bars in August of 2003 when a Grand Jury was convened to determine whether to indict her on charges of first-degree murder. Panelists heard from police officers, investigators, and forensic experts during three closed-door sessions. One criminalist testified that hairs found in Felix's clenched fist were 'consistent' with those of his wife, Susan, and that several of the hairs had roots, indicating they had been ripped from her scalp, probably during a violent struggle. Meanwhile, another forensic expert presented evidence that a bloody footprint found near the body was a match to Susan's right foot.

'I think there seems to be a reasonable conference [agreement] here that the crime was committed, that there was some clean-up within the pool house bathroom, and that for whatever reason, Susan Polk came around the back side of the crime scene, perhaps Felix was still struggling, and then exits the house,' the expert told the Grand Jurors. 'I make that argument because of the evidence at the scene, as well as that pool house bathroom, the towels on the ground that are bloody, the blood on the counter, and for the simple fact, no bloody shoes are found, no bloody female clothing is recovered.'

With regard to the lack of injuries found on Susan's body, ADA Tom O'Connor pointed to the testimony of Brian Peterson, the medical examiner who performed the autopsy on Felix Polk.

'It wouldn't be unusual that the attacker in this situation wouldn't have significant injuries,' Dr. Peterson told jurors.

In late August, the panel indicted Susan Polk on charges of first-degree murder in the stabbing death of her husband.

Eli was furious when he learned that the judge presiding over the case of the *People v. Susan Mae Polk* continued his mother's no bail status, and in January 2004 he sent a letter to the court objecting to the ruling.

'What has happened to my mom is unbelievable,' the teen wrote in a letter, dated 27 January, to the judge presiding over his mother's case:

> My mom has been charged with a crime she didn't commit. And now she has been unjustly incarcerated for over 15 months with no sign of the court's undoing the injustice that has been done.
>
> From what I see, the prosecutor's theory of what occurred is impossible. I know without question that if there were a

physical struggle between my mom and dad, my father would be the instigator, as he always was . . .

As I began to grow in my mind and body, I consciously and unconsciously searched for ways to figure out who was telling the truth and who was telling lies . . . I studied everything about both my mom and my dad . . . to seek what a normal kid my age could never even begin to imagine . . . My father's façade was well created . . . and if you're around it long enough . . . you start to break through it as you mature. So when I was roughly around the age of 15, I finally began to no longer see the poor, weak, aging man who was losing his family to a crazy, troubled wife.

If there was one thing my dad had never acted like, it was weak. My father definitely wasn't weak when he was beating me up or slapping my mom. He never acted powerless when he used to take my two brothers and I into the office, one at a time, and hypnotise us.

One of the few documents to provide a window into Eli's thoughts, the letter demonstrated the close connection between Eli and his mother. In the months ahead, Eli remained the only son to defend her account of his father's death. To many, his vows of support bordered on obsessive, and there was speculation that Eli and Susan's relationship was odd. Not only was Eli taking her side, but often he even used the same language that she did, and his letters to her were filled with professions of undying love – even expressing his willingness to take his own life for her. 'I love you enough to burn all I am and meet you in the afterlife,' he wrote to Susan while she was incarcerated at the West County Detention Facility. There was also speculation among members of the media that Eli and Susan could have entered into a suicide pact – in the event that Susan was sentenced to life in prison for Felix's murder, the two would kill themselves.

'You are everything to me,' Eli wrote in one letter to his mother. 'I will be there for you for the rest of your life. You are the strongest, smartest and most loving person I know. I will always be proud to have you as my mom. Most importantly, don't ever forget, or force out, the perfect person you are. Never again will I be as happy as I could with you in jail . . . You dying is a part of me dead as well.'

CHAPTER TWENTY

BUCKING AUTHORITY

Since her arrest on that October night, Susan was convinced that authorities had targeted her unfairly because of actions she took during her divorce proceedings with Felix. In her mind, the judges were part of a conspiracy and did not want to help her in any way.

'I believe the reason for this animosity is political,' Susan wrote in a letter she later sent to the court:

In October 2002, shortly before my husband's death, I sent a letter containing an excerpt from my diary to 7 (seven) judges in Contra Costa County accusing Judge Kolin of taking a bribe in a juvenile case involving one of my sons. There were other political statements in my diary, excerpts, which may have given rise to prejudice. I believe Judge [Laurel] Brady received a copy of this letter.

Judge Kolin was called as a prosecution witness at a bail hearing in 2004. He is a friend of Bud McKenzie, my brother-in-law's attorney, and so testified. Mr. McKenzie, according to Judge Kolin, asked him to help prevent me from getting bail. Judge Dan O'Malley essentially recused himself in October of 2004, stating he had been contacted by a number of De la Salle parents. The Briners, friends of Bud McKenzie with whom my son Gabriel lives, are De la Salle parents. Mr. McKenzie was a De la Salle parent. The O'Malleys are Carondolet parents, the sister school of De la Salle.

It seems apparent that there has been a great amount of discussion and influence among these parties, which has also prejudiced the bench. It should also be noted that De la Salle raised money for my sons following their father's death. The Psychology teacher at De la Salle, Mr. Otterstadt, was a former patient and trainee of my husband. I am informed and believe it to be true that Mr. Otterstadt organized the De la Salle community in relation to my husband's death and the case against me.

Susan went on to describe being 'attacked' by an officer of the court in August 2003, the day she attempted to file a Faretta motion — a preliminary step to representing herself. The motion is based on a 1975 decision that permitted a defendant to represent himself in a California murder case.

'I was attacked by Deputy Carin, and my arm was broken by him. He hit my elbow with a "blackjack", a metal rod,' Susan wrote.

Susan went on to claim that the officer assigned to investigate the incident 'appears to be related to Judge [Laurel] Brady's clerk.'

'He refused to take my statement, angrily declaring: "I'm not taking anything from you," betraying prejudice and animosity,' Susan wrote.

This beating is relevant to the homicide case in that I intend to show that the investigation was tainted, exculpatory evidence including my diary was destroyed by law enforcement officers. Other examples of tampering with evidence exist. The beating was an attempt to silence me. In fact, Deputy Carin said just before he broke my arm, "I told you not to speak in court," a major obstacle to a pro per defendant.'

Regardless of Susan's conspiracy theories, these early bail hearings made it clear that her contempt for authority in the court of law was a much larger problem, one that would prove highly ineffective if carried into the trial. Any progress she made would be reduced when she lashed out at the judges and their subordinates. Her paranoia became increasingly harmful to her case when coupled with her adamant refusal to obey the will of the court. When faced with the choice between controlling herself and lashing out at the bench, she always chose the latter, ensuring that she received no respect from the judges that controlled her fate.

It was a risky path for anyone to take, but for a woman accused of first-degree murder, it appeared almost suicidal.

More than two years of arguing over Susan's bail status (or lack thereof) did little to improve her situation. Finally, in the autumn of 2004, Judge Mary Ann O'Malley conducted a review of Susan's no-bail status. Prosecutor Tom O'Connor called Adam to the stand on 10 September to clarify a letter he wrote to the court with regard to bail for his mother, a letter which had ended with Adam saying that it was right for the court to release Susan.

'You know, I love my mom. She's always known that,' Adam said to O'Connor. 'I don't think that she's a person who belongs in prison. I don't think she fits into the general public of a prison. However, that being said, I don't think she belongs in the general public right now either.'

'And why is that, sir?'

'I think that my mom has psychological issues that need to be dealt with that could be detrimental to other people around her . . . and herself,' Adam said.

'Was it your opinion that prior to what occurred with your father that your mother was delusional?'

'A hundred per cent, yeah. I told her every day.'

'Did those delusions focus on one individual?'

'No, I guess the focal point of her delusions was obviously my father. But there's always something she's been delusional about for as long as I can remember [that] my father was a double agent for the Israeli intelligence.'

This idea of Susan's delusions was the focal point of O'Connor's argument that she should not be allowed out on bail. Focusing on her delusions about Felix's involvement with Israeli intelligence, her belief that the Briners were embezzling her money, and statements she made about the 'Jewish Network', O'Connor sought to portray Susan as a woman whose mental state was a risk to those around her.

On cross-examination, Susan's public defender, Jack Funk, an associate of Peter Coleridge, designed his questioning of Adam to convey that Susan's delusions had a singular focus on Felix. Susan's delusional behaviour did not make her a threat to the public at large, it made her a threat to Felix. Since he was no longer alive, Susan no longer posed a risk to the public.

'During your lifetime . . . do you know of any other time in which your mother has attacked or threatened any other person?'

'No.'

'And do you have any reason to believe that if your mother were released, upon whatever appropriate security, that she would threaten or attack any other person?'

'I believe the only answer I can give to that question is, I don't know. I don't think it's a fair question to ask me because I don't know what happened in the cottage that night . . . My honest opinion on my mom is that she is an 80 per cent sane and rational person and she's 20 per cent delusional, and that 20 per cent is completely unpredictable. There's no way for anybody to know what's going to happen next, and that's why I think she needs to be getting help somewhere . . . She should not be in prison. She should be getting help somewhere so she can come out and be a fully functional member of society.'

Shortly after the hearing in September 2004, Judge O'Malley set bail for Susan at $1,050,000, but Susan's time on the outside was brief. Within seven months of posting the monies, she was back behind bars at the West County Detention Facility for violating the terms of her release.

On 6 October 2004, Adam filed a 'wrongful death civil suit' against Susan seeking $1 million dollars in damages in addition to other declaratory relief. Eli Polk and Felix's twin brother, John, who was executor of the Polk estate, were named as codefendants in the suit. Andrew and Jennifer Polk declined to participate in the legal action, according to the court papers.

'As a result of the intentional wrongful death of their father, Plaintiffs Adam and Gabriel suffer damages by way of lost love, care, comfort, and support of their father, in an amount no less than $1 million, to be proven at trial,' the suit read.

In addition to monetary compensation, Gabe and Adam were seeking declarations from the court that John Polk be named proper trustee of the Trust and that Susan have 'no right, title, or interest in Trust, which may be funded by assets having a net total value of $1 million dollars.' Furthermore '"upon conviction of murder or finding of felonious and intentional killing" that Susan have no property right or interest in the Estate of Felix Polk or in any asset enumerated in the 1996 Polk Trust, and that she have no right or interest in Felix's share of any community property asset, including Felix's pension plan and the Orinda residence at 728 Miner Road.'

As a condition of her bail, Judge O'Malley set a no contact order forbidding Susan from having any contact with her son Gabriel, Dan and Marjorie Briner, Felix's friend Barry Morris, and family lawyer Bud McKenzie. Despite harsh warnings about the repercussions of contacting any of these individuals, upon learning of the filing, Susan sent a flurry of letters to her sons. Although Gabriel refused to respond to her, Susan sent him twenty-four emails during this time. Her actions landed her back in jail at the West County Detention Facility in April 2005 with $5 million bail.

Susan told the court that she was simply responding to the civil suit when she contacted her youngest son via e-mail. In a letter to the court, she railed at Judge O'Malley's 19 April decision to revoke her bail, claiming she had written to Gabriel only after her lawyers, Peter Coleridge and Jack Funk, advised her that the no contact order did not apply to legal correspondence.

'However, I was charged with 24 counts of contempt of court for 24 emails to Gabriel and reincarcerated and placed on a no bail hold by Judge Mary Ann O'Malley,' Susan complained in the letter.

Susan subsequently fired Peter Coleridge in May 2005, and announced her intent to act as her own counsel. Since her arrest, she had fired all three of her criminal attorneys – William Ousterhadt, Elizabeth Grossman, and now Peter Coleridge – supposedly because of disagreements over the handling of her defence. She had repeatedly refused to entertain an 'insanity' defence or one using 'battered woman syndrome.' She had spent much of her life running from a diagnosis of mental illness and she wasn't about to hide behind such a claim now.

Susan would represent herself *pro per*. In an interview with the *Contra Costa Times* in the summer of 2005, she told the newspaper that she was convinced she was not going to get the defence she wanted unless she represented herself. 'If I'm going to lose when represented by counsel, I might as well represent myself,' she was quoted as saying. 'At least I'll give them a fight.'

While self-representation is not a good idea for any defendant, in Susan's case it was a particularly bad choice. In Contra Costa County, women who choose to represent themselves are at a severe disadvantage in comparison to their male counterparts. The women who are housed in the West County Detention Facility are not permitted to use the jail's 'Male Only' law library, despite many administrative complaints from defendants facing felony charges. This restriction greatly limits the amount of research that they can undertake on their own.

This fact may have played a role in the abrupt change Susan announced in late July 2005 when she asked a judge to appoint Oakland defence lawyer, Daniel Horowitz, to her case. Horowitz had gained notoriety as a TV legal analyst during the Scott Peterson murder trial by stationing himself at the courthouse to offer legal commentary to cable stations in need of a sound bite. He soon became a regular on Court TV, providing analysis for the Peterson case and later in the Michael Jackson molestation trial.

Representing Susan Polk at her upcoming murder trial would be another opportunity for the lawyer to grab the media spotlight. While Horowitz had represented more than a dozen defendants in capital murder cases during his two decades as a lawyer, the majority of his practice was at the Federal level, involving white-collar crimes such as money laundering and embezzlement.

According to his profile, Horowitz was 'a defence attorney with an extensive computer and business background' and 90 per cent of his practice was devoted to litigation. Nevertheless, he was anxious to take Susan's case to trial. In August, he asked Judge Thomas Maddock to allow him to bring his cocounsel, Ivan W. Golde, on board for the case. Judge Maddock agreed, under the condition that the county pay only Horowitz's fee.

While Horowitz was lead counsel on the case, it was Ivan who actually persuaded Susan to meet with them. He made the initial contact while visiting a client at the West County Detention Facility where Susan was being held. During their brief conversation, Ivan convinced Susan to sit down with him and his partner, Dan, to discuss her case.

Born and raised in San Francisco's East Bay, Golde followed in his father's footsteps by attending law school and becoming an attorney. Unlike his dad, prominent Alameda County Superior Court Judge Stanley P. Golde, Ivan was not interested in a career on the bench. Instead, he had carved out a niche in the world of professional sports, providing legal counsel to members of the Oakland Raiders Football Club and to baseball great Ricky Henderson. Like Horowitz, Golde enjoyed the media spotlight. According to his web page, he had 'done battle with Nancy Grace on Court TV . . . and has commentated on the Scott Peterson and Michael Jackson high profile cases.'

Susan liked Golde. He was easygoing and down-to-earth, and the two shared a common background; both had grown up in Oakland and attended the same high school (although Susan's time there was far more limited than Golde's). During Golde's initial meeting with Susan, however, she had made it clear that she was not interested in being represented by counsel. She reiterated that position during the subsequent meeting with Golde and Horowitz, informing the lawyers she was not likely to change her mind.

Still, she listened intently to their advice during a series of additional meetings.

It is not known what finally led Susan to allow the lawyers to take over her case. Perhaps she was growing concerned about her ability to manage her own defence or maybe she sensed that Horowitz and Golde truly believed in her and were willing to do the work necessary to present the case she desired. Media reports claimed that Susan settled on the Horowitz/Golde team after they agreed to present a straight self-defence case and go easy during their questioning of Susan's youngest son, Gabriel.

Once on board, it was Golde who visited Susan in jail and responded to her countless phone calls. Golde quickly developed a friendship with Susan, but over time even he grew weary of her constant needs. At one point, her demands became so great that Horowitz assigned an office assistant named Valerie Harris, whom he had met at the Scott Peterson trial, to handle Susan's calls. At the Peterson trial, Harris had earned a reputation as something of a trial groupie because of her constant presence in the courtroom. Dan admired her interest in the case and asked her to join the firm.

When Adam Polk learned that his mother had asked

Horowitz and Golde to take her case, he admonished the lawyers to be careful.

'The first time I met Dan and Ivan, I told them, "Listen, in two months, you guys are going to be unemployed",' Adam later explained. 'My mother has, throughout her life, for as long I have known her, exhibited a pattern of warming up to outsiders and then completely turning on them.

'I have experienced it my whole life. She is a lady who values control and when somebody else maintains control over her life, I believe she contrives fantasies. Rather than use the word "delusion", I like to use "contrives fantasies" to gain control of the other people [outsiders].'

In spite of Adam's warning, the two lawyers forged ahead with their defence of Susan. In September 2005, Dan Horowitz and Ivan Golde filed a motion on her behalf, claiming Susan was the victim of legal manoeuvering that was tantamount to bribery and extortion in connection with the civil suit. Horowitz claimed that Bud Mackenzie, the lawyer representing the Polk estate, was trying to put a 'squeeze play' on Susan – raising the possibility that the Orinda house would go into foreclosure if she didn't act. However, when Golde went back to the attorney and offered to put up his own money to halt the pending foreclosure proceeding, Mackenzie reportedly said the house was not in danger.

The motion alleged that Adam Polk was aware that the Miner Road house was not at risk but wanted his mother to believe it was in order to push her to settle. It also claimed that Susan had received veiled threats from an unnamed party that Adam and Gabriel would 'testify with great anger and fear about the financial "situation"' if she did not agree to settle the suit.

While that motion as well as several others that the Horowitz/Golde team filed were denied, the civil suit was settled shortly thereafter, presumably in hopes that Adam and Gabe would be more friendly to the defence on the witness stand during the criminal case.

With the civil trial moving along, Horowitz and Golde began to hone their strategy for the murder trial. They publicly declared they could win Susan an acquittal at trial. Horowitz told ABC's *Good Morning America* that he had no intention of presenting an insanity defence or a battered woman/burning bed syndrome. Susan was a woman who was abused regularly by her therapist husband, and she truly believed Felix intended to kill her the night the two argued in the couple's guest cottage, the lawyer maintained. Dan Horowitz would argue a straight self-defence case on Susan's behalf – or at least that's what he intended to do.

CHAPTER TWENTY-ONE

SUSAN'S STORY

The temperature had already reached seventy degrees when I arrived at the West County Detention Facility on 1 October 2005, nearly three years to the day after Felix Polk's murder. I had come to the modern, tidy jail in Richmond, California, at Susan's invitation for the first in a series of jailhouse interviews for my show, *Catherine Crier Live*.

Much had happened since Susan's arrest in the autumn of 2002. The most significant was Susan's about face. For more than two years after Felix's death, she had publicly maintained her innocence – although she claimed she told her mother and her lawyer of her involvement five days after Felix's death. As the investigation progressed over the years, she eventually changed her story from innocence to self-defence. No one has been able to pinpoint exactly when the change occurred, but Detective Mike Costa later told Court TV's Lisa Sweetingham that he believed it was sometime in 2003 that he first heard Susan's new claim.

While Susan had privately detailed the events in the guest cottage to her mother and her then-attorney soon after her arrest in October 2002, the first time she publicly uttered the self-defence argument was in an April 2005 article in the *Contra Costa Times*. In the article, written by reporter Bruce Gertzman during a time when Susan was not represented by counsel, she insisted that she and her husband were arguing on the night of 13 October 2002, when an enraged Felix came after her with a knife. She fought back vigorously, ultimately killing him in an attempt to save her own life.

A uniformed jail official escorted me to the small interview room where I would meet Susan for the first time. The jangling of keys alerted me to her entrance into the small room on the opposite side of a Plexiglas partition. Her well-groomed appearance surprised me. After nearly three years in jail, she was slender and graceful, even in the baggy prison outfit that hung from her gangly 5'6"' frame. Her once long dark hair was now streaked with gray and cut in a stylish bob. She wore little makeup, just lipstick and white eye-pencil, artfully applied to enhance her beautiful, unblemished skin.

I watched as she slid into a sturdy, metal-framed chair on her side of the cubicle, placing her neatly manicured hands atop the small table we shared. Looking up at me through the divider, she flashed a half smile and then glanced around nervously. Susan and I were about the same age, and during the interview we found several commonalities. Like Susan, I too, had married young. And while I had long since divorced my first husband, Susan had stayed married and raised three children with Felix. She claimed it wasn't until her fortieth birthday that she realised she could no longer remain in the relationship. Felix was abusive and she wanted out.

I asked Susan what happened that night in the guest cottage. At times, her voice was so soft that I found myself leaning forward to hear her responses through the mesh opening just above the table.

'Well, we had things to talk about, um, and had arranged to meet later that night to have a talk,' Susan began in a quiet monotone. 'I got to the door. I knocked. The lights were on, um, around eleven, and it looked like he might have been reading because . . . he had a book.'

Susan explained that she had a can of pepper spray in her back pocket, which she had purchased at a convenience store in Montana. The clerk told her that one pump would stop a grizzly bear in its tracks, and she was confident the spray would protect her.

I asked Susan about her conversation with Felix. Were they trying to figure out where the two would live? Whether she would stay in the house or return to Montana?

'It was practical,' Susan said. 'He [Felix] offered to pay around three thousand dollars a month in spousal support and I wanted to discuss Gabriel, the kids, selling the house or not selling it. I wanted the kids to stay in the house. I didn't want to spend a lot of money in a battle. I didn't think it was worth it because I had been offering for months to just sign papers. It degenerated into an argument. He wasn't being practical and it just became one of those arguments.'

'How did he get the knife?' I asked.

There was a long pause, as if Susan was searching for an answer. 'I really don't know,' she finally said. 'What happened is he came over and backhanded me in the face as he'd done before. I pulled out the pepper spray. Sprayed him. He picked up the ottoman and charged at me with it, then grabbed me by the hair, threw me on the floor, punched me in the face again, and smeared pepper spray into my eyes.

'The next thing I knew, I looked up, and I saw a knife coming down, and I saw it go into my leg. I thought the reason I wasn't feeling it was because, sometimes, I've read, people don't feel it initially when they've been stabbed.

'It was like I flashed on "I am going to die. He is going to kill me. If I don't do something right now, I will be dead."

'I just thought of the one thing I could do and that was to kick him as hard as I could in the groin and hope at the same time I could get the knife from his hand. I kicked, pulled my leg back as far as a I could and kicked with as much force as I could into his groin, and went for the knife at the very same time, and his hand loosened just enough where I could grab the knife. And, um, I grabbed it, and I felt like I had to say something, and I said, "Stop, I have a knife."

'And then, um, he was going after the knife and I stabbed him in the side, and then he was leaning over, and I think at that point he punched me in the face again, and I reached around and I stabbed him in the back, and then he bit into my hand and bit down as hard as he could. There's actually teeth, tooth marks on both sides [of my hand] and then he went for the knife at the same time.

'And I thought, well, he was doing what I did and if I loosen up now, he's going to get it and kill me. And so then I stabbed him again.'

At one point, Susan remembered clenching the knife in both hands and repeatedly slashing at her husband. 'Stop, stop, stop, stop, stop!' she screamed, waving the blade from side to side to keep him at bay before driving it into his torso. 'Get off! Get off! Get off! Get off!'

'I opened my eyes, and I saw blood, and I thought that I had torn open his chest, but I think I would have seen some blood from the previous stabbing.'

Susan described watching as Felix staggered to his feet and mumbled his final words. 'I stood up and dropped the knife, and Felix just said, "Oh my God. I think I'm dead." And he wobbled back and forth like this,' Susan said, rocking back and forth to mimic Felix's movements. 'Like swayed, and then he just fell back and hit his head on the floor.'

Continuing, Susan described how the pounding of her temples was deafening as she worked to catch her breath. She needed to sit down. Striding to the short flight of stairs leading to the single bedroom, she perched on a step near to where Felix lay on the floor. The room was in a shambles. Blood was everywhere. Staring down at her husband, Susan said that scenes of their life together came rushing back. For one brief moment, she remembered the good times and the love they once shared. But those thoughts quickly disappeared.

It is not clear if Felix was dead at that moment. Susan admitted that she did not check for a pulse. Prosecutors would later insist that Felix was, in fact, alive and still breathing for nearly thirty minutes after the attack. They even suggested that Susan left her husband of twenty years to die alone when she returned to the main house some time later that evening.

Susan described how she crossed the room to the bathroom at the top of the landing to wash up. Her hands were covered with blood and she wanted to wash the pepper spray out of her eyes. The pool house had not been updated since it was first built in the 1960s. The tiny bathroom, reminiscent of a ship's head in size and shape, still had the original wood paneling and pull chain toilet. Turning on the faucet, Susan watched as rivulets of red streamed into the sink. It was clear she was not thinking of the consequences when she pulled the pair of blue towels from the towel bar, dried off her hands, and dropped the towels in a heap on the floor in front of the stall shower.

'When I came back, he was dead,' Susan related.

'Do you remember what you thought at that point?' I asked.

'Yes, I thought a number of things. I thought I should call the police. I thought that I had just written this letter accusing the juvenile judge of taking a bribe and I sent it on the way back from Montana to six or seven judges in our county, and I thought, I'm in big trouble.

'Because even if they believed me, which Felix had said nobody will ever believe me about anything, even if they did, they're not gonna maybe care. And I'd just seen what had happened to Eli in the juvenile justice system, and I thought, "Who's going to take care of Gabriel? Who's going to get him to school? Who's going to pay the mortgage? Oh my God!"

'And I waited, thinking the police would magically appear, that they'd heard me scream, they'd know, they'd come, and then it just became easier to just wait. And I just thought, "I need time. I need time to tell Gabriel what happened. I need time to make some financial arrangements for the kids. I should call a lawyer."

'Just, you know, I just put it off. So I went to the [main] house, and I just took about ten showers and took Gabriel to school in the morning and um, was just too tired to do anything. You know, too tired to make any financial arrangements, any plans, and then just tried to get up enough nerve to tell Gabriel and hinted around and . . .'

'Do you remember what you said as a hint?' I asked.

'Well, he was asking me, and I was just trying to tell him. I don't remember exactly. I said he [Felix] was gone. I mean we were always so connected. And then he accused me. Straight up. And um, then it was just, um, he could call the police, and um, the police came and that was that.'

'Was your mind working at the time? Were you thinking about denying? Is that a function of buying time?'

'I'd just been accused by Gabriel, it was just, um, I wanted to tell him what had happened, you know, and then all of a sudden he's accusing me, you know, he's jumping ahead. He's making these accusations. And I just didn't want to be seen in his eyes that way, and I just began to lie, and then there was the whole thing, seeing him, I still wasn't sure that I was going to lie until I was in the car, and I saw him in custody – he was in the car behind me, and I was told he was being detained.

'I had this thought that I had to do everything I could to keep him and me out of custody so I could protect him. And then I thought, well if they accused him, then I'd have to step forward immediately and say I did it, and so I had to keep track of what's going on here, and

I mean, I think a person who is that fatigued and in shock and that terrified is just not logical.'

It was then that Susan went on to describe how she first admitted her role in Felix's death five days after the struggle in the guest cottage to the lawyer who came to see her at the West County Detention Facility. She also insisted that in the months after Felix's death, she repeatedly tried to turn over the knife used in the attack to her defence lawyers but they had declined to give it to police.

'Listen, I tried to turn it over to every single attorney I had from day one,' she said. 'As soon as I found myself charged with murder I was like "oh my God". So I told them what happened. Nobody wanted to hear, nobody wanted to handle it.

'Seven months later, I was offered a deal – I said, "No, I'm innocent."'

Finally, in April 2005, while out on bail, Susan said she went back to the house with Peter Coleridge, who at that point was still her defence lawyer. While there, she pulled out the knife and told him that she wanted to place it into evidence.

'And he's like, "oh, you shouldn't have done that," and I'm like, "why not?" and he was like, "well now I've got to turn it in."'

Despite this dramatic recounting replete with extraordinary detail, elements of Susan's version of events that night would later prove doubtful – particularly those pertaining to the ottoman. Because Susan had waited until late 2004 to inform the authorities about the pepper spray, there was no longer sufficient evidence to verify her claim that any chemical residue should be on the ottoman. According to an official lab report, tests for traces of mace or pepper spray performed on the ottoman in March 2005 proved inconclusive. 'Due to the length of time elapsed before sampling, it cannot be determined if they were ever present or if they have changed to become undetectable.' In addition, 'the ottoman was not packaged in an airtight container' and 'some experimentation in the laboratory suggested it was unlikely to be able to recover spray residues after long-term storage.'

Susan's tale of that night was not the only thing that she had in store for me that afternoon. With help from Dan Horowitz and Ivan Golde, Susan had obtained a startling medical report from the US Navy that detailed the psychological evaluations of Felix in the days after his suicide attempt in 1955. Sitting across from me and staring through an inch and a half of Plexiglas, I asked her: 'Why was Felix hospitalised for a whole year after his suicide attempt?'

Susan paused, and looked directly at me before answering. Breathing in deeply, she began to explain how the naval records revealed that Felix had received treatment for a 'schizophrenic reaction', following his suicide attempt in the fall of 1955. This psychologist who had been treating patients over the course of more than twenty years had, in fact, been hospitalised himself for serious emotional troubles. Felix, who had accused Susan of being crazy for years, had his own set of psychological problems, problems that he never attempted to address.

'Well, what the naval records say is that he was unable to give a rational explanation for what he'd done.' She grew animated as she recounted her findings. First, she pointed to her own suicide attempt in January 2001. 'I was asked by the psychiatrist, "Why'd you do it?" And I said, "Well, in this moment of despair, I thought my husband would do the things he was saying he was going to do: destroy my life, take my children away, all these things. And I just had this moment of complete despair, and I'm very glad I'm alive and realise that I have options."

'My husband was very different. The records show he was unable to give a rational explanation for what he did. He talked about supernatural forces having been at work. He talked about hearing an echo when he spoke. He couldn't remember what had happened. He had amnesia. And his suicide note made it sound like he had other periods of amnesia.'

Susan said that Felix mentioned his suicide attempt during their early therapy sessions in Berkeley but claimed that he was in despair over the breakup of a relationship when he tried to take his life. As far as Susan knew, this was the reason that Felix was overly sensitive to being abandoned. At least, that is what she says he told her each time she threatened to leave the marriage.

However, after closer inspection of his suicide attempt, Susan learned that Felix's claim was untrue. Horowitz had located Felix's old girlfriend and gleaned from their conversation that there had been no break up. Felix, it seemed, had lied to his wife about the circumstances surrounding his suicide attempt. Worse, he had failed to mention his serious medical diagnosis or that this suicide attempt was the result of a 'schizophrenic reaction'.

'Psych records describe him as being hostile, as being in the lockdown ward.' Susan explained. 'They describe when he got transported to the hospital he got bruises along the way because apparently he got restrained. That's a picture of someone who was extremely disturbed, who was apparently almost mute. He didn't talk, you know.'

Susan told me of the journals that Felix kept. And for a moment, she considered my request to turn them over to Court TV. But in the end, she shared little of their content. 'He [Felix] described himself in words that he used to describe me and projected all of it because I wasn't really like that. I didn't feel that way.'

After our interview, I reviewed the naval records carefully. According to the reports, Felix was taken to a military hospital after his suicide attempt. He was 'confused' and 'depressed' and claimed 'amnesia' for the events prior to his arrival, medical records stated. He grew 'excited' upon awakening. In response to questions, he told doctors he had no recollection of his suicide attempt, or of writing the note that police found in a typewriter inside the family home.

Felix was transferred to the US Naval Hospital at St. Alban's, New York. Records show that he had to be restrained during the transport. Doctors at St. Albans diagnosed Felix's condition as 'Psychotic Depressive Reaction with Suicidal Tendencies'. Further studies revealed evidence of 'a schizophrenic process with much philosophical, abstract preoccupation with his lack of accomplishment, his emotional distance from people, and some concomitant disturbance in the psycho-sexual area.'

Under observation at the hospital, Felix talked of feeling apart in 'all relationships with others' and having the sensation that he was 'standing apart listening to an echo' when he spoke. 'His speech was at all times coherent and relevant, and no actual delusions or hallucinations were elicited during his hospitalisation at the naval hospital,' the records stated.

By all indications from the doctors there, Felix showed little sign of change or improvement during his lengthy stay at St. Alban's, where he was confined to a locked ward because of his 'depression' and 'hostility'. In fact, he remained depressed and talked of his confusion for much of the time he was confined. While doctors noted that Felix was not experiencing hallucinations or delusions during his hospitalisation, Felix described his thoughts as 'abstract' and spoke of 'dreams of glory'. He complained that he felt in a 'daze' and did things 'mechanically'.

On 18 January 1956, Felix was transferred to an open ward of the hospital on 'restricted' status, the records stated. The change had no appreciable effect on his condition. Three months later, he was placed on the Temporary Disability Retired list by reason of 'schizophrenic reaction', and later released from the hospital with a diagnosis of 'in remission'.

According to the naval records, Felix reported to the Naval Command at St. Alban's Hospital on 25 July 1957 for a 'trial visit' from the Montrose Veteran's Administration Hospital. Based on the visit, a three-man counsel listed its findings as a schizophrenic reaction. 'In remission.' The Clinical Board's findings noted that Felix was 'unfit to perform the duties of his rank – schizophrenic reaction.'

It was decided that the physical disability 'was not due to misconduct or willful neglect,' and that it was the proximate result of 'dementia, mixed type, in partial remission, slight impairment of social and industrial adaptability.'

At my request, several well-known psychiatrists reviewed the US Naval records and medical reports on Felix Polk. They reported back that if Felix had presented with the symptoms described in the reports today he would not be considered schizophrenic, but more likely a man who suffered from severe depression.

Nevertheless, this intimate look at his fragile emotional state was a key revelation, one that, if true, had dramatic implications – as a judge and a jury would eventually be examining his psychological state as well as Susan's. For years, Felix had openly questioned his wife's mental status, while shying away from his own problems. This report was yet another example of the psychological double standard that he employed. To Felix, his own mental issues were never significant enough to interfere with his ability to parent his sons; only Susan's problems were severe enough for that. In truth his psychological conflicts ran as deep as hers, and yet he refused to take the steps necessary to heal his wounds.

During another interview with Susan, she described for me the sexual abuse she allegedly suffered as Felix's teenage patient. 'What I remember is that he became extremely interested in me.'

Susan claimed that Felix made it clear right from the start that he was 'violating some sort of protocol' by seeing her as a patient. 'I think he was referring to a sexual interest in me and I think I was just blocking out as much of that as I could.

'What happened was he started giving me a cup of tea when I came in. I'm sure there was a drug in it because what I recall next is counting backward and then no memory of what took place, but just looking at the clock, and the times, and saying "What happened? What did we talk about?"

'And this feeling, this sense of loss. This gap. It was a very, very disturbing experience, to not be able to recall what had happened.'

I asked Susan if she'd ever raised the issue with Felix.

'I brought it up, and he looked nervous,' she said.

Susan's recollections of her early sessions with Dr. Polk seemed fuzzy at best; her words often became twisted when I asked her to clarify the abuse she allegedly suffered as a patient, and she failed to answer my question as to whether there was physical evidence to confirm her fears. After all, if she were a virgin when she first went to see Felix, then she would have most likely noticed some blood in her undergarments that first time.

'I recall the content of some of those hypnotic sessions, bits and pieces,' Susan answered in a soft voice. 'And I recall being told not to look.

'I guess at that time I didn't really think it was great that he basically had sex with me. And put me down . . . it just made me, you know, I was doing what I was told, but he was so overwhelming. So just, physical. It was just awful. And I really didn't remember that for years.'

Susan claimed that she completely blocked out the sessions in which she was 'raped' by Felix until she was in her forties. She described their sexual relationship as husband and wife as 'unpleasant' and alluded to years of 'rough' sex during their marriage. She said Felix enjoyed physically restraining her during intercourse, even as she lay crying.

'So what happened?' I asked.

'He essentially, what he told me was that if I ever left him he would kill himself, or he would kill me.'

'So even when you were seventeen he was telling you this?'

Susan could not really answer my question. In many ways, her responses were childlike, and she appeared at times to be no more than a teenage girl trapped in a woman's body.

'Felix wanted someone to dominate,' Susan maintained. 'He wanted a doll. There was no individuality left, there was none of me.'

From all the evidence that I had seen and what she told me in this conversation, I had little doubt that Susan was abused during the marriage, at least emotionally. Felix had misused his power and position as a therapist to wield control over his vulnerable patient. His selfish decision to begin a relationship with the teen had probably prevented Susan from getting the help she so desperately needed.

'My husband was a professional,' Susan explained. 'He was, I think, careful about what he did . . . I think it is hard for someone who hasn't been in a coercive relationship to understand how it is that a person stays in it.

'Because I kept hoping that it wasn't as bad as I thought. That he wasn't really as crazy as maybe he seemed to be. That when he said, "I'll kill you" with a smile, he didn't really mean it. And that's a huge hurdle to overcome . . . explaining to the jury that even though he didn't beat me with a crowbar, it was enough to scare me to death, that I was afraid for my life, but I was also afraid to leave.'

Going on to explain how she managed the finances for both the family and Felix's practice, Susan brought up Felix's questionable relationships. She tried to ignore her husband's inappropriate friendships with female patients over the years, but she detailed one incident specifically. 'I just chose to interpret them as not affairs, but as just friendships . . . But, in time, I guess the veil kind of fell from my eyes around when I turned forty, which is kind of a seminal period in a woman's life, anyway, right?

'It's like all of a sudden I'm like, Whoa, this is what's really going on, you know, I really actually turned forty and I said to myself, "Now, I should be prepared to face reality."' Susan laughed aloud. 'I just started to not lie to myself about certain things, including the relationship with one of his clients, another psychologist,' Susan said in reference to the woman whom Susan had seen her husband romantically embrace five years before his death.

Talking to her about Felix's alleged indiscretions, I couldn't help but wonder if this could have been the motive when she killed him.

Whether or not Felix actually did cheat, it was clear that he had maintained relationships with some of his patients that were eerily reminiscent of his inappropriate relationship with Susan. In Susan's situation, a revelation of infidelity might have pushed her over the edge, as this replayed her father's betrayal of her mother. This possible motive deserved some serious attention, as adultery touched at the very root of Susan's psychological issues.

Susan claimed that once she announced her intention to leave the marriage, Felix made all sorts of threats.

' "I'll drive you crazy." "I'll kill you if you leave me." "I'll destroy you." "I'll throttle you." "Pull you down the drain." "You'll wind up in an institution." "You are a bad mother." "You are so ugly.". . .

'I think he was very crazy, a little more than I realised . . . He was very, very split, you know, it was like night and day, Dr. Jekyll and Mr. Hyde. There were two sides to his personality. And he was extremely impulsive and malicious . . .

'It takes a certain kind of person to kill somebody's dogs or to threaten their children . . . he would sabotage their progress in school. He was just a very dangerous, damaged person.'

PART III
THE TRIAL

CHAPTER TWENTY-TWO

A MACABRE TWIST

Dressed conservatively in a grey suit, her short hair overgrown and brushed off her face, Susan unceremoniously entered the courtroom of the Contra Costa County Courthouse on 11 October 2005, for the opening remarks in her murder trial.

Onlookers watched from the gallery as Susan slid into a chair at the defence table between her lawyers, Dan Horowitz and Ivan Golde. Next to the tanned Horowitz, she looked pale and fragile, having lost a considerable amount of weight since her incarceration.

In the days leading up to the trial, her lawyers publicly proclaimed they would prove Susan acted in self-defence when she stabbed Felix in the guest cottage on 13 October 2002. They asserted that responding officers contaminated the crime scene that night by moving the body from its original position on the floor of the living room.

Pointing to police crime scene photos, Horowitz claimed that documented blood smears around the body and on the floor nearby indicated that Felix had been turned over by investigators, thus destroying potential evidence of Susan's innocence.

Superior Court Judge Laurel Brady had replaced Judge Mary Ann O'Malley on the bench after Susan complained bitterly of O'Malley's bias. Judge Brady, a square-shouldered woman with greying hair and a conservative manner, had been appointed to the bench in 1996 by then-Governor Pete Wilson. Susan was unhappy with her assignment as well. Brady had served as a prosecutor with both the Contra Costa and Solano County District Attorneys Offices, and had presided over numerous murder trials. She was married to Larry Brady, a longtime member of the Richmond Police Department who had recently retired after twenty-six years on the job. Using her preemptory challenge, Susan had asked that Judge Brady also recuse herself, but the court denied her request, ruling that Susan had filed it too late.

The trial had already been delayed two times by Judge Brady, who cited her 'extensive calendar' as the reason for the postponements. In addition, Susan's constant bickering with the judge, when she was acting as her own attorney, had nearly doubled the length of the hearings. Prosecutor Tom O'Connor had exhibited great restraint, despite the repeated delays. During his eleven years with the district attorney's office, O'Connor had won several convictions on charges of first-degree murder and he appeared confident he would secure another in the Polk case.

After eleven days of jury selection, the trial finally got underway that Tuesday with O'Connor's blow-by-blow recounting of the night that Gabriel Polk discovered his father's 'motionless body' covered in blood and lying on the floor of the family's guest cottage.

A commanding figure at well over six feet, O'Connor grabbed the courtroom's attention when he stood to address the jurors. In his opening remarks, he told the panel of six women and six men that the Polks were in the middle of a 'heated divorce' when Susan confronted Felix that October night. According to O'Connor, Susan was furious after learning that a judge had awarded Felix custody of their minor son and given him sole occupancy of the house while she was out of town. Even worse, Felix had managed to have her monthly support payments slashed from six thousand eight hundred dollars to one thousand seven hundred dollars.

It was enough to kill for, according to O'Connor. Felix's injuries were 'of a man fighting for his life,' he continued. 'In contrast, the defendant had almost nothing. Clearly, it was a one-sided battle.'

The prosecutor pointed out that Felix had been stabbed numerous times, sustaining six incise wounds and defensive-type wounds on his hands, forearms, and the soles of his feet. Police observed redness around Susan's eye and small cuts on her hand. It was most telling, though, that she publicly denied any involvement in her husband's death for some time, although she claimed to have privately admitted her role to family members and her lawyers soon after her arrest in October 2002.

'Now she claims she killed him in self-defence,' O'Connor said, resting his gaze on the jurors. 'The defendant is nothing but a cold, callous, calculating murderer. She got wind of what was happening in the divorce proceeding. She became angry . . . and came home [from Montana] to take care of business.'

Rising from his seat at the defence table, Dan Horowitz disputed the prosecutor's allegations. 'My client defended her life against an attack by a rage-filled, brutal, aggressive man who was also her husband,' Horowitz began in a soft voice.

Promising to dispel the prosecution's claim that his client killed her husband for financial gain, he said, 'This concept of the financial divorce is wildly unsupported.'

Susan wore a blank expression as her lawyer pointed out that she was the one who kept the family finances and was aware that once the court-appointed accountant reviewed the couple's financial background it would become clear that the information Felix had provided to the court was inaccurate.

'Susan Polk was going to get her money back retroactively,' Horowitz insisted.

The defence lawyer used his opening remarks as an opportunity to relate details of Susan's childhood and to tell jurors of her early sessions with Felix Polk as a fifteen-year-old patient. He described the therapist as a delusional narcissist who 'hyper-controlled' his wife and children and proclaimed that Susan and her family members would take the stand to testify as much.

At one point, he even drew a parallel between Felix Polk and fanatical cult leader James Warren 'Jim' Jones, the American founder of the Peoples Temple Church in San Francisco and later Jonestown in Guyana. It was Jones who organised the mass suicide of 914 of his followers, including nearly three hundred children, and convinced them to collectively drink a Kool-Aid cocktail laced with poison in November 1978.

Horowitz insisted that just as Jones gained control over his disciples, Felix won psychological control over Susan by molesting her under hypnosis at the tender age of sixteen, and then continuing the abuse with threats and beatings over the course of their marriage.

From the front row of the gallery, Horowitz's wife, Pamela Vitale, listened intently as her husband next introduced Felix's little-known secret: that he had been committed to a psychiatric hospital after suffering a 'schizophrenic reaction' in the mid-fifties while serving as a lieutenant in the US Navy. It was news to many in the courtroom that Dr. Polk had spent nearly one year in a locked ward of a US Naval Hospital. Horowitz promised more on Felix's hospitalisation through testimony from a defence expert who would explain how Felix's mental condition made him prone to 'outbursts of rage, violence, and anger'.

'Susan Polk defended her life against an attack by a vengeful, rageful, aggressive man,' Horowitz insisted. 'She was on her back. She fought him off and lived.'

In spite of Horowitz's strong opening, the trial did not get off to a good start. Jurors seemed skeptical of the defence's claim that police had mishandled evidence. In addition, Horowitz's explanation for Susan's initial denial and subsequent cover-up of the crime did not appear to ring true with the twelve jurors – especially after they heard the prosecutor describe her elaborate efforts to cover up the crime during his opening remarks. O'Connor pointed out that Susan cleaned and hid the knife used in the attack, got rid of her bloody clothing, and placed her husband's car at the train station in an effort to cover her tracks. Those were hardly the actions of an innocent woman, he insisted.

The following morning, jurors boarded a bus for the Polk's hillside residence to get their first look at the Miner Road crime scene. The group spent several hours viewing the pool area and the guesthouse where Gabriel found his father's bloodied body.

That Wednesday, the jury heard from prosecution witnesses, among them the 911 operator who took Felix Polk's call on 6 October, exactly one week before the murder, to report that his wife had threatened his life.

'I remember the caller saying, "My wife threatened to kill me,"' police dispatcher Randee Johnson testified.

Another witness, Deputy Sheriff Shannon Kelly, one of the first officers on the scene, testified that Susan denied having done anything wrong during the ride to police headquarters on the night of 14 October 2002. Although his role in the criminal investigation was limited, Kelly endured two hours of cross-examination by Horowitz, who was trying to cast doubt on police competence at the crime scene. This strategy proved lost on jurors, two of whom were overheard in the men's room trying to figure out why Horowitz had spent so much time with Kelly. Apparently the men were unaware that defence lawyer, Ivan Golde, was also in the bathroom at the time.

'They didn't see me,' Golde later complained to Judge Brady. 'I couldn't believe what I was hearing.'

The judge denied Horowitz's request to have the two jurors removed from the case, but warned the men to refrain from further discussion of the case. 'I know this is not like what you see on TV, but it is important,' Judge Brady told the jurors.

O'Connor closed the first week of testimony with a victory, as the judge accepted into evidence the letter Susan wrote describing Felix's alleged involvement with the Mossad. The defence was successful in convincing Judge Brady to admit a second letter that Susan wrote to her children in which she detailed the alleged abuse she suffered at the hands of Felix.

But the trial would take an unexpected turn when, four days into the case, Daniel Horowitz made a grisly discovery.

It was just before 6pm on Saturday, 15 October, when the lawyer punched in the security code for the locked gates barring entrance to his home at 1901 Hunsaker Canyon Road. He steered his red Honda S2000 up the winding dirt driveway. At the top of the remote hill was an expansive construction site, where Horowitz and his wife, Pamela Vitale, were building a lavish, seven-thousand-square-foot Italian-style mansion. Off to one side was a rundown trailer where the couple had been living with their dogs for nearly a decade while they oversaw the construction of their dream house.

The temporary home was cramped and without amenities. The couple had been pumping their water from a well on the property, where Dan intended to start a winery once construction was complete. It was no secret that Horowitz was wealthy, although it was unclear exactly how he had made his fortune.

Dan first met Pamela, a single mother of two, in 1994 when she moved to the Bay Area from Los Angeles County, according to a website maintained by Pamela's family. At forty-one, she was a striking brunette, two years Dan's senior and nearly three inches taller than the lawyer.

The couple was introduced by Pamela's sister, who arranged for Pam, an independent film producer, to read a script that Dan had written about one of his cases. Bright, ambitious, and sophisticated, Pamela was employed full time as a software-marketing executive and was raising a sixteen-year-old daughter and nineteen-year-old son. Later, she would apply her computer savvy smarts to Dan's law firm, maintaining databases and supervising the construction of their twelve-acre mountaintop estate.

Horowitz knew something was wrong the minute he spotted his wife's car in the driveway. She was supposed to be going to the Kirov Ballet in Berkeley that night. His suspicions increased when he found the front door of the trailer unlocked. Stepping inside, he gasped at the sight of his wife lying on her right side in a pool of blood, her body pushed up against the couple's sixty-five-inch television set. She was dressed in a T-shirt and panties, and there was a giant gash on her head. The carpet beneath her was red with blood, and the living room furniture had been moved about. The giant TV had been shoved nearly two and a half feet from its usual spot.

Hysterical, the lawyer called 911.

'Help me, she's dead!' he yelled into the receiver and then knelt down beside his wife's body. Cradling her in his arms, he tried to absorb the sight of her beaten and mutilated face.

'Who could have done this?' he raged.

The sound of a police car roaring up the driveway startled him to his feet. Racing outside, he shouted to the responding officers from the Lafayette Police Department. Almost immediately, they pushed him into the police car and ordered him to wait while a team from the Contra Costa Sheriff's Department inspected the crime scene.

That night, sheriff's officers took Horowitz to department headquarters, where he was escorted to a room normally used to interview child victims. Over several hours, investigators fired a series of questions at him, first trying to determine if he was suicidal. Next, they handed him a pen and paper and directed him to reconstruct his movements; they wanted a detailed accounting of his whereabouts that day.

Horowitz told officers he hadn't heard from his wife all day. He left home early that morning, around 7.30am, to meet a friend for breakfast. Upon arriving at his Oakland law office around 9.30, he tried to reach Pamela on her cell phone. She didn't answer. He met with a private investigator at 10.45 and finished up some work on the Polk case.

It was 2pm when he dialled Pamela for a second time with no success. Though he found it strange that she was not answering her phone, he wasn't alarmed. His wife was a former high-tech executive who had traveled extensively, both domestically and internationally. At 5'9"' and 178 pounds, she was no pushover. He assumed she was probably just busy with things at the house.

Horowitz told investigators that he left Oakland shortly thereafter. Later he made a deposit at the bank, and grabbed a Starbuck's coffee in town before heading to the gym. After his workout, he headed for home, where he found his wife murdered.

Though short and slender, Horowitz had a wiry strength. While he stood barely 5'8", with thinning brown hair and rimless eyeglasses perched atop a prominent nose, he had honed the physique of a person who worked out seriously at the gym. Like many defence lawyers, Horowitz had received his share of threats over the years. Staying in top physical shape gave him a sense of security. He informed police he was licensed to carry a gun.

An initial investigation by members of the Contra Costa crime lab determined that Pamela Vitale was savagely beaten with multiple objects during the attack that claimed her life. Evidence collected at the crime scene indicated that she was hit numerous times with several different weapons, although police declined to reveal further details of the brutal assault other than to say that Pamela's death was violent.

A coroner's report would later reveal that the fifty-two-year-old was found facedown on the carpet. She was struck more than two dozen times in the head, some of the blows so powerful they dislodged her front teeth and exposed sections of her skull. She had also been stabbed in the abdomen while she lay dead in a pool of blood.

News of the horrific killing quickly drew national media attention to Susan Polk, as speculation swirled that Vitale's death might somehow be linked to the Polk case. It seemed an eerie coincidence that both Felix Polk and Pamela Vitale had been brutally stabbed, although initial media reports stated only that Vitale had been bludgeoned to death. It was not long after Pamela's body was discovered that police began looking into the possibility the cases were linked.

Among those interviewed by investigators was Susan's middle son, Eli Polk, his younger brother, Gabriel, and lawyer Barry Morris. Investigators also questioned a number of the construction workers employed by Horowitz, as well as a neighbour, Joseph William Lynch, who had recently sold the couple four acres in Hunsaker Canyon.

A subsequent investigation revealed that Vitale and her husband had filed a restraining order against Lynch in Contra Costa Superior Court in June 2005. In the complaint, they charged that Lynch was mentally ill and a methamphetamine and alcohol user who routinely harassed them and other neighbours in the Lafayette area. Police were surprised to learn that the couple later elected not to serve Lynch with the court order after hearing that he had signed up for a drug rehabilitation program and was trying to clean up his act.

Lynch denied any involvement in the murder, claiming that Pamela and Horowitz were good people who had supported his efforts to get sober. 'Dan was trying to help me,' Lynch told the *San Francisco Chronicle*. 'I have a drug problem, an alcohol problem, and a big mouth. I'm clean and sober now. Dan and Pamela were really trying to help me.'

There was also mention of a former boyfriend of Pamela's who had been trying to get back together with her in recent months, but Horowitz expressed doubt about the man's involvement in his wife's death. 'I just think he knows what he missed out on,' the lawyer told a reporter for a local newspaper. 'But to think of him as a suspect would be a grave injustice.'

On Monday, 17 October, Dan Horowitz was at home making funeral arrangements when Judge Laurel Brady, at the request of Susan's other lawyer, Ivan Golde, dismissed the Polk jury and declared a mistrial in the case. Brady cited extensive media coverage of Pamela Vitale's murder as grounds for her decision.

'Ladies and gentlemen, it would be hard to miss, despite my

admonitions,' the judge told jurors over the sobs of Susan Polk. 'I have reached the conclusion at this juncture that it is not possible to continue the trial.'

Brady ordered all parties back to court on 2 December to set a new trial date, but no one – including Dan Horowitz – knew if he could put aside the turmoil in his own life and represent Susan. Horowitz acknowledged his own uncertainty in an interview with the local daily, the *Contra Costa Times*. 'I don't know,' he told the newspaper when asked about representing Susan Polk. 'I don't know if I'm alive. I don't know if I'm in hell.'

Outside the courtroom, Horowitz's cocounsel, Ivan Golde, pointed to 'a whole host of conflicts' that could arise since the same police agency that investigated Felix Polk's murder was now looking into the death of Dan's wife.

'You've got the same pathologist doing both investigations,' Golde told journalists gathered at the courthouse that Monday. 'This creates a huge conflict. I don't even know if we can try both cases now in Contra Costa County. We were doing well in there,' Golde said optimistically of their first week in court. 'We were winning this case. I hope we can pick up where we left off.'

Still, members of the Polk jury said they did not hear enough of the case to form an opinion as to Susan's guilt or innocence. 'The prosecution was the only one who had the chance to present information,' said juror Mark Zigler of Concord. 'There was not any reason to dismiss anything.'

Pamela Vitale had been seated in the front row of the courtroom on 11 October, when her husband delivered his opening remarks in the high-profile Polk murder case. Now, just seven days later, her battered corpse lay on a gurney in the coroner's office, awaiting an autopsy by Brian Peterson, the pathologist who performed the autopsy on Felix. Horowitz was not pleased to learn that Peterson was going to conduct the post mortem examination of his wife, since he had intended to dispute several of his findings at trial.

It was just after 10am on 17 October when the medical examiner removed a large gold and diamond ring from Pamela Vitale's left ring finger, and a gold band with a dark-coloured stone and multiple clear stones from her right ring finger. After placing the items in the office for safekeeping, Dr. Peterson began the two-and-a-half-hour post mortem examination on Vitale.

In his official report, Peterson listed the cause of death as 'blunt force head injury'. Pamela Vitale had sustained at least twenty-six crushing blows to the head and thirteen more to other parts of her face and body. 'There are extensive scalp lacerations and abrasions,' Dr. Peterson recorded. 'On the right side of the scalp, at least 8 distinct injuries are identified . . .'

An examination of the victim's torso revealed a post-mortem four-inch stab wound to the left upper abdomen that had perforated the stomach, exposing the intestines. There was also 'an H-shaped figure' carved into the skin of the 'posterior torso area'. Scratch marks on Vitale's breasts, arms, legs, and body indicated she had fought very hard for her life that morning. There were no signs of sexual assault. Still, a rape test was performed with negative results.

That Monday afternoon, police released an affidavit revealing that Pamela Vitale was not only bludgeoned but also savagely stabbed by a killer who wore gloves. In addition, crime scene investigators had located a 'large-sized blood shoeprint' on the cover of a storage container found at the crime scene.

Two days after the autopsy, police made an arrest in Pamela's murder. Surprising to some, the accused seemed to have no connection to the Polk case. The alleged killer was a sixteen-year-old boy named Scott Dyleski who lived with his mother and two families – eleven people in all – in a ramshackle house about one mile from Dan and Pamela on Hunsaker Canyon Road. Investigators linked Dyleski to a scheme with another youth to buy equipment for growing marijuana with stolen credit cards. The fraudulently obtained equipment was to be shipped to Dyleski's address but listed Vitale's home as the billing address. Homicide detectives speculated that Dyleski had gotten into a confrontation with Vitale when he went to her house thinking the package may have been accidentally delivered there.

Homicide detectives zeroed in on the teen just two days into their investigation after receiving a tip from a neighbour claiming that someone had obtained a credit card under his name and used it to purchase equipment often used to grow marijuana. In recent months, several of Vitale's neighbours on Hunsaker Canyon Road had reported mail being stolen from a common mailbox area along the road at the base of a hill. An investigation into the thefts had yielded no suspects until one resident, Doug Schneider, reported that Horowitz's remote hilltop address was provided as the shipping address for the hydroponics equipment that had been charged to his credit card on 12 October.

Police got a second break on 19 October when a youth came forward to confess to a marijuana-growing scheme with his former classmate, Scott Dyleski. The youth, Robin Croen, told police they had been using fraudulently obtained credit cards to purchase the hydroponics lights used for growing marijuana. Croen, a student at Acalanes High School in Lafayette, told police that he and Dyleski, a classmate, intended to grow the plants in Dyleski's closet.

According to Croen, the night before the murder Dyleski claimed that 'there was some sort of problem with the orders' and assured him that he 'just needed some more time to do something.' Police later learned that Dyleski and Croen, who was not implicated in the murder, allegedly conspired together in the mail thefts – including the one that lead to Vitale's death.

Croen also told police that Dyleski had scratches on his face when he saw him on 15 October – the day of the murder. Three days later, Dyleski showed up at Acalanes High School during lunch period and announced that he was going to tell his housemates about the credit card scam. 'He said he was going to admit it because somehow this would separate him from the [Vitale] murder,' Croen told authorities. The comment concerned Croen, who could not understand how their credit card scheme could be linked to the woman's murder. He asked Dyleski what he was talking about, and Dyleski 'said he was afraid his DNA was on her because she had grabbed him at some point (while he was walking in the woods). I asked how or why, but I didn't get an answer,' the youth told police.

Police subsequently alleged that Dyleski went to Vitale's home that Saturday, 15 October, to pick up the marijuana-growing equipment he ordered, but the package was not in the mailbox. Investigators suspected that Dyleski went inside the trailer to find out what happened to it, where he confronted Pamela Vitale and beat her to death. Dyleski had no way of knowing that the hydroponics equipment had never been shipped because the supplier suspected that something was amiss.

According to detectives, the gangly 5'5", 110-pound teenager was wearing gloves and a Balaclava mask (a mask which covers the entire face, with slits only for the eyes) when he entered the trailer home. Evidence collected at the scene indicated that he struck Vitale more than thirty times about the face and body with a broken piece of crown molding and other items before carving a 'gothic signature' in the shape of an 'H' into the small of her back.

After the murder, Scott Dyleski allegedly poured himself a glass of water, rinsed his hands in the sink and had a shower: a forensic examination of the bathroom faucets revealed traces of blood. Apparently unconcerned about the blood-stained crown molding he left, the teen used a little-travelled trail through the woods, arriving home sometime between 10.20 and 11.00 that morning. Croen wasn't the only one who noticed Dyleski's injuries that day. Several of his housemates later told police that they observed a gash on the boy's face that morning. When asked about the wound, Scott claimed he scratched himself during a morning hike in the woods.

A forensic examination of Vitale's laptop showed Pamela was on her computer, surfing the Internet for various things, including Court TV's website, for articles about Dan's criminal representation of Susan Polk, when Dyleski entered the trailer that Saturday morning. Logs show that at 10.12am her computer searches ceased.

On the evening of Wednesday, 19 October, investigators served two search warrants on the home of Dyleski's mother, Esther Fielding, 'looking for any type of murder weapon that would cause blunt-force trauma or other injury.' Posters covered nearly every inch of wall space in Scott's bedroom. Amid the clutter were drawings of symbols similar to the H-shape found carved into Vitale's back. Three computers were seized by investigators, along with several knives, bedding, and other items. In a van behind the house, police found a duffel bag with Dyleski's nametag. Inside, they found bloody clothes, shoes, and a ski mask that later tested positive for DNA from both Dyleski and Vitale.

The following morning, as friends and family were saying a final goodbye to Pamela at her funeral, her alleged killer was arrested and held in lieu of $1 million bail.

Six days after the killing, on 21 October, the teen was brought before a Superior Court judge and charged with first degree murder as an adult. Handcuffs encircled his bony wrists, and strands of dark, wavy hair covered much of his angular face as he was led into the courtroom. Dyleski said nothing during the brief court appearance.

Details of his brief and troubled life would emerge in the days and weeks ahead. Interviews with schoolmates painted the teen as a loner who was mercilessly teased about the way he dressed by his classmates at Lafayette's Acalanes High School. Friends said that Dyleski endured endless taunts for being 'nerdy' while growing up in the small, rural town as a Boy Scout, a basketball player, and a good student in elementary school.

But something inside Scott seemed to die in 2001 when his eighteen-year-old half sister, Denika, was killed in a car crash. The once easygoing student suddenly began shaving parts of his head, wearing dark eyeliner and black nail polish and dying his brown hair jet black. He began dressing all in black accessorised by heavy silver jewellery and a long black trench coat like the one worn by rocker Marilyn Manson, the self-proclaimed 'Anti-Christ Superstar' whose stage name merged that of Marilyn Monroe and Charles Manson.

One former classmate told the *San Francisco Chronicle* he believed Scott was trying to be noticed with his strange appearance and clothing. 'I always thought he was trying to get attention,' Kevin McDonald said of Dyleski. 'But he seemed like a nice guy, not someone who would ever do something like this.'

Dyleski had been reportedly studying hard for his GED, desperate to escape Acalanes High School and the teasing he endured. He was taking art classes at Mt. Diablo College in Pleasant Hill, the same junior college that Susan Polk had attended as a teenager, and had submitted some of his dark, imagery-driven art for grades. He was to celebrate his eighteenth birthday two weeks after the murder.

On 12 January 2006, Susan stood before Judge Laurel Brady and asked that she be allowed to fire Horowitz and Golde, her fourth attorneys, and represent herself in the murder trial. While the lawyers knew beforehand that she wanted them removed, Susan's action both surprised and disappointed them, after having invested so much into the high-profile case.

Interestingly, her decision to replace them seemed to have little to do with Horowitz's personal tragedy. As most lawyers who worked with Susan discovered, representing her was something of a roller-coaster ride. Just two weeks prior to her announcement, she had expressed concern for Horowitz's well-being and seemed happy to have him as her lawyer, but soon something soured her on his representation.

In the weeks leading up to the trial, Susan had made many calls to Horowitz's office with countless requests. Horowitz assigned Valerie Harris to handle the multitude of Susan's needs, but as time went on, that arrangement backfired. Susan began complaining about what she perceived as Dan's lack of attention to her case and accused him of failing to file legal motions on her behalf. Once she felt neglected, it was not long before she notified Horowitz that his services were no longer needed.

'She has a right to an attorney of her choice,' Horowitz told reporters outside the courtroom. 'But the judge may not let me out because we're so close to trial. I feel sorry for her [Susan]. What can I say? Going through Pamela's death was a horrible experience. It's not deliberate. She's not really trying to hurt me. She's desperate and scared.'

During the ninety-minute hearing before Judge Brady, Susan claimed that Horowitz had all but ignored her case since his wife was murdered. Though Horowitz had already filed some forty motions with the court, Susan still wasn't happy, claiming he had failed to file others for her. Despite the severity of the charges, Susan believed that she could represent herself in court. She asked that Harris, with whom Susan had formed a strong bond, be permitted to remain on her case as a consultant.

In addition to her complaints about Horowitz, Susan also filed a lengthy declaration on 12 January in which she outlined several grievances she had with the judge and police department. Among other things, Susan complained that Horowitz had failed to file her motion to disqualify Judge Brady and the entire Contra Costa County judiciary because they were all prejudiced against her. She also claimed that she had been subjected to discriminatory treatment by law enforcement since she had unsuccessfully moved to have Judge Brady removed from the case in August – including being 'the only female prisoner' to be transported in shackles.

Susan also claimed that Dan Horowitz was a suspect in the murder of his wife. Later, she told reporters that she believed that Horowitz may have been involved in Pamela's murder 'based on statements he

Above: Eli relaxing on the deck during happier times

Below: Susan's dogs were of particular importance to her and the subject of contention between her and Felix.

Above: Though Susan's relationship with Felix could at times seem normal, the years of conflict eventually became too much.

Below: One of the controversial bloody footprints found at the crime scene.

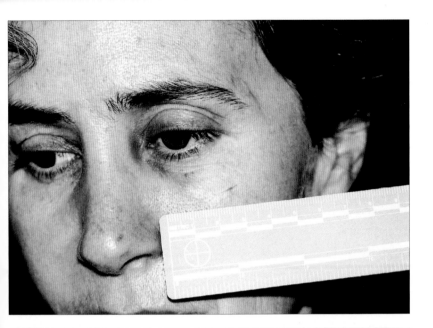

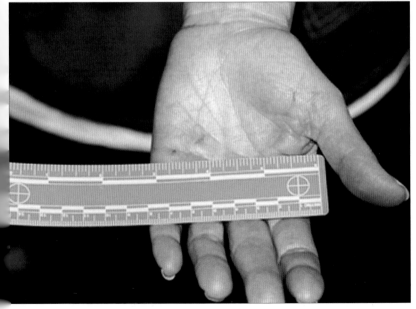

While at first she would claim that her injuries were the result of her dog's over aggressive behaviour, Susan later revealed that the bruising around her eye and the small cuts to her fingers stemmed from her struggle with Felix.

Above: A police department sketch of the Polk's Miner Road estate.

Below: My 2005 interview with Susan on *Catherine Crier Live*. It was during this discussion that she revealed Felix's naval records and told her side of that fateful evening.

Taken in the Polk's pool house, this sequence of photos shows Susan's attorneys, Dan Horowitz (with glasses) and Ivan Golde, reenacting the struggle between Felix and Susan on the night of Felix's death.

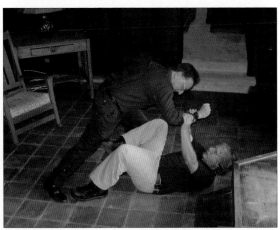

Above: Helen Bolling speaking with reporters outside the courthouse.

Below: Prosecutor Paul Sequeira preparing to address the media.

Above: Valerie Harris making a statement to reporters in front of the courthouse. While her professional relationship with Susan was strained by Susan's erratic behaviour, ultimately Valerie's presence was a big help to Susan as she manoeuvred through one legal mine field after another.

Below: Adam and Gabriel on the set of *Catherine Crier Live*.

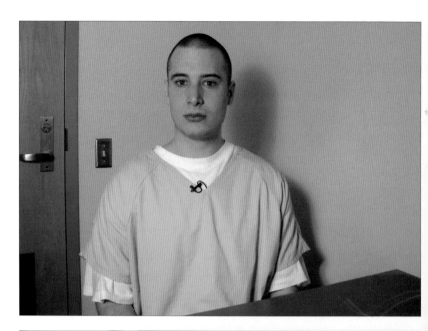

Above: Eli after learning of his mother's verdict.

Below: After the verdict: (*From left to right*) Prosecutor Sequeira, Gabriel Polk, Marjorie Briner, Adam Polk, Dan Briner.

made to me.' She even offered to testify on behalf of the murder suspect, Scott Dyleski, at his upcoming pretrial hearing. Though Horowitz declined to respond publicly to Susan's allegations, in part because a gag order had been issued, it was clear that he was infuriated by her remarks.

Not surprisingly, Judge Brady denied Susan's motion to have the entire judiciary of Contra Costa County removed at a hearing on 20 January, but she granted Susan's request to dismiss Horowitz. The judge set a new trial date for 27 February, giving Susan six weeks to prepare her defence.

'It is Susan's story,' a visibly pale Dan Horowitz said while waiting in the hallway of the courthouse after the hearing. 'She lived it and she wants to tell it. She has the absolute right to present her own defence.'

Ivan Golde chose to phrase it a bit differently: 'It's a very sad day,' he said.

CHAPTER TWENTY-THREE

GOING IT ALONE

On 27 February 2006, three hundred prospective jurors arrived at the Contra Costa County Courthouse in Martinez to begin jury selection in the murder trial of Susan Polk.

Surprisingly, Polk's original prosecutor, Tom O'Connor, had announced his resignation from the D.A.'s office just one week earlier to take a job in the private sector. A senior prosecutor, Paul Sequeira, was immediately assigned to take his place. Though new to the case, Sequeira told the media that he was rapidly getting up to speed and regarded the case as fairly straightforward.

With no lawyer by her side, Susan was relying on Valerie Harris and had a jury consultant to help with the selection process. Prospective jurors arriving at the courthouse were first directed to an assembly room where Judge Brady informed them about Susan's decision to represent herself. She asked jurors if they could fairly adjudicate the case under that scenario. Those who expressed doubts were immediately excused. The others were directed to the courtroom where Susan and Paul Sequeria would conduct their questioning.

As jury selection began, Susan seemed in control of her defence. Her questions were measured and appropriate, although in some instances she revealed too much about the specifics of her case and was admonished by the judge to restrict her comments. Soft-spoken and articulate, Susan's demeanour was more of a schoolteacher than a murder defendant. She showed up for court each morning in well-tailored outfits, gold-rimmed designer glasses – and a uniformed court officer on each arm. Though she appeared self-assured at the start, it wasn't long before it became clear that she was very nervous about her case and somewhat uncertain about how to proceed.

Late in the afternoon, Susan erupted into tears after a potential juror voiced alarm over the possible length of the trial, estimated at over two months, and Susan's decision to serve as her own lawyer – or to go *pro per*.

'I feel this is my one chance,' Susan defended, wiping tears from her cheeks. 'I'm taking a calculated risk, and I realise all of you have things you'd rather do.'

In the courtroom, Susan was timid one minute and more like an articulate, thoughtful law student the next. She could be confident, emphatically arguing legal points with the judge and citing information from a law book. Other times, however, she was apologetic and ill at ease. She grew visibly upset one afternoon when she misplaced one of her documents. After Susan spent several anxious minutes rifling through the stack of papers on the defence table, she finally gave up in exasperation and carried on from memory.

By the end of the second day, Susan had dismissed eight prospective jurors while the prosecutor had dismissed six through the preemptory challenge process. Susan's questioning made it clear that she was most anxious to have a juror who could be objective in adjudicating a case in which a defendant was acting as her own attorney.

While questioning one prospective juror, a building inspector, Susan crafted an analogy, asking him how he would react if he went to someone's house and found that the homeowner had fixed his own toilet and done his own construction and wiring, while following the appropriate rules.

The man said that wouldn't trouble him.

'And so, here in the courtroom, if I follow the rules, although I sometimes might make mistakes, would it annoy you that I'm doing it myself?'

'No. It wouldn't annoy me,' he said.

Despite his positive responses, Susan would later strike the building inspector from the jury because of his friendships with a local judge and members of law enforcement. She excused another potential juror after the woman told Judge Brady that she thought Susan 'was a fool' for choosing to go *pro per*. And she let a third man go after he joked about her decision to represent herself.

'It's like a game of wrestling, where a flyweight is with a heavyweight,' the retired draftsman chuckled. 'If I bet on it, I bet with the heavyweight.'

While Susan took the courtroom proceedings seriously, she invoked a little humour when one prospective panellist raised concerns over how Susan intended to cross-examine her sons and take the stand on her own behalf. With a giggle, Susan recounted a scene from a Jim Carrey comedy in which the actor played a defendant who was representing himself, leaping from the podium to the stand as he conducted his cross-examination.

'I'll actually have notes and questions for myself and an outline leading me through what I need to tell you,' Susan told the woman, a registered nurse, who was later selected to serve on Polk's jury.

By late Monday, 6 March, Susan and Paul Sequeria announced their agreement on a panel of six men and six women, among them a woman who had served in the US military, a retired female US Parcel Service worker, and a sales manager for the local plumber's union who shared one attribute with Susan – a young son. The jury selection process had taken a full five days.

Judge Brady could have started the case with opening remarks that same afternoon, but at the request of the prosecutor, she agreed to begin the following day, 7 March.

The case had drawn considerable attention from local and national media for a variety of reasons – the relationship between Susan and her therapist husband, the allegations of an abusive household, and the anticipated testimony from all three of the Polks sons – two were expected to testify against their mother and one was expected to take the stand on her behalf. The fact that Susan had fired four different defence lawyers and was now going to represent herself at trial made the case all the more interesting.

With people routinely questioning her sanity and judgment, the trial offered her an opportunity to prove the naysayers wrong and show that she could handle the task. Building from the material that

Horowitz had prepared, she would present a straight self-defence case, alleging that Felix attacked her with a knife that October night and that she had fought back before fatally stabbing him to save herself. Furthermore, she would present evidence that Felix died from a heart attack – not the multiple stab wounds she inflicted during their heated altercation – and would call an expert to support her claim.

On Tuesday, members of the media, law enforcement, and curiosity seekers occupied most of the fifty seats in the gallery. Others sat on chairs that had been set up along the walls or stood in the rear of the courtroom, awaiting the opening remarks from Paul Sequeira and Susan Polk.

Susan looked drawn and frail as she stood organising her papers at the defence table. Dressed in a white sweater and khaki pants, Susan's sporty attire contrasted sharply with the conservative dark suit and solid grey tie worn by her opponent, Paul Sequeira. The prosecutor looked to be about ten years Susan's junior, with thick, layered hair and wire-rim glasses that tended to perch on the end of his nose. Obviously comfortable in the courtroom, Sequeira made a habit of strolling across the commercial-grade carpet and sometimes leaning on the railing of the jury box.

Polk immediately surprised the crowd when she asked and was given permission to postpone her opening statement until she began her case-in-chief. It was just after 3pm when the prosecutor rose to address the jury. He told Judge Brady that his remarks would take about fifty minutes to deliver, but in reality the remarks took a lot longer, as Sequeira was interrupted repeatedly by Susan's objections.

'You are about to embark on a journey through a dysfunctional relationship that ended in murder and destruction,' the prosecutor began. 'Felix Polk was a Holocaust survivor. Susan was fifteen when she went to see him. They had a relationship that went wrong. The physical relationship began when she was seventeen or eighteen. They married when she was twenty-four and had their first son, Adam, in 1983. What was born out of dysfunction began to look like a normal, loving relationship.

'The defendant worked in the home raising children, but there were always conflicts. Wherever Susan went, there was a trail of conflict and confrontation. If there were problems in school, it was the teacher's fault. This also became the children's reality because it was easier to go along than to take responsibility for their actions.

'Susan also had a theory that Felix controlled the school. Gabe admits that he was sucked into this delusion. As time passed, Susan became more paranoid and began making things up. Then, five years before the murder, Susan's mental instability intensified on a trip to Disneyland. She had a full-blown break and claimed to have repressed memories. She claimed she was raped as a child by her father and brother, and described in graphic detail the rape scenes to her children.'

'I object, your honour!' Susan announced, rising to her feet. Judge Brady admonished Susan that she was not permitted to object during the State's opening remarks. But her words fell on deaf ears. In fact, Susan began interrupting the prosecutor at almost every turn. These interruptions set the tone for the entire trial. Throughout the proceedings, Judge Brady would attempt, often unsuccessfully, to control Susan's flare-ups and accusations, including allegations that she and the prosecutor were colluding against the defendant.

Turning his attention back to the jury, Sequeria took a deep breath and once again tried to complete his opening remarks. The prosecutor described how Susan's delusional behaviour soon focused on Felix. She believed her husband was in the CIA, the FBI, and the Mossad. She believed he had offshore accounts in the Cayman Islands. Susan told her three sons that Felix 'was a monster', the prosecutor charged, triggering yet another objection from Susan.

'Felix was a therapist who couldn't help his own wife with her paranoid delusions,' Sequeira continued amid more objections and yet another stern warning from Judge Brady.

'Until the murder, there was no extreme violence in the house,' the prosecutor went on. Citing the accounts of two of the Polk sons, the prosecutor argued that Felix was not the abuser and that both Felix and Susan provoked repeated confrontations in the household.

'Objection,' Susan yelled yet again.

'Mrs. Polk, I will not admonish you again,' Judge Brady warned angrily. The judge threatened to remove Susan from the courtroom if she interrupted one more time.

Jurors exchanged silent glances as the prosecutor continued.

'There was lots of grabbing and bumping but not extreme violence,'

Sequeira said. 'One time, Susan slapped Felix in front of a police officer. The boys will say that dad was an older guy and worked long hours. He came home late and tired and Susan would often verbally abuse Felix throughout dinner. Susan would challenge his manhood and poke fun at the size of his penis in front of the boys.'

'Objection!' Susan barked, seething with anger.

'I will remove you from this courtroom!' Judge Brady fumed, glaring at Susan.

For a moment, it appeared as though Susan would be barred from the proceeding. From Brady's tone, it was clear that this would be her final warning – and Susan seemed to understand the gravity of the judge's words.

From there, Sequeira continued his opening statement without interruption, weaving the complicated tale of the turbulent times in the Polk household. Painting a picture of dysfunction and psychological disturbance, the prosecutor detailed how Susan routinely belittled and emasculated the aging Felix. He walked jurors through Felix's final days, detailing the brutal battle for custody of Gabriel and the fight over Susan's alimony payments. To Sequeira, the Susan Polk who killed her husband was a cold, callous woman, not the victim she made herself out to be. She lied to the police about her involvement from the beginning, and she was still lying about her involvement as they sat there in the court.

'Susan then lies over and over and over and over at the police station,' he told the jurors as the defendant watched his every move. 'Does Susan say "he came at me with a knife and I attacked him in self defence?" No, she says she didn't do it. But then forensic science kicks in and her lies are not permitted.

'She destroys evidence. Bloody clothes. Gone! Knife. Gone! Car – moved! Lies and a cover up!'

Jurors listened intently to the prosecutor's theory. Sequeira detailed Felix's injuries, informing them of the savage nature of his wounds and showing the jurors dramatic crime scene photos. Despite the graphic pictures, no one flinched.

'Ladies and gentlemen, the evidence will show the defendant was upset. This festered until she made good on a repeated threat' to kill Felix Polk, the prosecutor charged. 'Dr. Polk, abuser or victim of the ultimate attack of murder?'

Following Sequeira's opening remarks, jurors were dismissed for the night, but Susan wouldn't leave without one parting shot at the court.

'I want a mistrial!' Susan demanded as the last juror stepped out of the courtroom. 'It's all lies,' she shouted furiously, ticking off each of the prosecutor's statements. 'Anyone who knows me knows I wouldn't talk about my husband's penis in front of the boys. It's laughable.'

Judge Brady angrily directed Susan to move on to evidentiary issues that needed addressing, but Susan wouldn't let things rest. She complained that her case assistant, Valerie Harris, was not being permitted to visit with her in jail and that she had still not received all of the case documents from Dan Horowitz.

Ignoring Susan, the judge turned to the prosecutor and instructed that he discuss the evidence with the defendant.

'Liar!' she shouted at the prosecutor.

'Lady, I know your act, and if you try to draw me in, and try to control me like you're trying to control the court, then I'll deal with Mrs. Harris,' Sequeira shot back.

'Then, I'll fire Ms. Harris,' Susan said as she promptly terminated her only assistant.

When court recessed for the night, Susan rehired Harris; she was back at Susan's side the following morning, watching intently as Susan interrogated her youngest son.

CHAPTER TWENTY-FOUR

THE CHIEF WITNESS

Susan's attention was trained on the witness stand, where Gabriel Polk sat in a suit and tie, ready to testify for the prosecution. Now nineteen years old, the teen appeared composed and in control that Wednesday morning. It had been three years since Susan last saw her youngest son. Susan's cross-examination of Gabe would mark the first time the two had spoken since Felix's death. A restraining order had barred any contact between the mother and son during the intervening period, and Gabe had refused repeatedly to read any of Susan's written correspondence.

Gabriel was the State's strongest and most sympathetic witness. That Susan had allowed the then-fifteen-year-old youth to find his father's dead body in the family's guest cottage would be a major obstacle for jurors to overcome as they considered her explanation of self-defence. Sitting before the jury, Gabe's once slender frame had filled out and what had been gaunt, sullen cheeks were now bright and healthy. He had grown into a handsome young man, with his mother's strong jaw and deep-set eyes framed by thick, dark lashes.

Susan, dressed in black trousers and a blouse, appeared unsettled as she sat at the defence table. She blotted away tears with a tissue and sipped on a glass of water she poured from the gold and black carafe on the table. Saying that she felt ill, she took two pain-killers after getting permission from Sheriff's deputies.

When asked by Sequeira to identify his mother, Gabe Polk looked in Susan's direction and pointed. The two seemed to avoid direct eye contact. In response to questions from the prosecutor, Gabe described how he stopped attending school as a youth because his mother insisted that administrators were 'out to get him' and were purposely giving him bad grades. Susan believed that his father was behind a conspiracy being perpetrated by members of the school faculty, that Felix had designated Adam for success and Gabe and his middle brother, Eli, for failure.

Jurors scribbled in notebooks as the teen responded to questions about Susan's breakdown during the family's visit to Disneyland. Gabe said he was nine or ten when the family made the trip and recalled his mother crying 'uncontrollably'. Later he was told that while on the trip she had remembered being abused by her father, mother, and brother as a child, and that she believed her parents had murdered a police officer and buried his body in the basement of her childhood home. On the stand, Gabe recounted his mother's recollections of the alleged abuse, which included 'very disturbing details', information he was ill-equipped to handle at the time.

Recalling Felix and Susan's dramatic accusations of molestation against their sons' day care providers, Gabe claimed that it was Susan who had convinced his father and brothers that he and Adam were victims of a satanic sex cult. Gabe went on to say that he now believed that his mother had 'brainwashed' him against his father and described her as 'full-blown delusional'. During his testimony, he recalled how she would sit at the breakfast table, scanning the newspaper for hidden codes and messages sent to her husband from the Mossad. She later elaborated on this, saying that this was how Felix communicated with undercover operatives. Gabe had no reason to doubt his mother's claims; he simply went along with what she was saying. It was easier to agree than to debate what she was telling him.

During the courtroom proceedings, Gabe seemed distant, wearing an inscrutable stare as he sat in the witness chair or raised his eyes to the ceiling when contemplating answers to the prosecutor's questions. Throughout the morning, Gabe used the word 'delusion' countless times to describe his mother's behaviour. He recalled a car ride with Susan six months prior to the homicide during which she began speaking of ways to kill Felix. 'She talked about drugging him and drowning him in the pool, hitting him over the head and drowning him in the pool, running him over with the car, or tampering with his car.'

Mentioning that she had been making threats for almost five years, Gabriel was accustomed to Susan's emotional outbursts and, at some point, stopped taking her seriously. 'She talked about killing him every day,' he said.

Still, Gabe said he was alarmed when she announced in September 2002 that she intended to leave him with Felix while she travelled to Montana to look for a place to live. He told the court that he found it odd that she would leave him with the man she deemed a monster, but after spending several days with Felix, Gabriel began rethinking his feelings about his dad. He was both surprised and pleased to find that Felix wasn't the ogre that Susan had portrayed.

'Dad's not such a bad guy,' Gabe told Susan during one call, recalling that his mother was 'furious' about the divorce proceedings.

One week before the murder, Gabe said he warned his father that 'he feared for his [dad's] life' because of 'all the things that his mother was saying.'

In response to questions from the prosecutor, Gabe said that he never witnessed any physical abuse in the home. 'The most I've ever seen my dad do to my mother was slap her once,' he said.' 'About six months before the murder, I saw my mom slap my dad and police came out to arrest her.'

'Objection!' Susan bellowed, voicing opposition to her son's use of the word 'murder'.

Judge Brady sustained that objection, as well as Susan's second protest over the word 'killing'. Susan argued that Felix's death should be referred to as 'the incident'. But the judge disagreed, and substituted 'homicide' as an acceptable alternative.

When Sequeira continued his direct examination, Gabe was asked to speak about his parents' relationship. Here, Gabriel's testimony corroborated Sequeira's opening statements, portraying Felix as the dutiful working husband and Susan as the aggressor who would get in his face within minutes of his return home. Susan often degraded her husband, calling him 'old' and 'decrepit', and making sexually explicit comments, including derogatory remarks about the size of his penis.

After Gabriel answered questions about the events of 13 October leading up to his gruesome discovery, the judge adjourned the proceedings for lunch and directed the defendant to begin her cross-examination when they returned. It had been a difficult morning for Susan, who spent much of Gabriel's testimony quietly weeping in her seat. Listening to her son vilify her was hard, but she left the court vowing to return with renewed composure and determined to get Gabriel to admit that his father had been a tyrant.

Questioning Gabriel proved to be an arduous process, one that lasted for five gruelling days. During that time, Susan challenged his recollections about his childhood, suggested he was hiding things when he couldn't remember any abuse, and elicited facts about his early brushes with the law. She asked innumerable questions about the relationship between Felix and herself and probed her son's affection for his brothers. She repeatedly broke down in tears when their memories differed and when he wouldn't corroborate her claims of spousal abuse.

Early on, Susan questioned Gabe about the alleged ritualistic sexual abuse of Adam at the day care centre in an attempt to demonstrate that the accusations came from Felix, not from her. Over Sequeira's objections, Susan played a tape of Felix's speech at the Berkeley Conference of the California Consortium of Child Abuse in 1988. It was at this event that he was introduced as a 'parent of a ritualistically abused child'.

Gabe sat impassively as his dead father's voice filled the courtroom. 'The children were raped on stage, raped in every form imaginable,' Felix told conference participants. Meanwhile jurors were transfixed by the audio-taped lecture in which Felix claimed that his eldest son, Adam, had witnessed a baby being stuffed into a plastic bag and 'hammered to death', and that cult members ate flesh, vomit, and blood in front of his son and other children.

'My rage is omnipresent . . . my fantasy, of course, is to kill them,' Felix's recorded voice resounded over speakers in the courtroom. 'And I'm a rather moral person. I want to kill them.'

'Did you recognise your father's voice?' Susan asked Gabe when the tape ended.

Gabriel responded affirmatively.

Afterwards, Susan asked about allegations that he, too, had been sexually abused while in day care and that both his parents had gone to police to file a complaint. Still, he insisted that he and Adam had no recollection of being molested while in day care. He maintained that Susan was the one who had created the whole scenario and ultimately convinced Felix that it was real.

'Did it ever occur to you that he might be making it all up?' Susan asked.

'I don't know,' Gabe replied.

While the questions were exhaustive, Susan never really probed Gabe's recollection of the night he found his father's body in the guesthouse. After three days of cross-examination, she asked the teen, 'On the night you found your father's body, were you scared?'

'I wasn't scared, I was completely devastated,' Gabe replied. 'But I wasn't scared.'

Questions like this made it clear that Susan's examination was going nowhere. She asked her son if he was 'completely truthful' with police during his interrogation, and if he recalled how many times he told officers that his mother 'had never been violent' with his dad. But she failed to delve further into the events of that day.

Instead, she pushed Gabe to portray his father in a negative light.

'You don't recall your father poisoning Tuffy, the family dog?' she asked.

'No, I don't.'

'Are you aware that your father woke up every day thinking about killing people?'

At times, Susan seemed determined to engage her son in a dialogue, invoking Judge Brady to issue a warning that cross-examination 'is not a conversation'.

Even the prosecutor expressed frustration after it became clear that Susan intended to question his star witness until she was content with his responses – no matter the relevance to the case.

There was a break in the case during the second day of testimony when Susan arrived for court and told the judge that she had a bad sore throat, vowed that she 'wasn't making it up' and asked for a postponement. The judge acquiesced and instructed everyone to return to court the following Monday, 13 March.

Still, Susan felt well enough to object to Marjorie Briner's presence in the courtroom before the adjournment. She argued that Briner, her son's guardian, was influencing Gabe's testimony. She also insisted that Briner stood to profit from the outcome of the trial because she was entitled to Social Security benefits as his guardian.

In a telephone conversation early in the trial, Marjorie Briner expressed Gabriel's concern over how he was being portrayed in the media. Some members of the press had been speculating over statements the teen had made during a telephone conversation with his brother Adam while at police headquarters that were being aired on Court TV. Briner explained that Gabe was anxious to clarify one remark in which he appeared to say 'Dad left us a pile of "money", when in fact, Gabe claims that he told Adam, "Dad left us a pile of *debt*".

'This young man is under a great deal of stress, and it's not unreasonable to have a support person in the court,' Sequeria argued with regard to Briner's presence in the courtroom, telling Susan that just because she thinks something is happening doesn't make it so.

Judge Brady ruled that Briner could remain in the courtroom, except when Gabriel was responding to specific questions about financial matters.

'I am going to need a therapist when this is all over,' Sequeira told reporters outside court that Wednesday afternoon.

That following Monday, Susan confronted the judge over the recent arrest of her middle son, Eli, on charges he beat up his girlfriend. On 9 March, police arrested Eli and charged him with misdemeanour battery based on claims that his then-girlfriend made to authorities at the Polks' Miner Road home.

Eli had been released on bail and was standing in the doorway of the courtroom when his mother asked the judge to issue a restraining order against his girlfriend.

Brady refused and instructed Susan to get on with her cross-examination. 'Mrs. Polk, your son is an adult, and if he feels a restraining order is necessary, there is an appropriate process for him to go through.'

'His life has been threatened,' Susan went on. 'There are physical marks on his face. He called police for help.'

Susan claimed that it was Eli who had summoned police that past

Thursday after his girlfriend entered the house without permission and assaulted him for not returning her phone calls. She then argued that Eli was entitled to an emergency restraining order from Brady because he was a witness in her case.

'I'm not going to issue a restraining order unless I hear from both parties,' the judge declared.

It was then that Susan spotted her son in the vestibule outside the courtroom. 'This is my son,' she shouted, pointing to the courtroom door. 'Look at his face!'

Susan directed her case manager, Valerie Harris, to retrieve Eli and bring him inside. But her son declined to enter, prompting Judge Brady to set a hearing date for 16 March to address the matter. She also ordered that Eli's girlfriend be notified of the court date.

A second interruption occurred when Judge Brady advised Susan that she was not permitted to have witnesses in the courtroom after spotting her mother, Helen Bolling, in the third row of the gallery. Susan appeared surprised at the judge's comment. Turning to look in the gallery, Susan smiled. 'Oh, there she is! Hi Mom!' she shouted, waving at the gray-haired woman in the ankle-high cowboy boots. 'I didn't know she was here.'

Judge Brady instructed Susan's mother to step out of the courtroom, explaining that she was a witness in the case and could not stay for testimony.

By the end of the day, Sequeira was throwing his hands up in exasperation. 'I give up,' he said, after Susan repeatedly questioned Gabriel about a pair of brass knuckles that he supposedly kept in his car, despite the D.A.'s objections.

'She's been cross-examining her son for three days and she's been talking about Tuffy and Ruffy and whatever else she's got going,' Sequeria complained. 'She's absolutely torturing that kid. And she's abusing her cross-examination privileges. She's abusing the process.'

Finding it pointless to continue objecting, the prosecutor stood silent as Gabe again explained that he carried the brass knuckles because he was scared of his mother and brother Eli. He said that Eli told him he would do 'whatever' it took to prevent him from testifying against their mother. Gabe took his brother's remark as a threat and obtained a restraining order against Eli. According to Gabe, Eli held 'a lot of resentment' towards both his parents and acted out a lot, both at home and in school.

Susan then turned to the family's time in Piedmont and Gabriel's difficulties while in middle school, where he admitted to being involved in fights and being suspended for 'drugs'. Responding to Susan's insinuations, Gabe blamed the constant arguing at home for his behaviour, for his acting up in school, and for the hard time he had making friends during childhood.

'Parents in the neighbourhood were scared of you,' he said. 'Scared of our family, generally.' Gabe went on to name one parent who refused to let her child play with him and his brothers because of concerns about Susan's mental state – or as Gabe put it 'you and your delusions'.

His sharp remarks did not appear to faze Susan, who plowed ahead, at one point displaying photographs of family trips to Disneyland and Gabe as a child playing with a friend and the family dogs, Max and Mitsie, in an attempt to elicit fond memories of their times together.

'Didn't you say "even if she is delusional, we love her because she's fun?"' Susan asked, holding up the 'Best Mom' plaque that her three sons awarded her in 1997.

'Yeah, we loved you. This [the plaque] was Dad's idea by the way,' he shot back. Susan wept when Gabe said he couldn't confirm her claims that his dad punched her in the face, dragged her up the stairs by her hair, and told her that he would never give her a divorce.

'He threw water in your face one time,' the teen acknowledged.

'One time?' Susan fired back.

Gabe admitted that his father may have picked up and thrown small items around the house during arguments with Susan but said that he never threw anything directly at her.

Continuing, Susan asked Gabe about his strained relationship with Eli, tearing up as the questions came out of her mouth.

'Do you recall telling your brother Eli that he was your best friend?'

'Yes,' Gabe replied in a monotone.

'Do you remember when you went to school wearing his oversized clothes and shoes?' Susan asked, referring to Gabe's time in elementary school. 'Do you miss your brother?'

There was silence in the courtroom as Gabriel contemplated his answer. 'Yes, I do miss him,' the teen replied, straightening himself in the chair. 'I still have affection for Eli, Dad, and you . . . I do have good memories. I do love you. But there's terrible memories with the good memories.'

'You still have affection for your brother?' Susan posed. 'Then why did you sue him?'

'I didn't sue Eli, I sued you.'

'Didn't you and your brother settle a wrongful death suit with me for $300,000?' Susan said, referring to the civil action that Gabe and Adam filed after her arrest.

Gabe was visibly upset when his mother brought up the suit in court, insisting that he wasn't allowed to talk about it because of a confidentiality agreement that both parties had signed. 'You know that,' he snapped at his mother.

'Couldn't you have just left him off?' Susan asked, referring to Eli.

Gabe told his mother that he was not a lawyer, but it was his understanding that he and Adam had sued her, and that since Eli took her side, he had to be named in the suit.

'These things are obviously very important to you but they don't seem to add or subtract from your case,' Judge Brady told Susan.

'I hope you don't think I'm picking on you,' Susan told Gabriel before court adjourned that night. 'You are aware that I loved all three of my sons the same?'

'Yes, I know,' he acknowledged. 'You appreciate Eli a lot more now because he buys into your delusions and we don't.'

On Tuesday, jurors arrived for a third day of cross-examination. Instead, they learned that Susan had asked for another delay.

'I'm sick and I think I'm getting bronchitis,' she sniffled.

The judge arranged to have her seen by a doctor; Brady also let Susan know that she was anxious to keep the proceedings moving along and hoped to resume court after lunch.

When Susan returned that afternoon, she reported that she had been prescribed antibiotics for her condition. She then requested an adjournment until the following Monday to get some 'much needed rest'. 'I was up half the night coughing,' she told the judge. 'This is a murder trial and I want to be at my best.'

Judge Brady was sympathetic to Susan's infirmity – she, too, was nursing a sore throat, but denied her request for what she deemed an 'unreasonable' delay and ordered all parties back to court on Thursday, 16 March. This adjournment was further evidence of the judge's extraordinary patience. Brady rarely lost her cool even as Susan accused her of conspiring with the prosecutor or showing bias against the defence in front of jurors.

At times, Brady's interchanges with Susan were akin to a kindergarten teacher scolding a young student, soothing the child until she calmed down. When it became clear that Susan could not be reigned in, Brady would order a 'time out', punishing Susan with fifteen minutes in a holding cell to regain her composure. Remarkably, Susan continued to push even as the judge reprimanded her. 'Well, then I'm taking papers with me to read!' she told Brady after being ordered to the holding cell one afternoon.

'No,' the judge shot back. There was no reading during a time out.

It seemed that Susan had mastered the art of knowing just how far to push before landing in serious trouble, and she continued to press throughout the trial. Sometimes the judge's latitude went too far as Brady allowed Susan to disrupt the flow of testimony and antagonise the prosecution. The end result was a highly irregular relationship between the bench and the lawyers, but in this case of many bizarre relationships, no one seemed particularly surprised.

On Thursday, jurors learned of yet another delay. An alternate juror had called in sick and, of course, there were more objections from the defendant. This time, Susan was upset that the leg shackles she was being forced to wear were causing runs in her pantyhose. Next, Susan objected to the prosecutor's request to interrupt her cross-examination of Gabe so that he could put Adam on the stand. Adam had been waiting in the wings to testify for the prosecution since the trial had begun and was on the State's list to take the stand after Gabe. But Adam was growing increasingly concerned that all the delays would prevent him from returning to UCLA in time for final exams and a scheduled trip to South Africa with his girlfriend.

Susan argued that it was unfair to disrupt her case merely to accommodate her son's holiday plans. Besides, she felt that Gabriel's testimony was too important to interrupt.

'You would think that the defendant might have some consideration for her child,' the prosecutor said.

'I object,' Susan shot back. 'That's an outrageous comment.'

'We will start fresh on Monday and hopefully move along,' the judge ruled, choosing to postpone the trial another day rather than replace the sick juror with an alternate. Already, one juror had been excused from the case and with the trial expected to last another two months, she did not want to risk losing another. This postponement would be the fourth delay since the trial began one week earlier.

Susan took two final shots at the prosecutor before the court adjourned Thursday. Out of earshot of jurors, she accused the D.A.'s office of 'coaching' her two sons to slander both her and Eli on the stand. She also accused Sequeira of prosecutorial misconduct, charging that he deliberately tried to provoke a mistrial with his supposed underhanded strategies.

'I'd rather have needles shoved in my eye than have a mistrial,' Sequeira shot back.

'I would be very careful about making such accusations without any proof,' Judge Brady admonished Susan.

Court reconvened on Monday, 20 March, with Susan continuing to question Gabriel about his childhood. 'I don't remember, I was five,' the teen responded to one question. 'I was just a little kid,' he replied to another.

'I think we're having a forest-for-the-trees problem,' Judge Brady told Susan at one point during her examination. 'A lot of time is being spent on minutiae about events that are extremely important to you – again, I'm not telling you how to try your case, but my concern is that [the jury's] attention will be lost for the important things.'

At the end of Monday's proceedings, the judge informed Susan that she would allow her just one more day to question her son. She refused to bend even as Susan demanded to continue for 'as much time as it takes to get to the truth.' Susan would have to finish her cross-examination by 5pm Tuesday.

The following day, Susan escalated her attack, engaging the prosecutor in a number of heated exchanges.

Before Gabriel even took the stand that morning, Susan accused Sequeira of 'making faces' in the courtroom. She claimed the prosecutor was rolling his eyes at jurors to imply that her cross-examination of her son was tedious.

'I can't freeze my face,' Sequeira replied dryly, remarking that he had an expressive face.

Judge Brady intervened, telling Susan that she had not seen any 'eye-rolling' on the part of the prosecutor, only a look of fatigue when Sequeira briefly shut his eyes in court.

'He is goading me,' Susan complained, talking over the prosecutor as he tried to defend against her latest accusation.

When he finally got the floor, Sequeira charged that Susan was making a 'farce' of the trial with her unending objections, demands for a mistrial and accusations of prosecutorial misconduct 'every fifteen minutes', and he implored the judge to revoke Susan's right to represent herself in court.

'We have gone far beyond the pale of what is reasonable,' he said, after jurors were cleared from the courtroom. 'This jury, God knows what they're thinking now.'

Even the court reporter voiced complaints about Susan's behaviour in court that day, at one point rising from her chair and telling the judge that it was impossible to record the proceedings with Susan repeatedly talking over the witness. When she complained a second time, Susan instructed the judge to 'admonish the court reporter!'

Sequeira froze in disbelief. He had never seen anyone instruct a judge to reprimand a member of the court staff. But Brady remained calm, giving Susan more latitude until she, too, reached her limit and threatened to revoke Susan's *pro per* status if she continued to ignore the court's rules.

'The jury is getting forgotten in this equation,' Brady warned. 'This pattern of behaviour that we seem to be going through is alienating the jury.'

'The defendant's style in this case is to be passive-aggressive,' Sequeira roared, accusing Susan of slyly introducing evidence in the pretext of questions. 'She flouts this court's authority at every opportunity so that it makes this trial somewhat of a farce.'

'Objection, your honour,' Susan yelled out. In a lawyerly tone, she informed the prosecutor that she was objecting to him raising his voice during his 'diatribe' and for taking 'inappropriate personal potshots' at her.

'Maybe he should start acting like a lawyer instead of being a baby,' she goaded.

It was an amusing quip and one that underscored the increasingly hostile relationship between Sequeira and Polk. For days now, Susan had been inciting direct arguments with the prosecutor, and Brady had done little to stop it. Like two siblings who loathe the sight of each other, they bickered back and forth instead of trying the case. In what was becoming the most entertaining aspect of the trial, Sequeira was routinely drawn into arguments with Susan. While her repeated objections were quite disruptive, it was surprising that she was so successful in eliciting a reaction from the seasoned lawyer.

The more she interrupted the court, the more it seemed that her actions were part of some coherent strategy, not just idle comments meant to annoy the prosecutor. While her behaviour was clearly ruffling his feathers, it was also distracting him from his arguments and disrupting the flow of discussion for the jury. Perhaps looking back on Sequeira's case during their deliberations, the jury would become confused by seemingly inconsequential and incomplete testimony. If intentional, this strategy's effectiveness would not be known for months, but one thing was certain: by reacting to Susan, Sequeira was playing right into her hand, allowing her to dictate the pace and manner in which the case was progressing.

During the afternoon questioning, Susan probed Gabriel about his relationship with Marjorie and Dan Briner, his surrogate parents since Felix's death.

'I consider myself their foster child,' Gabe told his mother. 'I consider them my parents.'

Gabe's remarks clearly rattled Susan. She immediately objected to his characterisation, insisting that Gabe was not a foster child, as that term is legally defined.

'I am doing extremely well now,' Gabe next told Susan.

Fuelled with rage, Susan sought to paint the Briners as greedy individuals who were trying to cash in on her son's circumstances. She claimed that they held Gabe back in high school so that they could continue to collect social security benefits. 'Isn't it so that if you hadn't been held back a year at school, your Social Security benefits would have ended when you turned eighteen?'

'You have no idea what you're talking about,' Gabe said, holding back tears.

Gabe told the court that initially he gave the Briners his entire twelve hundred dollar Social Security cheque. More recently, he paid half the money to help cover his room and board.

As the day wore on, Susan grew more and more confrontational. She demanded yes or no answers from her son and continued to pursue topics that were irrelevant to the murder case. Disturbingly, she grilled him about his alleged hatred of Felix.

'Didn't you say you wanted to "gut him"?' Susan asked tearfully.

'No, God no, I never said that.'

'Didn't you express absolute hatred of your father?'

'I've made mistakes. I have to live with that,' he said, anxiously rubbing his forehead. 'It's not easy that he's dead, that I can't say I'm sorry.'

It was just before 5pm when Gabriel Polk finally rose from the witness chair and waved goodbye to jurors. 'See you later,' he said, exiting the courtroom.

'I call for a mistrial!' Susan shouted, citing her son's banter with the jury.

On Wednesday, the crowd in the gallery had dwindled for Sequeria's second witness, former Orinda Police Chief Dan Lawrence. The prosecutor had rearranged his witness list to accommodate Adam Polk's holiday plans. He would call Susan's eldest son later in the trial and forge ahead with testimony from members of law enforcement.

Lawrence, who was now the chief of a neighbouring police department, was called to testify to the phone call he received from Felix Polk one week before his murder. During the call, Felix claimed that Susan had 'threatened to blow his head off'.

Sequeira's examination of Lawrence lasted just five minutes, however, Susan kept the law enforcement officer on the stand for more than one hour, arguing that Lawrence was an expert on police protocol and had expertise on domestic abuse cases. It seemed she was anxious to introduce jurors to the idea that victims of domestic abuse don't always report incidents to police, thus explaining why she had not reported the alleged abuse she now claimed occurred throughout her marriage.

'Isn't it true that women who are victims of domestic abuse back out, get scared, fail to appear, and make bad witnesses?' Susan asked Lawrence.

The police chief agreed, saying that Susan's scenario was possible.

Seemingly pleased with Lawrence's response, she next asked him why her husband wasn't prosecuted for his knowledge of underage drinking parties at the Miner Road house. She also wanted him to explain how Felix's influence with people in high places might have spared him from being charged.

Lawrence was unable to answer many of Susan's questions, including a number that stemmed from a letter she wrote to Moraga police complaining about their search of her home after Eli's arrest on felony assault charges. The letter alleged that officers had roughed her up, handcuffed her, and threatened to tear her house apart, thus colouring her perception of the police department and leaving her distrustful of law enforcement officers.

Susan argued that it was her mistrust of police that caused her to flee to Montana – instead of reporting Felix's murderous threats to authorities. She wanted to introduce her 'state of mind' through Chief Lawrence. Susan had sent him a copy of the letter and was anxious to introduce it into evidence.

But Judge Brady ruled that she could not question the police official about the search warrant because he was not there. Susan's accusations in the letter amounted to 'hearsay' and could not be proven through this witness. Nevertheless, Susan ignored the judge's instructions and continued her line of questioning.

Once Chief Lawrence had been excused, Susan questioned several more police witnesses, using their testimonies to present her theory that the sheriff's deputies had contaminated the crime scene by pouring water over Felix's head to make the dried blood look wet and to make his death appear more grisly. 'Doesn't that look like a puddle of water next to my husband's bloody scalp?' Susan asked Sheriff's Deputy Melvin Chamblee, one of the first officers on the scene. According to her, their carelessness and poor police work had resulted in a crime scene that looked much more like murder than the self-defensive struggle that Susan claimed it was.

She accused police of sloppy work, pointing out that officers were not wearing protective booties when they examined the crime scene. In addition, she also insisted that a photo of bloody footprints found at the scene appeared to depict two right feet, side by side. Meanwhile prosecutors maintained the footprint belonged to Susan and was the same size as the shoes found in her bedroom closet.

Dressed stylishly in a tan and green tartan kilt skirt, Susan looked lawyerly as she stood at the podium and thumbed through her papers. Displaying a photo of the bloody footprints found at the crime scene, she asked Chamblee if he saw, 'two right feet'.

The deputy studied the photo, and then hesitantly agreed that it was possible, although he could not be sure.

To Susan, Chamblee's uncertainty confirmed her claims of a tainted crime scene. Seeming pleased with her momentary victory, she shot a triumphant look at Sequeira. The prosecutor sat slouched in his chair, listening to Susan's questions.

'What size shoe do you use?' he asked the officer on redirect testimony.

'I use size 11,' Chamblee replied.

'Size 11? And that's men's?'

The officer smirked, eliciting laughter from the gallery and from jurors. 'Yes, men's.'

'Not that there's anything wrong with it, but do you wear women's shoes?' Sequeira asked.

'Not to work,' Chamblee grinned. His response brought a half smile to Susan's lips.

Nevertheless, the day was not without its challenges. Susan caused a ruckus when she complained that the overhead projector or LMO, pronounced 'ELMO', that both sides used to display photos and other exhibits was blocking her view of Juror Number 10. Susan had been watching this juror and another female juror over several days, seemingly convinced the two were quietly conversing during the proceedings. During a break, and with jurors out of the courtroom, she insisted that Judge Brady change places with her so that Brady could see the way her view was being obstructed.

Ordering Susan to the other side of the courtroom, the judge reluctantly stepped down from the bench and sat at the defence table, continuing her remarkable tolerance for Susan's antics. Still, she seemed more a ringmaster than an arbiter of the law as she worked to tame Susan. It was almost comical to watch the nearly fifty-year-old woman in the flowing black robe plop down in Susan's chair and study the jury box.

'Can I sit in the jury box to show you what view I'm not getting,' Susan asked the judge.

'No.'

After sitting in Susan's seat, Judge Brady determined that her view was fine. But Susan continued to argue, telling the judge that it was a serious violation of her rights if she couldn't see the jurors' faces and whether they were communicating with one another – which would be grounds for a mistrial.

'It will be moved after lunch,' Brady finally conceded.

Sequeira could not let the moment pass without voicing his objection. He told the judge that he had gone out his way to let Susan use the 'ELMO' and to teach her and her assistant, Valerie, how to operate it. 'Now she's just trying to delay and control!'

'Objection!' Susan shot back. 'Prosecutorial misconduct.'

Judge Brady closed her eyes and drew a deep audible breath. But the moment was quickly disrupted by Susan's finger pointing. Now, she wanted Brady to punish members of the gallery for snickering.

'She's just being obstreperous and obstructionist,' Sequeira barked, 'for the record.'

'Prosecutorial misconduct,' Susan retorted, 'for the record.'

Next on the stand was Sheriff's Deputy Shannon Kelly. Kelly was the officer who drove Susan to police headquarters the night Felix's body was discovered. He said that during the ride, Susan was 'unemotional' and claimed to have no knowledge of Felix's death.

'I didn't do anything,' Susan allegedly told the officer during the ride. 'Are you sure it's my husband? Did my son identify the body? Because his car isn't here.'

Susan jumped up when it was her turn to question the officer. 'Do you think if you had someone who was under arrest, and was accused of murder, sitting in the backseat of your car crying, and you had the music on, that you could hear them crying?' she asked from the podium.

'I could, depending on how loud the music was.'

'Have you ever heard the expression "crying inside"?'

'No,' Kelly replied.

The following morning, 24 March, Susan was brimming with complaints, but her latest grievance was not immediately clear to members of the court.

'I've informed the court of the harassment and outright brutality I've been subjected to while in custody,' she told Judge Brady. Judge Brady looked bewildered as Susan detailed her alleged confrontation more than two years earlier with a court officer. She claimed the deputy had pulled her from the courtroom and clubbed her on the elbow with a blackjack, thus breaking her arm.

'This incident has already been dealt with,' the judge advised Susan. 'I believe the facts surrounding it are quite disputed, but anyway, what's your point?'

'Instead of giving me medical treatment I was locked in a padded cell for hours,' Susan rambled on. 'Denied painkillers for the broken arm . . . I have been locked in cells with urine and faeces on the floor, urine soaked mattresses, broken sinks.'

The judge was losing her patience and instructed Susan to 'move it along'. Susan responded that she had been given 'secret' information from an officer who claimed there was a conspiracy in the works. Susan was going to be set up. A deputy was going to claim that she attacked him, providing a reason to discipline and harm her, Susan told the judge.

'I want bail, or to be moved to another county,' Susan demanded.

Judge Brady was incredulous. 'I can't act on information based on unnamed sources about vague allegations on some future event,' she told Susan. 'I need more evidence, statements from the officer, who has a legal duty to report that kind of information to his superiors.'

'I'm certainly not going to reveal my source,' Susan huffed. 'This officer is trying to help me.' Again, Susan claimed that she didn't feel safe and asked to be moved to another county.

When the judge denied her request, Susan angrily retorted, 'Well, I've made my record.'

Sequeira was in court for the bizarre exchange but remained silent. Once the matter appeared resolved, he informed the judge of his problems with several witnesses. One was sick and unavailable to testify. He was having trouble finding accommodations for several others who had flown in earlier to testify and had gone home because of delays in the proceedings. Now, all the hotels in town were booked because of the NCAA basketball tournament at the arena in Oakland.

'I object,' Susan interjected. 'This is a violation of my right to a speedy trial.'

Sequeira shot Susan a look, then asked the judge to instruct her not to discuss the State's delays in front of the jurors.

But Susan exhibited her usual defiance and continued to voice objections.

'Mrs. Polk, DO NOT interrupt me again!' Judge Brady threatened.

To which Susan replied, 'Well, you interrupted me.'

Susan was still ranting when the judge adjourned court for the weekend, stepped down from the bench and disappeared into the hallway. Proceedings would resume on Monday with testimony from more law enforcement officers. Among those scheduled to take the stand that week was the lead homicide detective, Mike Costa.

CHAPTER TWENTY-FIVE

FORENSIC
FACTS

O f all the police officers on the case, Susan was most interested in Detective Mike Costa. Susan watched from the defence table as the thickset detective climbed into the witness box Tuesday morning. Costa had recently retired from the force and had been flown in from his new home 100 miles away to testify. His first order of business would be to address the videotaped late-night interview he conducted with Susan at police headquarters on 15 October 2002.

Susan tried to get the judge to suppress the tape, claiming that she had not been Mirandized before the interview. When that failed, she insisted that the detective should have halted the interrogation after she complained of being 'very, very tired' and 'showed obvious signs of shock'.

Judge Brady denied her requests. 'There was a clear understanding of the rights and a clear waiver,' the judge told Susan during a sidebar that morning. 'It was probably the gentlest interview I've ever seen in a homicide investigation.'

Jurors waited in the hushed courtroom as Sequeira cued up the videotaped recording of the two-hour interrogation. Susan was now sitting at a table adjacent to the jury box so that she could watch along with the panel. The lights had been dimmed and the vertical blinds on the two windows on either side of the judge were pulled shut for the presentation.

As an image of Susan flashed onto the television screen, sobs could be heard from the defendant – emotional at the sight of herself in the interrogation room. She was dressed in a pair of shorts and a polo shirt; an official police jacket was draped over her shoulders. The jury could not see her at the counsel table, but they could hear her whimpers, which grew louder as the videotape played on. She was so upset that her case manager, Valerie Harris, slid a box of tissues in front of her.

'Do you want to talk to me about what happened?' Costa's voice boomed from the TV monitor.

'I do, and I am very, very tired,' Susan responded. She appeared toned and at least ten pounds heavier in the videotape and her hair was styled and neat – nothing like the overgrown, bushy mop that she wore to court each day.

'So am I. I haven't been to bed all day either, but we have to do this.' Susan wore a puzzled look, 'What *did* happen?'

'Well, that's what I'm hoping you can tell me.'

For the next two hours, Susan repeatedly denied any involvement in her husband's death, even as the detective presented evidence to the contrary.

In the courtroom, Susan managed to quiet down and now sat beside Valerie wiping tears as jurors listened carefully to the interrogation tape.

'And you don't know what happened to your husband?' Detective Costa asked for a second time.

'No.'

'Something happened, obviously. That's why we're all here. That's why you're here. You've had ongoing marital problems for sometime now, living in different places, money difficulties. So something happened, Susan.'

'That doesn't mean that I killed him.'

'Was he seeing any other ladies?'

'I don't even know that he's dead,' Susan replied. 'All I know is I was lying in my bed reading and I heard Gabe get on the phone and ask to speak to a police officer, so I got out of bed and asked him "What's wrong?" He accused me of having . . . killed his dad.

'I did not kill my husband,' Susan insisted. 'I am not that kind of person.'

Jurors listened to Susan dance around the detective's questions, spending an inordinate amount of time detailing the couple's financial woes and how Felix had terrorised her during their marriage. Finally, she told Costa about the call she received from her husband while in Montana, alerting her to a judge's ruling to cut her spousal support and award Felix custody of their youngest son. 'And I said, "Are you kidding?" '

Her reaction to the phone call was crucial to the state's case. Prosecutors claimed that the conversation triggered Susan's murderous rage, prompting her return to California and killing her husband. The videotaped interrogation was intended to demonstrate how she initially denied any role in the homicide – an outright lie.

On the stand, Detective Costa reported that his investigators had confiscated a number of incriminating items during their search of the Miner Road crime scene, including Susan's computer, which contained her diary and the knife with 'red dried stuff' on its tip. Although that knife would not match Felix's stab wounds, the prosecution tried to show that investigators had come away from the Miner Road home with physical evidence that could be used against Susan.

During his testimony, Susan demanded that Costa be reprimanded for conversing with a juror while seated in the witness box. According to Susan, her case manager, Valerie Harris, had witnessed the exchange and Susan wanted the detective admonished.

Out of earshot of the panel, Costa admitted to Judge Brady that he had enquired about the climate in the courtroom. 'Is it me, or is it warm in here?' he had asked the juror seated closest to him in the jury box.

'Don't talk to the jurors,' Brady instructed. 'You know better.'

But Susan couldn't leave well enough alone. 'Are you acquainted with courtroom decorum?' she asked the detective once jurors had returned to their seats.

Brady immediately reprimanded Susan for improperly raising the subject in front of the panel.

Despite her lack of experience in the courtroom, Susan did a commendable job of cross-examining Costa about his investigation. Her first line of enquiry focused on whether police had looked into her claims of spousal abuse.

When the detective replied that they had not, Susan went after him.

'It was a murder investigation, wasn't it?' she asked derisively.

'Yes,' the detective agreed.

'And you didn't check any of these things out?' Susan demanded.

'Not personally.'

'Did anybody?' Susan asked, firing off questions like a veteran lawyer. 'Yes or no?'

'Not to my knowledge,' Costa replied.

'Were there any individual sources, not from the defendant's mouth or pen, that you came across that gave you a domestic violence background?'

'No.'

'Not even Eli?' Susan asked, referring to her middle son.

Costa said he hadn't heard any accusations, not even from Eli.

Susan criticised the detective for not conducting more interviews with her son. She also raised questions as to why police had only confiscated some of the knives from her kitchen and not others. She even got Costa to concede that approximately thirty law enforcement officers had 'trampled' around Felix's body that first night.

'That could be – not all at once I assume,' Costa said.

Susan also elicited admissions from the detective regarding Felix's computer. Costa told the court that his officers found only the monitor and the keyboard in the trunk of Felix's Saab. Susan suggested that her husband's computer might have contained evidence to support her claims of spousal abuse. She also noted that police had not interviewed her eldest son, Adam, until October 2005, just days before her first, aborted murder trial got underway.

For all the salient points, Susan suddenly lost momentum when she veered into an outlandish enquiry that put her own mental stability in question. It was a pattern throughout the trial that repeatedly overshadowed her productive moments.

'Didn't I accuse my husband of being a Mossad agent?' she asked, referring to an entry in her computer diary. 'Did you follow up on that at all?'

The detective said he had not.

Susan next pointed to her written claim that Felix had betrayed his country by failing to turn over information provided to him about the September 11 terrorist attacks. Susan later admitted that she gave that information to her husband while under hypnosis and in a trance.

'Did you report it to the FBI?' Susan asked Costa.

'Not to my knowledge.'

'Do you believe there is no such thing as the Mossad?'

'Do I believe? Yes, they exist.'

'Normally, if there is some kind of treasonable activity, doesn't that get reported?'

'Yes.'

'Are you aware that my husband believed he was a psychic?'

To raised eyebrows from jurors, Costa said he was not.

'Do you believe in psychic phenomenon?'

'No, not really.'

'No?' Susan was incredulous. 'Are you aware that most Americans do?'

'No, I was not aware of that.'

'Did anybody tell you that I am supposed to be a medium?' she persisted.

Costa had not heard that, nor had his investigators looked into accusations that Felix intended to overthrow the US government, as Susan claimed in her diary. This elicited jeers from the gallery. Still, Susan continued firing questions at the detective about her husband's supposed anti-American activities. Claiming that two private investigators had looked into Felix's dealings, she said that the pair had stumbled upon writings that detailed his plan to bring down the US government and take over the country.

Susan grew surly when the detective suggested that Felix had several restraining orders against her at the time of his death. 'To your recollection, how many restraining orders do you think my husband had . . . ?'

'Maybe two,' Costa replied with an air of confidence.

'Oh really? Two? How about zero?' Susan snipped.

'At least one I can think of,' the detective assured the court.

Susan retorted in a mocking tone to chortles from the gallery. 'Oh you do, do you?' She got him to admit that he was incorrect in his belief that Felix had gotten some type of order of protection as a result of his 911 calls to police.

Her attack continued when the detective said that, during the course of his investigation, he never learned that Felix was violent. Susan pointed to two letters she wrote detailing Felix's alleged abuse; one that was found on her computer hard drive and another that police confiscated from a safe hidden beneath the wet bar in the master bedroom.

'How'd you guys get my safe open?'

'Again, I don't know anything about a safe and I don't know who might have opened it,' Costa said, claiming that he did not know about the safe.

Susan handed the detective a copy of the letter that she claimed was locked inside the safe. 'You don't recall that the letter contains a history of my husband's threats, violence . . .'

'Objection!' Sequeira interrupted.

'Ms. Polk, this is inappropriate,' Judge Brady said, sustaining the prosecutor's objection.

'Did you investigate whether my husband did the things in that letter? For example, did you investigate whether he raped me when I was a patient in his care?'

'Objection!' the prosecutor jumped up again.

Talking over Sequeira, Susan quoted the evidence code.

'Do not argue with me,' Judge Brady snapped.

Brady's admonishment did little to deter Susan. Handing the detective a crime scene photo depicting the safe lying open on her bed, she asked, 'It's not likely I'd keep my safe on the bed.'

'No,' the detective agreed.

Once Susan jarred his memory with the photo and had him read the letter while on the stand, he vaguely recalled entering it in his police report.

'So how can you say nothing ever came to your attention about spousal abuse,' Susan demanded. She was visibly annoyed with Costa and his claims.

'No other sources indicated your husband was violent,' the detective retorted. He admitted that he had not read Susan's complete diary. To do so would have violated the terms of the search warrant that detectives used to seize evidence from the house. Susan was incredulous, charging that detectives read the diary before the warrant was even signed.

In spite of this setback, Susan pressed on. At one point during the cross-examination, she trotted out police photos of the overturned ottoman that detectives claimed was kicked out from under Felix after he was struck on the head during the attack. Susan argued that the position of the ottoman, upside down and on the opposite end of the living room from its cover, proved her claim that Felix had used it as a weapon and thrown it at her early in the fight. Marching to an easel set up in the courtroom, she sketched a diagram of how police claimed to have found the furnishings. To Susan, it was apparent that officers had 'staged' the crime scene.

'Why is the ottoman cover across the room from the ottoman at the "so-called" crime scene?' Susan asked Costa. She was so thin in her black slacks that it looked as though they would fall from her hips if she moved too quickly.

Costa studied the photo. 'It was due to the fight.'

'Is an altercation between a 110-pound woman and a 170-pound man a fight?'

'Yes,' the detective replied matter-of-factly.

'And how much do you weigh,' Susan asked.

'Too much,' Costa grinned. 'Two-hundred-and-fifty-pounds.'

Susan asked that the clerk and bailiff bring out the ottoman for jurors. She continued to suggest that police had moved it in an attempt to bolster their theory of events in the guest cottage that October night.

Susan's own omissions would prevent her from questioning Costa about the pepper spray she said she used on Felix that night. More than two years passed before she told authorities about the spray, and the window of opportunity for effectively testing the ottoman for residue had come and gone. Had the authorities been able to find evidence of the chemical, it would have given credence to Susan's argument that Susan felt threatened by Felix that night, and she went to the guest house armed with the spray for protection.

Unable to use that argument, she was forced to focus on the 'inconsistencies' in the crime scene. She asked again about the bloody footprints she believed were made by 'two right feet'.

'I think you're wasting your time,' the detective told her. 'It's a question for a criminalist.'

'Oh really, you're a detective. You've accused me of murder. I'm asking you for your professional opinion as a detective.'

Refocusing Costa's attention on the photo, Susan intimated that the only way the bloody prints could have been made is if somebody had taken a shoe, 'stuck it in some wet blood and then stamped them on the floor.'

Still, the detective maintained that he did not see 'two right feet'.

Unwavering, Susan pointed to blood found on the soles of Felix's feet and inquired as to why investigators hadn't found any bloody footprints from him on the floor of the living room.

'There was nothing in this case that led me to believe that this scene had been staged,' Costa huffed.

Late Wednesday afternoon, Susan learned that Costa was asking to leave the trial so that he could refill a medical prescription for an unspecified condition. Although she had been questioning him for two full days, she insisted that she needed one more day to complete her cross-examination. Susan recommended that Costa have the prescription called in to a local pharmacy.

The detective complained, saying he didn't feel he should have to do that. He also pointed out that the questions she was now posing were out of his area of expertise and would be better answered by a criminalist.

Despite Costa's argument, the judge told him to contact his doctor about phoning in the prescription so that Susan could continue the cross-examination.

'Well, what's his condition?' Susan demanded, after the matter was resolved.

'It's completely irrelevant,' the judge told her.

'I think it's relevant, I mean, is he on psych meds?'

'It's a physical condition,' the prosecutor jumped in. Sequeira was anxious to move the case along to accommodate the out of town witnesses he had waiting to testify.

'Is it visual?' Susan wanted to know.

'It's totally irrelevant and I don't want her to make references to it in front of the jury,' Sequeira told Judge Brady.

'I had no intention of doing that, but now I'm curious. This *IS* a deviant prosecutor,' Susan charged.

Her remark elicited laughter from the gallery.

'All right, that's it,' Judge Brady warned. 'We're done. Ladies and gentlemen of the gallery, this is not for entertainment.

'Mrs. Polk, there will be no mention of this issue in front of the jury.'

By Friday afternoon, Sequeira was asking Judge Brady for help. 'I'm at my wits end,' he announced. 'At this point, it's becoming absurd. She won't follow the rules. She won't stop interrupting. I don't know what else to do. I'm asking the court for guidance.'

Finally, Sequeira tried helping his opponent. Susan kept questioning about a 16 March 2001, letter in which she alleged domestic violence. The judge had ruled the letter inadmissible when offered through the detective but explained that Susan could enter it later during her own testimony.

During a break, Sequeira offered Susan advice on how to question the detective about the letter. 'You can ask him if they investigated claims made in the letter.'

'I understand your point,' Susan replied. 'But the jury has to see the letter to understand what I'm referring to.'

'Ms. Polk, for the fifth time, he cannot testify to the contents of that document,' Brady told Susan. 'Move on please.' Sequeira just shrugged.

Susan was now completely on her own at the defence table, having fired her case assistant, Valerie Harris, the previous afternoon. She did not provide Harris a reason for her second dismissal since the trial began.

Harris later told reporters that Susan simply said, 'I think I have to do this alone.' Those close to the case later learned that Susan was angry that Harris had given her dog away after Eli was arrested and incarcerated at the same detention centre as his mother. She could find no one to care for Dusty.

Having Harris off the case would present additional challenges for Sequeira. The prosecutor had been using Harris as a middleman after citing his unwillingness to deal directly with Susan. He would later admit that trying the case against Susan was extremely challenging – something he would have been ill-equipped to handle as a younger man.

Meanwhile, Susan would also suffer. Valerie had been selecting Susan's clothing for court each day. The chore was not without its challenges. On days that Susan didn't like the outfit, she would refuse to get dressed. Now, she would have no one to bring her clothes and came to court in prison attire. Court watchers remarked that even in jail garb Susan still managed to look elegant. She had a natural flair for making sweat pants and a T-shirt look stylish.

On Tuesday, 5 April, the prosecutor called former Contra Costa criminalist Song Wicks to the stand. Wicks had collected and evaluated evidence at the Miner Road crime scene on the night of 15

October 2002. He testified that he found Felix Polk's body splayed on the tile floor of the couple's guesthouse when he arrived at the crime scene that night. When Sequeira brought up Susan's accusations that he and other members of the sheriff's department had moved furniture to bolster their theory of the homicide, Wicks scoffed indignantly.

'Who had the most time to spend at the crime scene – the detectives, the criminalists, or the defendant?' Prosecutor Sequeira asked Wicks.

'The defendant.'

'Would your job have been made easier if you had the defendant's bloody clothing?'

'Objection!' Susan shouted from the defence table. She was quickly overruled by the judge.

'It could have allowed me to draw conclusions, if I had the defendant's clothing,' Wicks said over a second objection from Susan.

Anxious to get the query out before Susan could object again, Sequeira shouted his next question. 'Did you find any bloody clothing anywhere?'

'No,' the investigator replied.

Judge Brady interrupted. 'Mr. Sequeira, I am not hard of hearing. Please moderate your tone.'

'Sorry,' the prosecutor apologised, glaring at Susan, who sat grinning at the defence table.

'I'd like to just finish without you interrupting,' he told her after she voiced yet another objection. But Susan continued, claiming a conspiracy.

By late Wednesday, Sequeira had regained his sense of humour and was mockingly referring to Susan as 'Madame Defendant'.

'The sarcasm can be done without,' Susan scolded. 'Ms. Polk is fine.'

During her cross-examination of Song Wicks, Susan accused the criminalist of plotting to frame her for her husband's murder and claimed that he and some thirteen other law enforcement officials were responsible for dousing water on Felix's bloody head to 'create a more dramatic photo opportunity'. Once again, she brought up the ottoman, accusing Wicks of having moved furniture at the crime scene. Addressing the bloody footprints, Susan went a step farther than she had with Detective Costa, suggesting that Wicks or other officers on the scene that first night took a shoe from her bedroom closet and 'stamped' footprints into the blood encircling Felix's head to further implicate her in the homicide.

Wicks shot Susan an incredulous look.

'When you frame someone for murder, you don't think you are going to have to come up with an explanation, do you?' Susan retaliated.

'I don't know,' the officer shot back. 'I have never framed anyone for murder.'

Wicks agreed with the prosecutor's charge that a person who defended herself against an armed attacker wouldn't need to dispose of her bloody clothes – as Susan had allegedly done.

When forensic pathologist Brian Peterson took the stand, Susan levied similar accusations at him, attempting to show that he too was also a member of the elaborate conspiracy to frame her for Felix's murder. 'You have a bias to produce evidence for the prosecutor, isn't that correct,' she asked the pathologist when he took the stand later that week. She went on to insinuate that he was paid by the Contra Costa Sheriff's Department to render results favorable to the county.

'That's absolutely ridiculous,' Dr. Peterson balked. 'Everybody is paid by somebody.' He insisted the sheriff's department would have to be 'stupid' to try and force him to alter his findings.

Peterson said the stab wounds found on Felix's hands, arms, and feet were the result of the victim trying to defend himself from a knife-wielding attacker. 'There might be times when you want to get your feet between you and the blade,' he explained. 'Otherwise, it's pretty hard to get wounds on the bottom of your feet.'

When asked by Sequeira if the wound on Felix's head was the result of falling or getting 'whacked,' Dr. Peterson said, 'I believe it was more consistent with being hit with something.' This statement directly contradicted Susan's claim that Felix had struck his head on the tile floor when he fell backward shortly before his death. According to Peterson, there was no medical evidence to support Susan's purported chain of events, and instead, he reiterated his opinion that Felix's wounds to the head were the result of being hit rather than a fall.

In addition, Peterson and Susan differed on the subject of what had actually killed Felix. While his post-mortem examination revealed that Felix suffered from advanced heart disease that could have played a role in weakening his ability to stave off an attack, he testified that Felix Polk died as a result of stab wounds to his stomach, lungs, and the area close to his heart – not heart disease. Susan, on the contrary, maintained that Felix's injuries from the knife were not life threatening and that his death was the result of a heart attack he suffered while aggressively assaulting her in the guest house that night. In order to support her views, Susan intended to call another forensic pathologist to challenge Peterson's testimony when it was her turn to present evidence.

Over the course of the trial, Susan had worked diligently to discredit Felix's professional reputation. On 27 March, Neil Kobrin, the clinical psychologist and former president of Argosy University, was called by the prosecutor to testify about a phone call he received from Felix in the days before his murder.

'He [Felix] said that his wife, Susan, was going to kill him and that he was at a hotel hiding out,' Kobrin told the court. He also said that Felix told him that Susan had a gun.

Susan responded by raising allegations that ranged from Felix's supposed affair with his patient turned colleague, to cocaine abuse. She pushed Kobrin to acknowledge that he was aware of Felix's many indiscretions. Unfortunately for Susan, Kobrin could not substantiate the claims.

Once Kobrin's testimony had concluded, only one witness remained before the prosecution would rest its case. On Tuesday, 17 April, Adam Polk took the stand, ready to face his mother for the first time in several years.

Sitting on the witness stand with thick curly brown hair and a soft, cherubic face, Adam told the court that his father did not abuse his mother, while also shooting down Susan's claim that Felix had threatened to kill her during their marriage.

Adam's testimony for the prosecution lasted just thirty minutes.

But the well-spoken college senior would be on the stand for three days responding to questions from his mother, and it did not take long for the twenty-three-year-old's testimony to degenerate into a family therapy session gone haywire.

'Do you recall saying that you would come into court and say the worst possible things about me unless I give you irrevocable power of attorney?'

Adam told his mother, 'You're a cruel, heartless person and you should be ashamed of yourself.'

Susan presented her son with the letter he wrote for her bail hearing in which he called his mother 'a gentle and intellectual mother who enjoyed movies, cooking, and baking cookies.'

Adam testified that he wrote the letter to win her favour and gain the use of Susan's car. He also claimed that the letter was 'intended to manipulate Eli into giving me access to you.'

'I was in a precarious position for mediating for my two younger brothers' financial future,' Adam continued.

Susan's eldest son admitted that he had promised his mother he would testify at her trial if she called him. But Adam claimed that he never agreed to take sides. He would simply tell the truth, which Susan assumed would be in her favour.

Like Gabriel, Adam denied his mother's claims of spousal abuse, calling Susan 'bonkers' and 'cuckoo for Cocoa Puffs' during her questioning of him. Judge Brady, usually reserved, covered her mouth and fought back a smile during the bruising exchange.

Later, he recalled that Susan broke down in tears when he first went to visit her in jail two days after her arrest. 'What happened?' he asked his mother. To which she replied, 'Things just got out of control.' Adam testified that Susan then said, 'you can have everything, I'm just going to plead guilty.'

He said his mother had a change of heart after she learned that she was being charged with first-degree murder after stabbing Felix twenty-seven times. Adam claimed that his mother said that she had not stabbed her husband that many times and was convinced she was being set up.

'They might as well execute me because I'm being framed for murder,' Susan allegedly told Adam at the jail that day.

During the heated cross-examination, Susan repeatedly brought up unfavourable incidents from Adam's past in an attempt to discredit his testimony, at one point calling him 'a bar room brawler'. Adam sat twirling a marker and staring at the ceiling as Susan once again played the fifteen-minute audiotape of his father telling an audience about his alleged sexual abuse by a satanic cult while a toddler in day care.

Pressing the stop button on the tape recorder, Susan asked her son if he thought that she put those ideas in his father's head.

'I don't think it's a huge leap, that it's outside the realm of possibility.'

On Thursday, after three days of questioning, Susan was informed that this would be her last day of cross-examination. Frustrated, Susan resumed her questioning of Adam over his father's daily treatment of her, but as the day wore on, Susan's time was running out, and she angrily complained about the 'unfair' constraints. Still, she continued to ask him about topics that Brady had ruled inadmissible or irrelevant.

At 4.15 that afternoon, the prosecutor requested an adjournment. 'Your honour, I'm feeling quite faint, can we take a break for the day?' It was not clear if Sequeira was ill or if he had just had enough of Susan's courtroom antics.

'I think we can get a little more out of this witness,' the judge replied, signaling Susan to proceed.

Less than fifteen minutes later, Brady ended the cross-examination. She was angered by Susan's flagrant disregard for her instructions to avoid questions about Adam's alleged prior bad acts and Gabe's relationship with the Briners.

'Okay, we're done for the day,' Brady ordered, instructing court officers to remove jurors from the courtroom.

Rising to her feet, Susan shook her finger at the judge and shouted at her from the podium. 'I move for a mistrial for judicial misconduct on your part! You're putting time limits on me, you're not allowing me to recall him [Adam] . . .'

'SIT DOWN MS. POLK!' Brady instructed, as jurors filing out of the courtroom looked on in stunned amazement. 'Recess until 9am Monday.'

Susan continued her ranting even as deputies rushed to the defence table and shut off her microphone.

CHAPTER TWENTY-SIX

DEFENDING
HER LIFE

On Monday, 24 April, Susan arrived at court ready to begin her
case. A blue, long-sleeved T-shirt and chinos replaced her drab
prison attire. She looked very thin and bony; reports were circulating
that Susan now weighed less than 110 pounds. It was not clear who
delivered the clothing to her at the detention centre, although her
former case assistant, Valerie Harris, was amid the journalists and
spectators cramming the gallery that morning.

Susan's trial had already filled thirty-four days when she informed
Judge Brady that she had subpoenaed more than one hundred
witnesses and anticipated her case would take another three weeks to
present. On Susan's extensive list were both her mother, Helen, and
her son, Eli, who was still being held at the West County Detention
Facility in Richmond on charges of misdemeanour battery and
violating a restraining order. These charges stemmed from the
incident with his girlfriend, but Eli also faced a probation violation for
the high-speed chase that resulted in charges of evading a peace
officer. Authorities had agreed to push back his trial date from 2 May
to 16 May so that he could testify in his mother's case. Also on the list
were the doctor who examined her in January of 2001 after her failed

suicide attempt at Yosemite National Park, a high-tech crime investigator, a psychic, and a forensic pathologist who would testify that Felix Polk died as a result of a heart attack – and not from the multiple stab wounds she had inflicted.

During her one-hour opening statement, Susan called Felix 'Dr. Frankenstein' and told jurors that he drugged, molested, and manipulated her during their twenty-year marriage. She quoted from Thoreau and Dickens and referred to other literary works to illustrate that many narratives have surprise endings and that innocent people are sometimes wrongly accused of horrific acts.

In her speech, Susan maintained that she went to the guest cottage 'just to talk' with her husband that fateful night and that Felix fell back and hit his head during the violent struggle.

'I was framed,' she said. 'I did not stab my husband twenty-seven times, nor did I hit him. He fell.'

Susan promised a 'nail biting, edge of your seat thriller' defence. 'You may think you know all there is to know,' she told jurors. 'But it's my turn now.'

As her opening progressed, Susan insisted that she was a medium and claimed her husband had used her psychic talent to gain information that he reported back to his 'handlers'. Though she warned Felix about her vision of the 9/11 terror attacks, he failed to report her prediction to authorities. Despite her unique abilities, Susan explained that hers was an ordinary situation, one that could have happened to anyone in an unhappy marriage.

'What happened to me could happen to any family,' Susan said. 'The D.A. will have you believe that I was controlling . . . that I was a Lolita.'

This was a case of systematic spousal abuse that had gone on for far too long. To Susan, the events were clear: she had not killed Felix that night in the guest cottage; he had a heart attack. Further clouding his death was the conspiracy that she alluded to concerning her family members and law enforcement.

During the final minutes of her remarks, Susan revisited the parallels found in literature. Jurors had heard only one side of the story, but before they could truly pass judgment, before they could decide her fate, they had to hear her version of the twenty-four years. When that happens, 'it will be up to you to write the ending.'

Jurors immediately took a liking to Susan's mother, Helen Bolling. Petite and high-spirited, Helen had the panel in hysterics with her humorous responses to Susan's questions. Barely five feet tall, she almost disappeared in the witness chair beneath the judge. Clutching her daughter's childhood writings, school assignments, and photos, Helen adjusted herself in the seat and waited for Susan to begin.

'You've only been married once?' her daughter asked, referring to Helen's marriage to her father, Theodore Bolling.

'Oh yes, once was enough, it cured me,' Helen cracked, as the courtroom erupted into laughter. Susan's seventy-three-year-old mother grinned as she told jurors that she was 'almost a virgin' when she married Bolling. 'You know what I mean,' she smiled.

During her testimony, Helen boasted of her daughter's creativity and imagination. Her pale blue eyes sparkled with pride as she pulled out the awards, prize-winning writings, and photographs of Susan's youth that she brought to court that day. Her props, and the homespun stories that accompanied them, provided jurors their first glimpse into the tender side of Susan Polk – a side that most had not witnessed in the courtroom.

'Did you see any signs that I was going to grow up like the D.A. says, a homicidal.'

Helen interrupted her daughter mid-sentence. 'No.'

Helen did not hold back her dislike of her son-in-law, and in defence of Susan, told the story of her own life-and-death encounter. While she did not identify her attacker, who had throttled her violently, she described how she had to react in an instant to save her life. Helen 'played dead' to thwart the attack, but her daughter had not been as fortunate. Susan had no choice but to resort to violence against Felix's onslaught, she said.

'Boo-boo Susie' as she lovingly referred to her daughter, was not the violent type. Helen maintained that Susan didn't have it in her to deliberately harm anyone. As far as she was concerned, it was her son-in-law who had provoked the assault.

She claimed Felix 'had an exterior of being acceptable. Hidden under that, is all that shit. Excuse me, I beg the court's forgiveness, that's not proper language.'

Helen drew a deep breath before completing her thought. 'Felix had a way of persuading you into thinking he was a good guy.'

She told jurors Susan had attempted suicide shortly after beginning therapy with Felix but provided few details.

When asked about the possibility that Susan could have been behind the allegations of the ritualistic sexual abuse of Adam and Gabriel, Helen balked. 'That was from Felix. It didn't come from my side of the family. When we hear about Satan, we run like hell.'

On cross-examination, Helen told Sequeira that her 'falling out' with Susan happened over time. She denied accusations that she and her husband had abused their daughter during her childhood. 'Absolutely not!' she replied. But Sequeira pressed the issue, wanting to know why Susan would make such claims during her police interrogation on the night of her arrest.

Helen sat poker-faced as the prosecutor played the videotape of that portion of the interrogation for jurors. 'Maybe when she gets angry at people, she has a falling out with them, she makes up things about them. If she did it to you, she did it to Felix, too.'

Susan jumped up and objected. 'Torture of my mom on the stand. It's not right.' Her repeated protests were overruled by Brady.

Helen continued to defend her daughter, even after viewing the video clip in which Susan called her father a 'pervert' and accused her mother of abusing her. She argued that Susan was a victim of Felix's mind control and was just spitting back beliefs that he had drilled into her. Proof of this was the fact that now, almost four years after his death, Susan no longer believed her parents abused her during her childhood.

On redirect, Helen said she forgave Susan for 'the lost years'.

'Of course, you're my daughter. You'll be my daughter until my last breath. Furthermore, I think people are placing too much blame on you.'

Susan's mother expressed disappointment with her grandsons Adam and Gabriel, accusing the boys of being concerned only with themselves in the days and weeks after their father's death. She described them with their 'palms up', implying that they were looking for money.

Outside court, Helen continued to defend her daughter. 'All I have to say is you live practically as a hostage for forty-eight years, and then let's see how you do.'

In retrospect, Helen would be seen as Susan's best witness. Her testimony gave a fascinating look into the early years of Susan's relationship with Felix. In order to win this case, Susan had to convince the jury of the profoundly disturbing psychological impact of Felix's seduction. Since she was the only witness who could testify to Susan's behaviour before and after she met Felix, Helen was in a unique position to provide insight into the unhealthy relationship between the couple. Her charm and straightforward manner made her words convincing, but with so much of the trial remaining, it was unclear what impact this testimony would have on the verdict.

At 4.30pm, with Helen's testimony concluded, Judge Brady suggested they adjourn for the day and put off Eli's testimony until the next morning, but Susan insisted that her son had been waiting in a holding cell all day, and she wanted to use her remaining time to begin her direct testimony. Ten minutes later, a clean-shaven Eli strolled into the courtroom. Susan broke into tears immediately. Her son was wearing the county's bright yellow jumpsuit, but his hands and feet were not shackled. Taller and broader than his two brothers, Eli also possessed his mother's angular features and strong jaw.

'On the whole, did you have a happy childhood?' Susan asked him when he took the stand.

'For the most part, yes.' Eli pulled out a letter he had written to his mother in November 2002 and read it aloud:

Dear Mom,
I miss you a lot. Whatever happens, I will always hold close what you taught me . . . Going to Dad's funeral this Saturday. I don't think I am going to say anything. What could I possibly say? Nothing good.

Jurors looked on as Eli's eyes welled with tears and he began to cry. 'I pray that one day I will have control over my life,' he read between sobs. 'I want so badly to tell you not to change . . . but jail changes a lot of people.'

The following morning, Eli was back on the stand describing the time he 'split his mother's lip,' testifying that he 'threw a punch' at his mom after he found her crying in her bedroom, with his dad by her side.

'I'll kill you, I could just kill you, Susan,' Eli claimed he heard Felix threaten. 'It just popped into my head. Next thing I knew, I was throwing a punch.'

Eli claimed the incident followed a violent display by his father, who, he said, had dragged his mother up the stairs to the bedroom by her hair. Later, Felix rewarded Eli for punching his mother by taking him out to dinner at a Japanese restaurant. 'It's not your fault, it's her fault,' Eli claimed his father told him after the incident, which sent Susan to the emergency room for stitches.

On Tuesday, because of scheduling conflicts, the remainder of Eli's testimony had to be postponed, and instead, the jury heard testimony from the psychiatrist who examined Susan after her 2001 suicide attempt at Yosemite National Park. Dr. Alan Peters told jurors that he assessed Susan after she was transported by ambulance to Columbia General Hospital in Sonora on 20 January and transferred to the psychiatric unit where he was on duty. She had overdosed on aspirin, Vicodin, and Scotch, he said.

At the time, Dr. Peters said he diagnosed Susan with post-traumatic stress disorder. He believed her state of mind was a result of her failing marriage to Felix and Eli's punch. Referring to his case notes, Dr. Peters related that during his one-hour examination, Susan was articulate, cooperative, and aware of what was real and what was fantasy.

'Your manner was quite proper and composed, there was no delusional thinking,' he said in response to her questions. 'You were overwhelmed and increasingly despairing over how you were going to manage.'

Referring to Susan's description of the 'power struggle' she was facing with her husband, Dr. Peters said that she was 'constantly on the losing end. You were isolated off within your family as being the quote-unquote "crazy one" ', the psychiatrist told Susan in court.

On cross-examination, the witness admitted that Susan was also recalling sexual and physical abuse, supposedly inflicted by her parents, and that Felix Polk expressed concern for his wife and was anxious to take her home. He also testified to a notation in Susan's record that Felix had requested Susan be committed to the psychiatric hospital for observation. Dr. Peters said that Felix had made no such request to him.

In addition, Sequeira pointed out that it was Felix who called the ambulance that day, arguably saving Susan's life.

'One could say that, yes,' Dr. Peters replied.

On Tuesday, after calling Eli's former rugby coach to testify about her son's character, Susan then called David Townsend, a forensic computer expert, originally hired by Dan Horowitz, to discuss the tests he performed on Susan's home computer. Townsend, a former police officer, claimed that someone had twice accessed the files containing Susan's two-hundred-page diary before officers had obtained a search warrant. This contradicted Detective Mike Costa, who, under oath, denied reading the diary, but it remained unclear who might have done so. While this accusation suggested a violation of police protocol, his tests showed that, though the diary was accessed, it did not appear to have been altered. Townsend's examination also revealed that law enforcement did not document the required chain of custody for the computer.

The court adjourned for lunch but when the session resumed, it was Eli who returned to the stand. He testified that his father was a violent and controlling man who regularly tried to convince his children that their mother was crazy. Wearing a pained looked, he sat hunched in the witness box, listening to an audiotape of himself reacting to news of his father's death the day after Felix's body was found.

Eli's sad demeanour on the stand did not match his commanding figure. Broad shouldered, at just over six feet tall, nevertheless, Eli appeared vulnerable and in need of emotional support. Unlike his two brothers who seemed defiant and expressed a loathing for their mother, it was clear that Eli had a special connection to Susan. Eli's subdued appearance also stood in stark contrast to his lengthy juvenile rap sheet that included various assaults and encounters with the police.

'Did you love your dad?' Susan asked her son.

'Yeah, he was just a damaged person . . . Looking back, he was a really unstable person,' Eli described his father.

For the remainder of the afternoon, Eli confirmed Susan's claims regarding Felix's tyrannical behaviour, his purported links to the Jewish mafia, and accusations that his brothers had turned on Susan out of greed.

'He tried to get you on medication,' Eli said. 'He talked to the kids about how to handle you. His whole thing was you were crazy and you imagined things.'

Eli insisted his mother had every reason to believe that Felix was linked to the Mossad. 'We'd be at dinner and he'd talk about his patients,' Eli recalled. 'He said he had a patient in the FBI who was an assassin. He said he saw numerous people involved in the FBI and the CIA.'

Eli also contended that two of Felix's friends regularly spoke of their ties to Israeli Intelligence and the Mossad.

On Wednesday, Eli's testimony was again interrupted when a surprise witness was wheeled into the courtroom and announced her need to speak out on Susan's behalf.

Seemingly out of breath, seventy-seven-year-old Elizabeth Bradley's appearance momentarily created what could only be described as a 'Perry Mason moment'.

'Oh my God!' Susan gasped. 'Eli, do you remember who this is?'

Eli did not recall the Polks' former neighbour from Berkeley, but he sat quietly as Mrs. Bradley addressed the court from her wheelchair.

'I didn't know when I should come,' she said, speaking to Susan at the podium. 'But I arranged for a taxi and my son to get off from work, and my cardiologist arranged for some extra medications in case I had a heart attack or stroke, so I came without notice and here I am.'

Her shoulders wrapped in a shawl, Bradley guided her motorised wheelchair to the front of the courtroom. Her son, Edwin, trailed behind and held a microphone to her lips when she stopped in front of the clerk's desk and addressed the court. 'I'm obliged to come to the aid of a very special person.'

Initially, Sequeira objected to the surprise witness, saying that her name was not on the required list. In response, Susan told the court that she was unaware that Mrs. Bradley was planning to attend the trial. Her former Elmwood Avenue neighbour had written to her in jail, upset over the way she was being portrayed in the news. Producing Bradley's letter for the prosecutor, Susan said that they had spoken about her coming to court but nothing had ever been firmed up.

'Elizabeth, did we discuss your testimony at all?' Susan asked the elderly woman, whose frail body shook intermittently from palsy.

'No.'

'Today is a very special day, isn't it?' Susan said, addressing her neighbour.

'Yes, 26 April is my seventy-seventh birthday. And I have to apologise for my difficulty speaking, because I'm in the middle of some major oral surgery. If you can't understand me, let me know and I will try harder.'

During thirty minutes of testimony, Bradley explained that she had been moved to act because the news media 'was demonising Susan in such a way, I was shocked. There was no comparison to the Susan I knew.

'She was an outstanding citizen of the neighbourhood and we loved her,' Bradley tearfully recalled.

Elizabeth Bradley said that she was a single mother raising two children when Susan and Felix moved into the neighbourhood with their three sons nearly twenty years ago. 'We were neighbours and friends. I babysat when Susan had to go shopping. I was like an aunt to the children. They were so adorable. I loved being around them and Susan.'

'You're being too kind, Elizabeth,' Susan said in between sobs.

'I saw no meanness in the children, except that Eli took a terrible amount of sibling abuse from his older brother, Adam. And his older brother was the apple of his father's eye.'

Bradley charged that it was not Susan, but Felix, who was emotionally agitated. She recalled one day that she was visiting the Polk house when Felix unleashed his rage on one of his sons. She was not sure which boy it was but said the beating sounded brutal.

'[T]his little boy was screaming something awful. I wanted to cry out but I couldn't say anything. But the beating was cruel.'

While Bradley disapproved of the physical handling of the boy, she did not interfere, believing that Felix was a therapist and 'must know what he is doing'.

'I spent a lot of time around that family and one thing I can tell you, in my lifetime, I never met a more diligent mother, housewife, and assistant to her husband.'

'Thank you for your courage and integrity in coming today,' Susan said.

'I couldn't live with myself if I didn't. It breaks my heart. You deserve a better life.'

'I have a brave son like you do, Elizabeth. I have a good life.'

'No further questions.'

Bradley looked to the prosecutor. Sequeira had no questions

for the elderly woman. He simply rose and thanked her for coming to court.

Jurors wiped away tears as Susan's old neighbour rolled her wheelchair out of the courtroom, waving to Susan. 'Bye, bye, honey. God bless you.'

Bradley failed to add anything new to the case at hand, but the theatrics meshed brilliantly with Susan's showmanship. Susan maintained that she had no idea Bradley would come, but she adapted amazingly well to the moment, presenting a surprise witness who had nothing good to say about Felix and nothing bad to say about Susan.

Once back on the stand, Eli continued to bolster his mother's claims of spousal abuse and her belief that a conspiracy was at work to wrongly convict her of murder.

'He admitted to striking Andy, his son [from his first marriage], and said that's just the way he was raised,' Eli testified. 'He told me his first wife [Sharon Mann] was crazy and delusional, and that's why they got a divorce.'

The following day, Susan ended her examination and turned the witness over to the prosecutor, but by Friday morning she was demanding a mistrial. Furious at the way Sequeira was cross-examining Eli, she accused the prosecutor of being in cahoots with the judge to discredit the only one of her children to testify on her behalf.

'This is unfair treatment!' Susan said, jumping up at one point to object to Sequeira's questions about Eli's criminal past.

'Shame on both of you!' she ranted, directing her anger at both the prosecutor and the judge for their 'tricky, nefarious, and devious' actions.

'I fully recognise that watching your son be cross-examined has got to be extremely difficult,' Judge Brady said, adding that the prosecutor's questions were permissible.

During two days of cross-examination, Sequeira questioned Eli about his run-ins with the police and his on-again off-again relationship with his mother. He intended to poke holes in Eli's claims that his mother was a victim of abuse, and not a coldhearted killer who stabbed his father in a premeditated rage. Using excerpts from Susan's diary, Eli's letters, and his disastrous trip to Paris with Susan when he was a teen, Sequeira stressed the often rocky relationship between mother and son.

Susan's middle child did little to hide his disdain for the assistant district attorney and the court in which his mother was being tried. His responses to Sequeira's questions were peppered with sarcasm and he accentuated the word 'sir' when he replied to the queries.

With regard to the argument between his parents that had prompted him to strike his mother in the face, Sequeira asked, 'Why didn't you hit the abuser?'

'I don't know.' Eli replied. He maintained that it was the first time he was ever violent with his mother.

Susan, meanwhile, raised objections when the prosecutor handed her son a copy of the police report that documented another instance of aggression toward his mother. She accused Sequeira of violating the rules of discovery, alleging that he had not provided her with a copy of the report he had just handed Eli. The judge overruled her objection, clearing the way for Sequeira to question Eli about the incident.

The report documented a call to police from Susan after another argument with Eli that turned violent. According to the report, she told police that her son had shoved her out of the house, locked the door, and then took her car without permission.

Eli claimed he couldn't recall the incident.

Grinning, Sequeira moved on. He next enquired about the fight he had with a fellow teen in the parking lot of a fast-food restaurant that resulted in a felony assault charge. Though Eli insisted it was just a 'fistfight', the prosecutor noted that witnesses told police that Eli struck the victim with a flashlight – a claim Eli denied.

'I hit him four or five times,' Eli said.

'You broke his nose and cut his face up pretty good, didn't you?' Sequeira noted.

'I object!' Susan jumped up yet again. 'He's attempting to interject hearsay information that hasn't been established.'

'Would you like to see the medical records?' Sequeira smiled, rummaging through the papers on his table.

'He doesn't even have them!' Susan shot back, watching as the prosecutor fumbled to retrieve the document.

'He's attempting to confuse and mislead the jury,' Susan complained to Judge Brady out of earshot of jurors, 'when the most important part of this young man's testimony is that his father was violent, and that his father threatened to kill me.'

But Sequeira wasn't finished with Eli's rap sheet. There was the October 2003 incident in which he shot a passing motorist with a pellet gun. The bullet lodged inches from the man's spine.

Eli insisted he struck the man by accident. He wasn't aiming at anything in particular when he fired the weapon toward the road. 'I was sorry. Accidents do happen. That was a terrible one.'

Sequeira also cited the high-speed car chase in which Eli attempted to elude officers, reaching speeds of 130 mph in his attempt to ditch the bag of marijuana he had in his Camaro.

'And then I pulled over,' Eli insisted of the October 2003 incident.

'You had a flat tyre.' Sequeira pointed out.

'I was between homes,' Eli protested. 'Things were going very badly. I made some mistakes.'

Sequeira also called the jury's attention to Eli's troubles in school, noting that he had been suspended from Miramonte High for making racist and homophobic remarks. It was a calculated strategy to portray Susan's ally as the bad seed. Using Eli's record against him, Sequeira cast sufficient doubt on his credibility, demonstrating the witness to be an unreliable person whose words were equally unreliable.

Continuing on, Sequeira raised questions about Eli's allegiance to Susan, pointing out that he seemed to side with his mother when it was convenient. Supporting Sequeira's claim was Eli's aborted trip to Paris with his mother, as well as the March 2001 police report in which Eli sided with Felix, telling officers that he witnessed Susan kick his dad during an argument.

'I did what my father told me to do,' Eli defended. He now related that day's events differently, saying that his father had attacked his mother, shoved her up against the refrigerator and ordered him to tell police that she had instigated the fight.

Sequeira paused to let jurors digest the information. 'And sometimes you do what your mother tells you to do?' he asked.

'Yes.'

'And you told a third version, too, didn't you?'

Tossing his hands in the air, Eli blurted out, 'I don't know. I'm lost.'

Striding to the witness box, Sequeira presented the young man with a transcript from a July 2003 conversation with his mother's former defence investigator in which he claimed that it was his father who kicked his mother that day.

'It seems like there's been a mistake, a miscommunication,' Eli announced after reading the notes from Susan's former lawyer, Elizabeth Grossman. Eli argued that Grossman was not really working for his mother. He then provided the prosecutor with a rambling explanation that made little sense to those in the courtroom. 'It had to do with a conspiracy, a civil conspiracy, as well as the conspiracy to have my mother convicted.'

Sequeira froze in front of the witness box. 'Are you telling this jury that Liz Grossman . . . is part of a large conspiracy to get your mother convicted and to steal from the estate?'

Eli looked directly at Sequeira. 'I never said large. It takes two people to conspire.'

'You're right,' the prosecutor said in a raised voice. 'It takes two!' Pacing before the jury, Sequeira directed Eli to identify the members of the alleged conspiracy for the court.

Dumbfounded, Eli looked to his mother, who was at the podium demanding the questioning of her son be halted immediately.

Judge Brady cut Susan off mid-sentence and directed Eli to answer the question.

Repositioning himself in the chair, Eli listed the alleged participants. There was his Uncle John Polk, John's lawyer, Bud MacKenzie, the Briners, and his dad's friend, Barry Morris. 'They've used their connections in this court and others to control things the best that they can.'

'Am I, me, Paul Sequeira, just some guy who works for the D.A.'s office, am I working for this big conspiracy?'

'I have not seen documentation, proof . . . no one has said anything to lead me to believe that,' Eli said. He also declined to speculate as to whether members of law enforcement were also involved, or that they had 'staged' the crime scene, as his mother alleged.

All eyes in the courtroom turned to Susan, who was now chuckling. Addressing the prosecutor, she insisted that she never accused him of being a party to the conspiracy. 'But, I've had my doubts,' Susan giggled. 'You, too, your honour.'

'Ms. Polk, I do not find anything amusing about this,' Judge Brady reprimanded. 'And I don't think the giggling is appropriate. Stop it!'

Friday's court session adjourned when the prosecutor announced that he had no further questions.

CHAPTER TWENTY-SEVEN

NO MURDER
AT ALL

The following Monday, court resumed with Susan's redirect examination of Eli. She would keep her son on the stand until Thursday afternoon when Judge Brady announced she had heard enough and halted the questioning. During those four days, Susan trotted out numerous e-mails that her sons exchanged after their father's death and instructed Eli to read them aloud. 'I hope you do join the team and then I can see you soon,' Gabe wrote to Eli in January of 2004.

'I'm disappointed in you,' Gabe wrote in another correspondence. 'Get your shit together. You're siding with a person who murdered our dad.'

Gabriel was not the only brother sending e-mails to Eli. In January 2005, Adam sent one saying he would entertain his mother's request to write a letter to the court, pronouncing, 'I don't believe my mother killed my father in cold blood, but in self-defence.'

In response to questions from Susan, Eli maintained that his elder brother had threatened to disinherit him if he did not join the wrongful death civil suit that Adam and Gabe filed against their mother.

'If I could just apologise for my language beforehand,' Eli asked jurors before reading Gabriel's final e-mail correspondence aloud. 'Eli, if you believe all that shit, you're a fucking psycho, and I never want to see you again,' Eli read from the page his mother handed him. 'I really should start calling you Susan. Grow the fuck up!'

Looking up from the paper, Eli accused Sequeira of 'smiling at him'.

The accusation caught the judge off guard. Straightening herself in her chair, Brady glanced at the prosecutor. For the record, she noted that he was sitting at his table, resting his cheek and chin in his hand and gazing away from the witness box.

'I object!' Susan barked. 'The district attorney is making faces at my son.'

Brady drew a breath and instructed Susan to move on with her questions.

'Was it like a smiling face?' Susan asked Eli with regard to Sequeira's supposed grin.

'Mrs. Polk,' the judge interrupted, warning Susan to move on.

'It was like a smirk,' Eli replied.

Brady instructed Eli not to respond after she had ruled.

'I object!' Susan yelled out.

'Is there any way to take this show on the road?' Sequeira interjected, shaking his head in frustration.

'It is a show,' Eli agreed.

Banging her hand on the desk, Brady terminated the proceedings. 'All right! We're done for the day!'

Humorous though it was, the episode reflected Brady's growing frustration. Whereas once the judge had been willing to tolerate Susan's behaviour, she was becoming much less lenient. Furthermore, Susan continued to bait Sequeira, and her efforts were clearly taking a toll on everyone involved.

On Tuesday, Susan directed her middle son to read letters he had written to her in jail. She was anxious to point out the sections in which Eli referred to his willingness to take the stand and 'tell the truth' about Dad, but she didn't anticipate the unsettling impact that many of the letters would have on the courtroom. As Eli spoke about his mother's innocence, his voice sounded less and less like a son, and more like a lover. The impact was palpable, as the jurors shifted in their seats.

'I miss you so much it is driving me crazy,' Eli read aloud from one. 'You are everything to me . . . The truth about Dad needs to come out.'

'P.S. I wake up and see your face,' the note continued. 'I love you enough to burn all I am and meet you in the afterlife.'

Susan cried aloud as her son recited the words to jurors. He had already told the court about the framed photo of his mother that he kept in his locker at Byron Boys' Ranch. He had made the frame in wood shop and hung it in the locker so he could see her face every day.

The testimony that day was disquieting, and Sequeira recognised that Susan may have alienated the jurors with her son's writings. Once again the prosecutor had uncovered a weak spot to probe, and the following morning he did just that, announcing his intent to introduce short stories that had allegedly been written by Susan about a wife who murders her husband and a mother who has a sexual relationship with her son.

According to Sequeira, he learned of the stories six weeks earlier during a phone call from Susan's landlord in Montana, former Congressman Chris Harris, who claimed he and his wife came upon the writings while cleaning the cabin. Harris said the writings were tucked under a mattress in the cabin that Susan had rented from him in the autumn of 2001, but he was unsure if his wife had kept them. From the handwriting, Harris's wife had determined that a woman had written the stories.

Susan argued there was no basis to introduce the material into evidence, as the landlord did not even have them in his possession. 'There's speculation that I wrote the dirty story and that I wrote the murder story,' Susan barked. 'That's totally slander. He [Paul Sequeira] should be ashamed of himself! There isn't anything they wouldn't say or do to defame me!'

Judge Brady postponed a ruling on their admissibility, saying there were 'some issues' that needed to be considered.

Angered at the judge's response, Susan launched into an attack on Sequeira, at one point blurting out, 'The man needs a spanking and the judge should give it to him.' Judge Brady did not respond. Instead, she instructed the deputies to return Eli to the courtroom to resume testimony. Eventually she would rule the stories inadmissible.

In response to questions, Eli portrayed himself as the only one of Susan's three sons to come to court and 'tell the truth', claiming that his father had hypnotised all three boys during twice weekly therapy sessions at the house. He contended that Felix served them tea and put them in a trance. 'I remember not remembering what had happened.' He also believed that Felix was behind the accusations regarding Adam's sexual abuse by a satanic cult. 'It seemed like it was definitely dad's thing.' And he agreed with his mother that his two brothers were part of a conspiracy to 'loot' the Polk estate.

During his final moments on the stand, Eli told jurors that he believed his father's death could have been prevented if someone had simply reported his abuse to authorities.

'Isn't it true your dad did try to prevent it and now he's dead?' Sequeira asked. He reminded Eli that Felix had called authorities several times in the days before his death, saying he was afraid for his life.

'First of all, I believed *he* attacked her that night, and she defended herself,' Eli argued. It was his contention that Felix was simply trying to set his mother up; that he had 'every opportunity' to fix his marriage and had failed miserably.

'Your father's dead, isn't he?' Sequeira asked.

'I'm not going to answer that question.'

By late afternoon, Judge Brady had had enough. Susan's repeated objections and requests to interrupt her son's testimony with other defence witnesses now seemed like an attempt to keep Eli on the stand – and out of jail – for as long as possible. Brady called an end to Susan's examination just before 4.30pm that Wednesday, directing her to pick up her case in the morning with testimony from Montana real estate agent, Janna Kuntz, and retired forensic pathologist, Dr. John Cooper.

The following morning, Susan's first witness, Janna Kuntz, testified about conversations she had with Susan in September 2002 while the two were out viewing properties.

'It was not a good marriage,' Kuntz responded to a question from Susan. 'You were very unhappy and you wanted to move away, get away.'

The estate agent told the court that she was under the impression that Susan's husband was 'a very emotionally abusive human being'.

'Did I express rage?' she asked the estate agent, referring to the day she learned Felix had won custody of their Orinda home and their minor son, as well as a significant cut in her support payments.

'I wouldn't describe it as rage. It was more like, "Can you believe this? He's gone and done something again."'

Under cross-examination, Kuntz agreed that her feelings about the Polks' marriage were based solely on Susan's statements. She had never met Felix Polk and could not speak to his character from personal experience. In spite of the one-sided nature of Kuntz's testimony, her appearance was a relief, as she brought a sense of normalcy to the otherwise chaotic proceedings.

The harmony was short-lived. For her next witness, Susan called Dr. Cooper, a self-employed forensic pathologist from Austin, Texas. Dr. Cooper had reviewed the autopsy report and was in court to dispute the medical examiner's claims that Felix Polk died as a result of blunt force trauma and bleeding from his extensive injuries. Susan's former defence lawyer, Dan Horowitz, had considered hiring Dr. Cooper when he was in charge of the case, but he opted not to after deciding that the expert witness was a bit of a 'kook'.

Susan seemed infatuated by her expert witness, smiling and batting her eyes at the fortyish Texan with the round cheeks, dark hair, and lispy Southern drawl as she stood at the podium. The doctor told jurors that he was an independent forensic expert who was often retained by prosecutors to provide expert testimony at trial. Though he claimed that defence lawyers with 'wild theories' often contacted him, he said he usually denied the jobs because 'I don't want to look foolish'. During his career, he performed nearly two thousand autopsies and said he hoped to retire soon to pursue his interest in the medical practices of indigenous cultures.

Dr. Cooper contended that Felix's heart problems were a 'time bomb' and that heart disease, not multiple stab wounds, caused his death. He reached this conclusion after spending more than fifty hours reviewing materials related to the case, including the autopsy conducted by Dr. Brian Peterson, police crime scene photos, grand jury testimony, and letters from Susan that detailed her version of events the night Felix died.

'I believe Dr. Polk died of a coronary event while assaulting his wife,' he testified, noting that the autopsy found that two of Felix's arteries were 75 per cent blocked and his heart was swollen at the time of death.

Dr. Cooper characterised Felix's stab wounds as 'relatively trivial' and claimed they did not cause his death because the 'severity of the injuries was really not that great.'

'In your opinion, was my husband killed?' Susan asked, reading from a list of prepared questions she had in front of her on the podium.

'No,' Dr. Cooper affirmed. 'I came to the conclusion that the manner of death should be categorised as natural.

'The stab wounds were not enough for death without the coronary disease. He could have gotten medical attention and survived these injuries,' he concluded.

Rising from his seat in the witness box, the forensic expert strode to the front of the courtroom, his cowboy boots peeking out from beneath dark-coloured slacks, and fell to his knees. He was about to provide jurors with a live reenactment of the events of 13 October 2002, as he believed they occurred based on his review of the evidence, and his interpretation was vastly different from that of Dr. Peterson.

Kneeling before the panel, he explained that in order to inflict wounds to Felix's stomach in the direction they were made, Susan would have to be beneath him, and not standing, when she plunged the knife into his abdomen. Furthermore, Dr. Cooper was critical of Peterson's findings, particularly his decision to list the exact number of injuries – twenty-seven stab wounds – found on Polk's body on the autopsy report. It was his contention that Peterson was anxious to dramatise the findings in light of the media attention the Polk case was receiving.

'I would have just said "multiple stab wounds", because when we fill out these reports we know we're going to be quoted . . . I've read the stories in the press.'

'Objection!' Sequeira cut the witness off mid-sentence.

'I've read them!' Dr. Cooper shot back, to which the judge issued an admonishment.

Dr. Cooper testified that he found no evidence to support the prosecutor's claim that Felix was rendered incapacitated early in the struggle by a blow to the head. Holding up a photo of Felix's head injury, he showed jurors that there was no indication that blood had flowed from the injury to areas of Felix's neck and back. Blood droplets would be present if Felix had stood up after he sustained the blow, he maintained.

'He hit his head on the tile floor after he fell back from his cardiac arrest,' he concluded.

He testified that Felix's death was the result of coronary deficiency and that the stab wounds were a contributing factor. This, he asserted, was a clear example of self-defence. Sequeira immediately objected that the witness was not qualified to make a legal assessment. It was one of many objections made by the prosecutor that morning, but his objections never stopped Dr. Cooper from testifying. Ordinarily, a witness stops speaking when a lawyer interrupts; in this case, Dr. Cooper just kept talking. This odd behaviour proved quite frustrating for both Sequeira and Judge Brady, who finally called for an early recess.

'I've been doing this for a very long time,' Brady told the witness out of earshot of jurors. 'I've never had an expert witness respond to either party during an objection. Whether you agree with the objection or not, it is for me to deal with.'

'I'm sorry,' Cooper replied.

But Susan could not let the matter rest. Once again, she charged that Brady and Sequeira were conspiring, this time to 'intimidate' her witness.

'I'm outta here,' the prosecutor announced, throwing his arms in the air.

'He's playing chicken,' Susan accused.

'She's right!' her mother, Helen Bolling, shouted from the gallery, an outburst that prompted a court bailiff to expel the elder woman from the courtroom. Once in the hallway, Bolling told reporters that she viewed her daughter's murder trial as 'unfair', labelling it a 'phony trial'.

That afternoon, Dr. Cooper continued his testimony, listing seven reasons why he believed that Dr. Peterson's autopsy was not 'objective'. There was the 'physical improbability factor' with Felix standing five inches taller and fifty pounds heavier than his wife and 'direct evidence' such as the injury on Susan's face and strands of her hair in Felix's death grip. According to Dr. Cooper, the 'defensive wounds' on Felix's body supported the theory that he was attacking Susan with his right hand while blocking the knife with his left. He noted that the wounds had a leftward slant and clumps of Susan's hair were found in his right hand. Cooper insisted that the data indicated that Felix 'didn't turn and run'. The fact that Felix ripped out strands of his wife's hair, punched her in the face, and bit her on the hand was proof that he was the party responsible for the assault, the expert argued. 'To me, he did not try to avoid violence, he was trying to perpetuate it,' he said.

In addition, there was also the 'distribution' and 'multiplicity' of the stab wounds coupled with 'the relative position of the two combatants'. Blood from Felix's chest and upper thighs had flowed to his knees, but not his shins, supporting his claim that Susan was under Felix during the attack. Furthermore, Cooper pointed out that the county's medical examiner would have found evidence of blood flowing down the back of Felix's head and neck if he had been struck first on the head by Susan that night. He called the State's theory that she had initiated the attack with an incapacitating blow to the head 'a bogus suggestion', noting that Felix's head wound lacked bruising.

The pathologist agreed with Susan's assertion that Felix's body was moved after his death, evidenced by blood smudges found on the floor near the corpse. This comment drew objections from the prosecutor, who took issue with the scope of Dr. Cooper's testimony. Sequeira argued that while Cooper was qualified to render medical findings, he was not an expert in criminal investigations and should not be espousing theories as to how the crime played out. Judge Brady agreed with Sequeira and sustained the objection.

In the minutes before court ended that Thursday, Dr. Cooper made a stunning admission: He did not write a report of his findings, nor did he have any notes to turn over to the prosecutor. Essentially, he had come to court without any of the supporting materials he had used to render his expert opinion in the first-degree murder case.

'Once one knows the truth of the case, one does not need to remain neutral,' he told Sequeira. 'One goes with the truth.'

Sequeira's frustrations, which he had previously directed only at Susan, came out, as his patience with Dr. Cooper disappeared. The prosecutor retorted, 'You don't think it's not good professional practice to write a report so people can review what your findings are in a murder case?'

Dr. Cooper challenged Sequeira to 'subpoena' him, claiming he had not prepared a written report for fear that it would be used as a tool to prevent him from testifying. He also noted he had not been asked by the prosecutor to prepare one.

'I don't consider it appropriate for you to know all of the details of what I'm going to testify to,' Cooper added.

The discussion was clearly becoming a problem. Sensing a number of issues with Dr. Cooper's testimony, Judge Brady intervened, halting the cross-examination and clearing the jury and the witness from the courtroom. She informed Susan that protocol required expert witnesses to provide the other side with supporting documents used to render a decision in a case. Susan told Brady that she hadn't made copies of her written correspondence and claimed there were no notes. When Brady appeared skeptical, Susan launched into a frenzied attack, repeatedly cutting the judge off mid-sentence and accused her of being 'wrong'. Ultimately, Judge Brady sided with Sequeira on the matter and ordered Dr. Cooper to produce his report based on the evidence the next morning.

The following morning, Dr. Cooper failed to produce the discoverable materials he had used to prepare his testimony. Brady demanded an explanation. Initially Dr. Cooper claimed to have left them on the plane – after telling members of the court that he had driven up from Texas to testify on Susan's behalf. He then suggested that a burglary may have occurred in his motel room. From the witness stand, he said that at one point during his stay, he returned to find the door to his room stuck shut, leading him to suspect a thief. Perhaps the documents were among the items taken, he put forward.

Judge Brady was incredulous. 'I must admit I am very troubled by the turn of events this morning. Don't you have copies in your office?'

Dr. Cooper's answer was vague, and after some back and forth, he suggested the materials could be at his home in Austin.

'Are you married?' the judge enquired.

'Yes.'

'Then have your wife FedEx them to court,' Brady suggested.

'Um. My wife is out of town,' the expert replied.

'Do you have pets?'

'Yes, dogs.'

'Who is feeding the dogs?' the judge asked.

'Um . . . I don't know.'

'I don't believe you and order you to have the letters faxed to the court by Monday.'

It was then that Paul Sequeira lost his temper. The prosecutor, who for weeks had tried to keep his composure, rose to his feet and launched a formal complaint, saying that through all of Susan's continued attacks and outbursts, he had done his best to remain in control. 'But this latest shenanigan is unacceptable,' he remarked. 'How is this happening? This is outrageous! The witness is going back and forth on the existence of these letters. Not only that, but he's testifying way outside the area of his expertise. He's creating verbal crime scene reenactments for the jury.'

While Sequeira was criticising Susan and her witness, Susan attacked Brady's ruling regarding the papers. In Susan's opinion, she should not have to provide the prosecutor with the disputed papers if he did not explicitly ask for them beforehand. In addition, she also disputed the judge's assertion that the laws of reciprocal discovery covered the materials, arguing, incorrectly, that discovery 'is a relatively new concept and still being developed'. Susan claimed that Dr. Cooper's testimony 'was completely independent, unbiased, and neutral, and she attacked the prosecutor, calling him a "cry baby".

'He doesn't like Dr. Cooper's testimony, so he does a little dance in front of the media and says I'm in violation of discovery,' Susan quarrelled.

'I want you to listen to me, Mrs. Polk,' Judge Brady intervened. 'If you make any more insults, I will sanction you.'

Despite the threat, it was not immediately clear what the judge had in mind. The situation embodied the paradox that the judge faced throughout the trial: Susan was already in custody, so what other punishment could Brady hand down? It was a difficult situation for Brady, but it was becoming increasingly clear that Susan needed to be reigned in. Susan's respect for the court had been far from exemplary, but now her witnesses were giving testimony that seemed dangerously close to perjury, conduct that could produce serious consequences for Susan.

Monday morning, Judge Brady made an announcement. Out of the presence of jurors, she informed the court that Susan's expert witness had 'skipped out' on the trial. 'He is indicating not only is he not going to return, but he will be unavailable by telephone for this week and he will be travelling,' Brady said, referring to a three-page e-mail she received from Cooper over the weekend.

'In all my years that I've been doing this, I have never heard of anything like this before,' she added. 'I've never had an expert witness take on the role of an advocate and then indicate he has chosen not to come back – that is just not an option.'

Like Judge Brady, Sequeira also expressed his shock after reading the letter that day. 'I've never seen an expert run off like a scared rabbit before he is cross-examined.'

Cooper cited 'the hostile behaviour of the prosecuting attorney' as a key reason for his decision to withdraw from the case. 'It was regrettable that I was unable to fulfill my designated role in the case during the week I had set aside for it,' he wrote in the letter that was made public later that afternoon. Dr. Cooper told Judge Brady that it was a 'pleasure' to appear in her courtroom and assured her that his grievances were not 'in any way intended to reflect unfavourably upon the Court . . . I hold Mr. Sequeira completely responsible for last week's debacle. Perhaps he has forgotten that justice isn't always about winning.'

Cooper charged the prosecutor with crafting a 'dramatic smokescreen about some discovery issues that have no bearing on the physical evidence and certainly have nothing whatsoever to do with the fact that an innocent woman is being held on false charges.' He also expressed 'outrage' at the county medical examiner, Brian Peterson, accusing him of 'irresponsible, unprofessional, and to my way of thinking, immoral conduct.

'Allow me to review the facts as I see them: Susan Polk is on trial for murder because Dr. Brian Peterson . . . saw fit to present a distortion of the autopsy evidence to the Coroner, to the District Attorney's office, to the Grand Jury, and ultimately to the trier of fact in a murder trial.' Dr. Cooper wrote. 'Not only has Mrs. Polk been indicted on false pretenses, but she has also suffered from protracted false imprisonment and estrangement from her sons as a result of Dr. Peterson's false representations.

'I see this man to be nothing more than a public menace,' Cooper said of Peterson.

Meanwhile, Judge Brady informed jurors that morning that a 'scheduling issue' had arisen, and the court would hear from Dr. Cooper at a later date. Court officials had reached the runaway pathologist by phone and, after advising him of his obligation to come back to court to finish his cross-examination, set a date of 16 May for his return.

In the meantime, Susan called her first hostile defence witness, Gabe's foster mother, Marjorie Briner. She believed that Briner and her husband, Dan, had 'brainwashed' Gabe into testifying against her. Now, she was anxious to paint the middle-school teacher as a member of a money-hungry conspiracy out to rob the Polk estate.

'I have not gained a single cent from your estate,' Briner insisted during a testy exchange. She also balked at Susan's claim that she had turned Susan's children against her by labelling Susan as 'crazy and delusional'.

'From the very beginning, Dan and I tried to stay as neutral as possible,' Briner replied. 'I tried never to use those words. Because those were words that made you very upset.'

Polk and Briner repeatedly interrupted one another, prompting the court reporter to insist they halt the cross-talk so she could transcribe all of their remarks.

'Mrs. Briner, have you ever heard of Pinocchio?' Susan asked.

Briner insisted that she had 'nothing to gain' by testifying against her.

'Nothing?' Susan was incredulous. 'Didn't I put you on notice that I was going to sue you for fraud?'

Smiling, Briner acknowledged that fraud was among the threats Susan had made over the months.

'And wouldn't a guilty verdict get you off the hook?'

During the heated examination, Susan accused Briner of perjury, in response to the schoolteacher's claim that Susan had been verbally abusive during phone calls and in letters she sent from jail. Furious, Susan commanded Briner to sift through two mountainous stacks of letters that sat before her on the wood railing and point out an instance of 'verbal abuse'.

'We haven't even come close to the area of enquiry I've allowed,' Judge Brady admonished. 'Move on, this is not relevant.'

'I object,' Susan shot back. 'Perjury is always relevant.'

Week three of Susan's presentation also included testimony from a former colleague of the slain therapist and a former patient who had participated in his group therapy sessions with Susan thirty years earlier. While their brief time on the stand bolstered Susan's portrayal of Felix as a controlling husband, her monotonous questioning diluted the effectiveness of their testimony.

Psychotherapist Karen Saeger, a former colleague of Dr. Polk's at the California Graduate School of Professional Psychology, testified to 'two Felixes'. 'One was tightly coiled like he could spring at you, the other was charming and charismatic,' she said. Saeger claimed that Polk had a 'widespread reputation' at the college for his 'taboo' relationship with his patient/wife.

Afterwards, Kathy Lucia told jurors of Susan's dependence on Felix during their group therapy sessions at his Berkeley office in the early 1970s. 'He was trying to control you, I felt,' Lucia said in response to Susan's questions.

Unlike her mother or Eli, Saeger and Lucia were two seemingly objective witnesses, who supported Susan's claims concerning inappropriate treatment that she had suffered in Felix's hands – especially during her young, vulnerable years. Indeed, it was on this issue that Susan should have pressed harder. At times, it appeared that she failed to realise the chord of sympathy that she could have struck with the jury had she focused on Felix's emotional manipulation of her at a young age. Regardless of his alleged abuse, he had clearly violated professional and ethical standards in his treatment of Susan, and this behaviour left his character open to question. Unfortunately, Susan found it difficult to exploit this weakness, as her evidence about Felix's behaviour often became muddled in her confused accusations of abuse and conspiracy.

By Thursday, the jury had still heard very little testimony relevant to the murder charge when Susan recalled her son Eli to the stand to refute Marjorie Briner's testimony.

'Is she a liar?' Eli responded to his mother's enquiry. 'That's just an understatement of her character. She is disgusting, what she's done.'

Week four got underway with Susan's list of witnesses interrupted once again by testimony from her 'runaway' forensic pathologist, John Cooper. Dr. Cooper returned to court on 16 May, and delivered portions of his case file to Judge Brady. After a review of the documents, Brady turned over in excess of fifty pages of documents to the prosecution, holding back portions she ruled to be Susan's 'work product'. Among the materials was a letter Susan sent to Dr. Cooper from jail that detailed her version of the events of 13 October 2002, and was accompanied by a rough sketch. Excerpts of that letter were read aloud in court and released to the public later that day.

Sequeira's cross-examination of Dr. Cooper focused on the witness's prior courtroom conduct and his contradictory conclusions regarding the County's autopsy report. The nondescript carpet muffled the clicking of his cowboy boots as he strode to the witness box that Monday as courtroom spectators poked fun at the Hawaiian shirt beneath his dark suit and tie.

Dr. Cooper was again defiant as he faced off with the prosecutor that morning, repeating his conviction that the murder charges against Susan Polk were 'false'. He told jurors that an 'injustice' was being carried out in Contra Costa County and he could no longer remain a neutral witness.

'You haven't sat here and heard all the evidence,' Sequeira rebuked. 'You don't know if she's being held on false charges.'

'I see that the autopsy evidence exonerates her.' Dr. Cooper reiterated that while the stab wounds Felix sustained were a 'contributing factor', he died as a result of a heart attack suffered during his 'aggressive' and 'angry' attack on Susan. 'I believe it is sound logic to say if he weren't involved in an altercation, he wouldn't have died,' Cooper said.

Dr. Cooper contended that Susan's account of the murder, as depicted in letters she sent him, was 'honest' and an 'excellent fit' with the autopsy report depicting Felix's injuries. 'My assessment is that she is a reliable eyewitness.'

'Are you aware that Susan believes she is a medium?' Sequeira asked, striding around the courtroom.

'My understanding is that she's got considerable psychic ability and there's no reason to doubt that,' Dr. Cooper replied matter-of-factly. 'Maybe you don't believe in psychic ability.'

'Really? So you believe she's psychic?'

'I have no reason to doubt it.'

Though the questions seemed tangential to the witness's expertise, Sequeira's strategy was clear. Dr. Cooper's strange conduct during his first appearance had already tainted his credibility, and now Sequeira was attempting to sully his scientific reputation further by showing his belief in psychics. It was a clever line of questioning as this placed the doctor in something of a catch-22. On one hand, Cooper could not disagree with Susan's claims that she was a medium, since such a statement could make it seem as though other elements of her story were suspect. On the other hand, by saying that he believed in her abilities, Cooper inadvertently cast doubt on his own scientific credentials. The doctor emerged from the ordeal looking less and less like a man whose medical word could be trusted.

Sequeira next asked him about Susan's assertion that her former lawyer, Daniel Horowitz, had a role in his wife's murder.

'I object!' Susan said with a grin. 'I never exactly said that. Although, I do think that maybe it's so.'

On redirect examination, Susan got down on the floor to reenact the events of 13 October 2002. As she lay prone on the courtroom floor demonstrating her position during the attack, she asked Dr. Cooper, 'If I were able to kick him in the groin and disarm him, it would be consistent with the fact that I don't have stab wounds?'

Yes, the pathologist affirmed.

Sequeira was dubious. Walking to the overhead projector, he flashed photos of Felix's bloodied body and of the deep, swollen defensive wound on his right hand. He then contrasted the images with photos of Susan's injuries; a red bruise encircling her right eye and supposed bite marks on her hands. 'Somehow she got the knife away without sustaining one nick or cut on her whole body?'

'Yes,' Dr. Cooper replied.

Over two days of heated cross-examination, Cooper maintained that Susan's lack of bruising did not trouble him, and in fact, was consistent with the crime scene.

'I object,' Susan said at one point during the question. 'I did have injuries, they were relatively light compared to my husband. My crime is that I survived.'

'The odds were definitely against her,' Dr. Cooper added. 'It's unbelievable that a woman that size would attack a full-grown man – the chances of her survival are minuscule.'

'Yes, it's, and I'm using your words, it is unbelievable, isn't it?' Sequeira grinned.

'I would say miraculous. It's not unbelievable, because it happened,' Dr. Cooper maintained.

CHAPTER TWENTY-EIGHT

SUSAN'S SOLILOQUY

On Wednesday, 17 May, Susan called her most compelling witness to the stand.

'Mrs. Polk, your next witness?' Brady directed.

The gallery brimmed with journalists and trial watchers looking on in complete silence as Susan announced with a nervous giggle, 'Yes, I'm going to testify, so the defence calls myself.'

Raising her right hand, Susan swore to tell the 'whole truth'.

Over the prosecutor's objections, Judge Brady ruled that Susan's testimony would be a straight narrative; a Q & A with both questions and answers coming from Susan would be too confusing.

'This is not carte blanche,' the judge warned Susan before inviting jurors into the courtroom to begin hearing the testimony. 'This is not an opportunity for a speech. This is a privilege, not a right. You may not like it, but the reality is now that the defendant – you – do not dictate how we proceed in this courtroom.'

'I object,' Susan said, telling Brady that it was her legal right as a *pro per* defendant to voice objections. 'It may appear impertinent or argumentative or unruly to some members of the audience, but it's not. This is not a playground. This is a battle for truth. This is not a movie. This is not a script.'

Jurors filed in that morning to find Susan outfitted in prison issue greens and seated in the witness box. 'I'm not going to go into every detail,' she assured them. 'Everyone wants to get on with their lives.'

Despite this disclaimer, Susan began her testimony with a two-hour slide show depicting her life. She narrated the show herself, with the help of on-again, off-again case assistant, Valerie Harris, on the overhead projector. Throughout the slide show, Susan's demeanour seesawed between weepy and mournful to thoughtful and contemplative as she identified photos of herself as a young girl, as a twenty-five-year-old bride, and as wife and mother, posing with her husband, children, and the family dogs. She broke into sobs when an image of her son, Adam, popped up on the screen.

'I think he said what he said to survive, and that's what he had to do,' Susan told jurors of the twenty-three-year-old who called her 'evil' on the stand. 'I think you saw a different Adam. The real Adam, the one I knew, sent me poems [in jail], came to see me, and was extraordinarily loving.'

Jurors were riveted by Susan's narrative, which she delivered in a soft, folksy manner, her hands folded in her lap, along with a copy of her diary marked with yellow Post-Its. Throughout her testimony, she would refer to the diary that documented the actions of her husband and others who had come out against her.

As she spoke, Sequeira sat quietly in his seat, listening to her testify for much of the morning without voicing a single objection. Instead, he allowed Susan to talk about her relationship with Felix and her realisation at the age of forty that she wanted out of the marriage. The twelve-member panel had already heard much of what Susan would testify to through other witnesses and in her opening statement. Still, she insisted the jury needed to hear 'her story'.

Susan said the onset of Felix's alleged abuse came soon after they were married, and she retold for jurors her story of premarital doubts about their relationship, saying that she later felt 'ashamed' of her decision to marry 'my therapist'. Despite her reservations and subsequent abuse, she never spoke up because she 'thought telling someone would precipitate getting me killed ... I kept thinking I could fix it. His refrain was that nobody would ever believe me if I told them anything.'

Susan told jurors the first time she left Felix was in March 2001. He had a restraining order against her so she rented a room at the Claremont Hotel. She compared the experience to 'recovering from an accident'. The peace and quiet was broken only by repeated calls from Felix. Susan held up a photo she took while at the hotel, showing the bruise she allegedly received on her wrist during an argument with him. Later that month, at her then-lawyer's request, Susan documented the alleged spousal abuse she suffered from October 2000 to March 2001 in an attempt to secure a restraining order against her husband. She recited the five incidents for the panel, contending that Felix had slapped, punched, and abused her, once tossing a drink in her face.

Moving on from her abuse, Susan recalled her January 2001 suicide attempt and her decision to move out of the Orinda house and rent a cottage in Stinson Beach. During that trip, Susan decided not to return home but experienced a change of heart when Eli and Gabriel begged her to come back. It was while she was living in Stinson Beach that she began her diary, vowing to look at life with more humour. Normally, Susan said, she would run from the room crying when Felix would bully her. Now, she would not let herself become unglued; she would adopt a more sarcastic attitude when he tried to intimidate her. But according to Susan, her new approach only succeeded in further enraging her husband.

'I finally made up my mind,' she said. 'I wasn't going to behave like a caged bird. I would live my life. I could go shopping if I wanted to.'

Upon her return to Orinda, Susan observed that her three boys had changed. They were growing increasingly chauvinistic, more like Felix. To remedy the situation, Susan arranged to travel with her sons to show them the proper way to act around a woman, taking Gabe to Thailand and Hawaii, and Eli to Paris.

At lunchtime, jurors filed out of the courtroom, notebooks and pens in hand, but they were pretty much the only people who were guaranteed seats upon their return. Interest in Susan's testimony was so great that court officers returned from the lunch break that afternoon to find a line that stretched from the second-floor courtroom across the hall to the public bathrooms. In a rush for one of fifty seats in the gallery, Susan's own mother, Helen Bolling, was pushed to a spot in the back of the courtroom to hear the remainder of her daughter's testimony that day.

While listeners had been riveted by Susan's testimony in the morning, their interest would wane before she was finished for the day. What had begun as a poignant story of a flawed relationship between a fragile teen and her much-older therapist would soon degenerate into an outlandish tale of brutality, and spies and conspiracy theories. After the lunch break, Susan described how she had been repeatedly raped and drugged by her therapist husband who used her as a 'project' to further his studies of hypnosis and ESP. Susan maintained that as a teenage patient, Felix spiked her tea with drugs, lulled her into a trance, and coerced her into sex. He later demanded that she make predictions on world events that he could pass along to his Israeli operatives.

'I wanted a normal life. I didn't want to be a medium. I didn't want to live like that,' Susan said, claiming to have predicted both attacks on the World Trade Center and to have thwarted the assassination of Pope John Paul II.

'Looking back over my life, I became convinced that he was actually poisoning me,' Susan told jurors, recalling that at one point she started experiencing numbness and tingling in her extremities. 'Felix smiled and said it was MS,' she said. But when a doctor discounted that diagnosis, Susan surmised that her husband likely was poisoning her. To be sure, she stopped accepting food and beverages from him, a tactic that put an end to her symptoms.

It was soon after her surprise fortieth birthday party that Susan realised she could no longer stay married to Felix. 'I looked around that room and saw mostly patients, patients who were his friends,' she recounted. 'I thought, my God, what am I doing? I'm married to this guy who's twenty-five years older, he's my dad's age, he was my therapist. I was ashamed of his values.'

When Susan told Felix of her desire to leave the marriage, he allegedly threatened to harm their children and hinted he might alert one of his patients, a lawyer who moonlighted as an assassin, about the situation. 'It was a recurrent theme,' she added. 'Whenever I brought up divorce, he would say, "You better think of the consequences to the children" and "You better think of the consequences to the dogs."'

The comment about the dogs seemed to strike a particular chord with Susan, who shuddered when she recalled the fate of the family's

German Shepherd, Maxi, a dog that Felix had supposedly poisoned. When she confronted him about Maxi's untimely death, he fingered the neighbour as the guilty party.

By day two, Susan's plodding narrative and penchant for minutiae grew even more tiresome. She had been on the stand almost six hours and had yet to discuss the events that led to her indictment. Surprisingly, Sequeira had only voiced a handful of objections, the majority of which were related to hearsay testimony, but as the day wore on, even he appeared to be wilting.

Susan's gentle tone grew brusque as she role-played both sides of the argument she had with Felix when she tried to leave the house for Stinson Beach in March 2001.

In a gravelly voice intended to be that of her husband's, she asked, 'Where do you think you're going?'

'To the beach,' she then replied in a soft tone to indicate she was speaking.

'No, you're not,' Felix fired back, allegedly striking her in the face as she attempted to flee the house.

Susan contended that for much of their marriage, Felix forbade her from having friends, leaving the house without his permission, and shopping for herself.

On Thursday, Susan told jurors she wanted to clear up an inaccuracy in previous testimony provided by Dr. Peters, the one who evaluated her after her Yosemite suicide attempt. It was Dr. Peters who had agreed during cross-examination that Felix's call to 911 had saved her life that day.

Susan said she wanted to make it clear that she had called Felix, not because she was reaching out to a supportive husband, but simply because his was the only phone number she could remember in her alcohol and drug-induced haze.

Calling the jury's attention to the actual timeline of these events was not a bad idea. Dr. Peters portrayed Felix as ultimately caring about the fate of his depressed and troubled wife. If Susan could make it seem as though this phone call was her doing, it might make Felix seem more the callous husband who cared little about his struggling wife.

Ultimately it was uncertain what impact the clarification had on the jury, since, on Friday, Susan interrupted her direct testimony to recall her eldest son, Adam, to the stand. It was an interesting move and her underlying motivation for it was not immediately clear. Susan seemed more concerned with trying to win her son's affection and stir his emotions with remembrances of the past, than with providing evidence to counter the State's claim that she murdered her husband in cold blood.

'Adam, you've testified that I'm crazy,' she continued.

Adam told his mother that he was the first person to suggest to his father that she was mentally ill. 'I was the one who brought it to the table. He refused to believe it at first.'

'Are you aware that your dad tried to have me committed?'

'All that I'm aware of is that you'll say anything you feel like, drag him and our name through the mud, to serve your cause.'

Susan cried as she read aloud from a Mother's Day card from her eldest son: 'Mom, I know we've all had our share of troubled times, but I will always love you.'

'Did you mean that?' Susan asked.

'Yes, I do love you,' Adam said flatly. 'And I will always be there, but I've stated it before, you need some help.'

Susan asked her son if he was aware that the psychologist who examined her right after her 2001 suicide attempt testified that she was not crazy.

'I have a much better vantage point,' he replied. 'I've spent twenty years in this situation. You're a sick, sick person who's in dire need of a very controlled environment for a very long time. If that doesn't happen, I won't feel safe, and I'm sure a lot of other people won't feel safe.'

On Monday, Susan continued her testimony with a long-awaited explanation of the events of 13 October 2002. Her story of that night began by explaining how she went to the guesthouse to talk to her husband. When he answered the kitchen door, he was wearing black briefs but refused to put on pants, saying that he couldn't be bothered.

Upon entering the house, Susan sat as far from Felix as she could in the tiny cabin-like guesthouse, intending to discuss their finances and a plan for Gabe's education. During the conversation, Susan made a sarcastic comment that infuriated Felix, and he hit her in the face.

'I staggered back and pulled out the pepper spray. I sprayed him right in the face, and he was just angrier.'

She reached for the metal Maglite torch sitting on the coffee table beside the leather chair and 'tapped him on the right temple', indicating that the 'tap' 'did not stop him at all'. He was 'absolutely enraged' and raced at her with the ottoman, eventually grabbing her by the hair and dragging her to the floor. She was on her back, knees up, and Felix was on top of her.

'He rubbed the pepper spray off his hands and into my eyes,' Susan contended. 'It was oily and orange-ish. My eyes were burning. I was thinking, Oh my God. I'm dead. I'm in the worst possible situation. . . . He punched me again in the face. I was completely stunned. I opened my eyes and I saw the knife coming down and it went into my pants,' Susan said, without explaining how, or where, Felix had obtained the knife.

'It's hard to see the cut 'cause I sewed it up later,' Susan insisted, holding up a pair of jeans she pulled from a brown evidence bag. Several coins tumbled from the pockets as she scanned the jeans for a tiny 'nick' the knife made when it entered her left pant leg. 'I saw it come down and go in,' she insisted, putting on her eyeglasses to aid in her search of the garment. Susan noted the jeans were her favourite pair and she had washed them after the tussle. She also showered several times that night.

The bailiff held the jeans up for jurors as Susan described the 'flash' she experienced as Felix was stabbing at her with the knife. 'I thought, unless you do something right now, you're going to die. He's going to kill you.' With this realisation, Susan briefly contemplated letting herself die but quickly changed her mind, and pulling her leg back, she delivered a swift kick to Felix's groin with the heel of her foot and then grabbed for the knife, which nearly fell from his grip as he reacted to the sharp jolt. 'It was a very strong kick,' she said. 'He was stunned.'

Susan claimed she warned her husband, 'Stop, I've got the knife.' But he kept coming at her. She recalled stabbing her husband just five or six times. After repeatedly demanding that Felix 'get off' of her, he finally rose to his feet and said, 'Oh my God, I think I'm dead.'

'He rocked back and forth on his feet. He swayed . . . and he just fell straight back.'

Susan ran to the bathroom to clear the pepper spray from her eyes. When she returned, Felix's eyes were open, staring up at the ceiling, but he was not breathing. At that moment, memories of their years together flooded back. She recalled their first meeting, the day they wed, the children they raised, but the good memories soon gave way to bad, and the façade of their relationship crumbled as she thought about the years of abuse and marital difficulties.

According to her version of events, Susan remained in the cottage for about thirty minutes, carrying on a conversation with her dead husband, asking the questions in death that she never managed to ask in life. Standing on the stairs, she spoke to him, trying in vain to understand this man who had been a mystery to her for more than twenty years, at one point yelling at the body, 'How could you do that to your children?'

Susan's testimony proved surreal. While she had long highlighted different aspects of that night, she had never fleshed out the full picture to the court, never provided any of the details that made her narrative seem human. Now, the court was transfixed by her story, picturing her huddled around the body and trying to make sense of her tenuous situation. It was a vivid image, one that displayed her many inner contradictions. Though she professed to have loathed her husband for years, she could never completely let go of him. In this ending, his death was too abrupt, their relationship too flawed to simply be over, but somehow it was.

Once she moved past the initial shock of her situation, her next thoughts were more practical. 'I'm going to be in big trouble,' she realized. She didn't call police. Instead, she left through the kitchen door and returned to the main house. Holding up a pair of black clogs, Susan identified them as the pair of shoes she was wearing that night. 'I don't wear athletic shoes,' she said plainly. 'I have no idea whose shoes those are in the blood. They're not my son's.'

That night was sleepless for Susan, who said that she drove Felix's car to the BART station so that her son wouldn't see it in the driveway and go to the guesthouse in search of his dad. The following morning, Susan drove Gabe to school, took him out for lunch, ran some errands, and did some housekeeping. 'I kept putting off calling the police. I wanted to have a nice day with Gabriel. I just didn't want to tell him what happened.'

Later in the day, when Gabe asked about Felix, she claimed she had no idea where he might be. 'It was like living in two worlds. My husband was dead in the cottage and I was acting and pretending like he hadn't died,' Susan testified. 'I wanted to hang on to some semblance of a normal life for a few more hours.'

She said her son knew better. 'He knew. I knew he knew. I just wanted to deny. The look in his eyes,' Susan's eyes filled with tears. 'He thought I'd killed his father . . . But Gabe knew there was something wrong. I just wasn't the mom I always was,' Susan sniffed. 'Gabe is so sensitive. We were all so close; we finished each other's sentences.'

Addressing Gabriel's earlier claim that Susan had asked Gabriel if he was happy that his dad was gone, Susan claimed that she never actually said those words, but in actuality said, 'He's gone. You aren't happy, are you?' Susan recalled. 'I was buying time to put off telling him he's dead.'

According to Susan, it was this initial lie to Gabriel that enabled her to carry her story forward, even as officers presented her with evidence to the contrary.

'At some point, I decided to lie,' she said. 'I thought my best shot at getting out of custody, to take care of my dogs and my son, was to lie. So I did. Once I denied it, that was it. I just kept doing that.'

In spite of her lie, Susan admitted that she 'would have confessed' if police indicated they were going to arrest Gabe for the crime. 'I was relieved that Adam was coming for Gabe,' she said.

Susan went on to maintain, 'I didn't murder Felix, and I didn't want the stigma of people thinking I murdered him. I just hoped I wouldn't be charged, but I was.'

As the afternoon progressed, Susan presented jurors with 'explanations' for the accusations made in court by prosecution witnesses, but the more she talked the more it appeared that she was fabricating stories. For example, she insisted that Gabe had misconstrued her discussion of purchasing a shotgun, saying that it had nothing to do with murder. In her version of the story, she was shopping for a weapon on the advice of huntsmen in Montana who told her a shotgun would provide good protection from bears during her frequent hikes in the woods. Similarly, she also challenged Gabe's testimony that she threatened to drown Felix in the pool unless he wired millions of dollars into her bank account. Instead she claimed that she had simply expressed concern that his father would get too drunk one night and 'drown' in the pool.

On Tuesday, before the jury was brought into court, Susan asked that she be allowed to have lawyer Gary Wesley of Mountain View present during her cross-examination by Sequeira. Susan told Brady that if she agreed to allow him to act as assistant counsel, he would be in court solely to make objections on her behalf. Sequeira immediately objected, arguing that the lawyer was unfamiliar with the case and had not been in court during the thirteen weeks of trial. Allowing the lawyer to join at this late date would be 'setting up a disaster' and could lay the groundwork for an appeal on the basis of 'ineffective assistance of counsel', he said.

'I'm extremely concerned about his competence. He can't possibly know the ins and outs of this case,' Sequeira went on, insisting that Susan Polk 'knows the case as well as anybody.'

Brady raised an eyebrow when Wesley stepped before her and admitted that since graduating from Santa Clara University Law School in 1978, he had never tried a murder case. Nevertheless, he had tried all felony cases 'short of murder', and ultimately, Brady allowed Wesley to act as assistant defence counsel during Susan's cross-examination. This was not, however, a blank cheque; there would be ground rules. He could not offer any unsolicited advice. The judge also warned Susan that she would not be permitted to raise objections if she agreed to Wesley's participation.

Brady fought back a smile when Susan agreed. 'I'm going to hold you to that,' the judge grinned.

Wesley told reporters outside court that afternoon that he came on board at the request of Susan's case manager, Valerie Harris, and had been providing informal advice to Susan for several weeks. As if to demonstrate his familiarity with the case, he offered a criticism of Sequeira's cross-examination of Eli Polk, calling it improper and accusing the prosecutor of crafting questions to 'bait' the young man on the stand.

Susan ended her fourth day of direct testimony that Tuesday with what could only be described as a presentation of her kitchen knives. In a testimony akin to a sales presentation on the Home Shopping Network, Susan detailed each piece of cutlery, as a lanky deputy displayed them in his gloved hands. Though she was expressly forbidden to handle the utensils, she appeared happy to provide details about them to members of the jury. Jurors craned their necks to glimpse the family's bread knife, a butcher knife, and a set of steak knives.

'That knife was everyone's favourite knife,' Susan said of one steak knife, smiling as she explained how all three of her sons liked that one best. 'It was always disappearing . . . And that [a different knife] was the knife he [Felix] had in the cottage that he attacked me with,' Susan said of the one with the black handle. 'Afterwards, I picked it up, brought it back into the kitchen, washed it, dried it, and put it away.'

Once Susan had finished with the detailed history of the Polk family cutlery, she moved on to an entirely new and until now, unmentioned subject. Susan attempted to raise allegations that her husband had engaged in inappropriate contact with his daughter from his first marriage. She provided no evidence and there is no evidence whatsoever to support these allegations. Nevertheless, it was Susan's intention to introduce these allegations only by her own testimony. For much of her first four days on the stand, Sequeira had allowed Susan's testimony to go into the record with few objections, but the period of relative calm in the courtroom came to an end with this latest development.

'I move for a mistrial based on being called a liar!' she demanded during a sidebar with the judge.

Susan flew into a rage after Sequeira objected to this line of testimony. Susan claimed that Jennifer had alluded to the abuse in letters she sent her father. But she could not produce the writings because someone had supposedly stolen her 'Jennifer files'.

'I was impressed that we have gone for four days very smoothly,' Judge Brady said. 'But this display in front of the jury with such a sensitive matter, especially when I'm learning for the first time that those letters just don't exist anymore.'

'That's not true!' Susan interrupted.

'Stop interrupting me,' Brady instructed. 'I'm not done.'

'It is an outrageous abuse of your power to keep me silent on his abuse!' Susan shouted at Brady.

'Nobody's going to keep you silent,' Sequeira mumbled aloud.

Unable to quell Susan's rants, Brady adjourned for the day.

Before being led away that afternoon, Susan learned that Eli's trial had resulted in a conviction on three of the six counts he was facing in connection with the March 2006 fight with his girlfriend. Valerie

Harris was the one to deliver the news that a judge had just sentenced Eli to nine months in jail on the charges.

The next day, Susan's cross-examination by the prosecutor began. That Thursday, Susan quickly charged Sequeira with using 'doctored' photos of the crime scene and Contra Costa detectives with 'staging' the scene to look like murder. She contended that pictures of her husband's 'defence wounds' appeared to have been magnified to make them appear more dramatic than they really were.

'They [detectives] were primarily focused on ensuring it did not look like self-defence,' Susan insisted when shown photos of the white numbered place markers encircling Felix's bloodied body to indicate shoeprints found by police.

'Well, it looks as if someone, maybe a female deputy, because they're really small shoes that fit in your shoe size range, maybe walked around the body and then walked to the bathroom,' Sequeira said in a raised voice. 'Is that how it happened?'

'I think you guys goofed,' Susan implied. 'I mean, to put two shoe prints, right-side shoes, side-by-side, like, what, I jumped up and did a whirligig?'

Later on, Sequeira stood before an easel, listing the names of all of the people that Susan had accused of lying about an aspect of her case. There was Gabriel, along with several members of the police department under the column labelled 'Liars'. During the questioning, Susan pointed out that Felix had also lied and insisted the prosecutor renumber to put Felix's name at the top of the list. Sequeira obliged, and changed the order to read: 1. Victim, 2. Gabe, 3. Sgt. Hanson. Appearing at once ridiculous and true to Susan's form, the display succeeded in demonstrating her confused paranoia. In Susan's eyes, it was everyone against her – not because she was wrong but because she was persecuted. With this single gesture, Sequeira managed to show the entire court the skewed lens through which Susan viewed the world, while giving the members of the jury a concise look at the 'enemies' that Susan claimed to have in the case.

As the cross-examination continued, Susan responded to questions about her motive for destroying potential evidence in the case. Sequeira asked why she laundered and repaired her blue jeans, got rid of the pepper spray, and washed the knife that Felix allegedly wielded that night, stripping it of potential fingerprints to prove her claim he had provoked the attack.

'Did you use that knife the next night?' Sequeira asked Susan. 'Did you warn Gabe, "Hey, don't use that knife?"'

'I don't recall.'

'Is it possible that Gabe used the knife to eat his dinner? The same knife that was used to kill his father?'

Susan recoiled at the implication, claiming she had no idea if the knife was ever used again.

'In emergencies I get very fastidious. That's just who I am. I cleaned it and put it away,' Polk said. 'If you think that makes me a murderer? I mean, c'mon. But it makes a good story, so I guess you like that part.'

'It's about the truth, Mrs. Polk.'

Expressing frustration with the District Attorney's implication that she 'snapped' inside the guest cottage that October night, Susan insisted that 'snapping' was not in her nature, but it was in Felix's. Susan also pointed out that she had successfully argued against a court order requiring that she submit to a psychological evaluation before going to trial.

'I'm not going to play crazy,' she told jurors. 'I'm not going to say I snapped when I didn't. And I'm not going to pretend this D.A. isn't out to frame me for murder and this judge's rulings are not biased, when I believe they are.'

'You've used the words "shocked" and "appalled" many times, Mrs. Polk,' Sequeira told Susan during recross-examination. 'But do you recall saying in an interview on Court TV that you talked about it in a joking voice – the different actresses that might play you in a movie?'

The prosecutor was referring to an April 2006 interview that aired on *Catherine Crier Live*, conducted by my senior producer and coauthor, Cole Thompson. During the conversation, Susan said for the first time that she might be losing her case in court. In a moment of levity, she also joked about the possibility of a movie being made about her life, leading her to speculate that Winona Ryder should play the younger Susan, while Susan Sarandon should play her older self.

Though at the time the humour seemed harmless, Sequeira was seeking to use that televised interview to portray her as someone who pokes fun at a murder victim.

'Is it a crime to be able to find some humour in my situation?' Susan asked the prosecutor, charging that the Court TV producer 'sandbagged' her with the question. Breaking into a girlish giggle, she admitted that she still believes that Hannibal Lector is 'too nice' a character to portray Felix.

'This is funny to you?' Sequeira huffed.

'I thought so,' Susan chuckled. But her demeanour quickly changed when she realised that jurors were not laughing along with her. Turning on the tears, she reminded panellists of her serious nature as a child, her difficult years as a wife, and her mother's mantra.

'Have a sense of humour!' Susan said her mother always told her.

'I could look at my life as a tragedy. Or I could see it as a triumph,' she said as the tears flowed and she gasped for breath. 'And I made a conscious choice that no matter what happened in my life, I wasn't going to be a victim.'

Before resting her case on Thursday, 8 June, Susan would call a colourful assortment of witnesses to testify. Among them was Laura Castro-Shelly, a fifth-degree Shaolin black belt who used the 'fight or flight' response to explain the relatively few bruises Susan sustained during the fight with her husband.

'I believe it's animalistic,' Castro-Shelly responded when asked how a woman of Polk's size and stature could survive such a brutal attack by someone so much larger than she. 'You become a lioness in the wilderness. You will protect yourself. You will protect your babies . . . You will fight back knowing this could be your last breath.'

Susan also sought to direct the court's attention to the role that psychics can play in crime investigation, calling Roger Clark, a retired Los Angeles sheriff's lieutenant and self-described psychic detective and expert in crime scene analysis to testify on her behalf. The former police lieutenant took the stand to bolster Dr. Cooper's assertion that Felix died from a heart attack and not the massive injuries he sustained in the guest cottage. Similarly, Susan called psychic detective Annette Martin to testify; however, Judge Brady limited her testimony to a discussion of how her intuitive abilities are used by members of law enforcement – adding little to Susan's defence. Susan touted Martin's abilities, claiming she had a 100 per cent success rate on the hundred cases she assisted on. 'She testified because she cares about me,' Susan later said.

Next to take the stand was family therapist and domestic violence expert Linda Barnard who supported Susan's claim that she was a victim of 'physical, emotional, and verbal abuse' during her relationship with Felix. The expert admitted she had not conducted a psychological evaluation of Susan in jail, but instead, had based her conclusions on four meetings with the defendant at the West County Correctional Facility and a review of the case documents, including recorded interviews, medical records, and naval records on Felix Polk. In response to questions, Dr. Barnard asserted that Susan suffers from post–traumatic stress syndrome as a result of the ongoing abuse she endured during her relationship with Felix.

'Can you describe for the jury what a delusional disorder is?' Sequeira asked Barnard during the subsequent cross-examination.

Referring to the *Diagnostic and Statistical Manual of Mental Disorders* (DSM), she described someone who might be out of touch with reality, hold false beliefs, and experience hallucinations.

Clutching his own copy of the diagnostic manual, the prosecutor read aloud from a section on 'persecutory type delusional disorder'.

'This subtype applies when the central theme of the delusion involves the person's belief that he or she is being conspired against, cheated on, spied on, followed, poisoned or drugged, maliciously maligned, harassed. Small slights may be exaggerated,' the prosecutor read on. 'The focus of the delusion is often some injustice that must be remedied by legal action.'

After a dramatic pause, Sequeira read the final line of the passage aloud: 'Individuals with persecutory delusions are often resentful and angry and may resort to violence against those they believe are hurting them.'

'Is this an accurate portrayal of the disorder?' he asked.

Dr. Barnard nodded in agreement.

Sequeira didn't ask if the description applied to Susan's conduct, the jury would make the obvious connection on its own.

On the morning of Tuesday, 13 June, Susan presented her closing arguments to the jury, ignoring the remarks prepared for her by Valerie Harris and some of her supporters. For months, Harris and several others, including former Miner Road homeowner Roger Deakins, had been holding roundtables at the Polk house to plot defence strategies. Deakins had come to court during several days of testimony to show his support for Susan. But once again, Susan would do things her way.

Before she began, Susan unsuccessfully protested Judge Brady's imposition of a three-hour time limit on the closing remarks. She also tried to convince Brady to charge the jury on just two possible outcomes – either first-degree murder or an acquittal based on self-defence. But Brady ruled to let the jury consider the 'lesser included' offences of murder in the second degree and involuntary manslaughter.

Meanwhile, Helen Bolling waited in the gallery, lost in a game of numbers. 'Numbers are fascinating,' she told Cole Thompson, who secured a seat next to her in the rear of the courtroom. Bolling attracted sneers from the trial watchers, so called gavel groupies, when she continued to crinkle the plastic wrapper of a lemon candy she was fighting to open, seemingly oblivious to the amount of noise she was making. Helen looked up in time to see her daughter searching the gallery for a familiar face.

Susan's frantic expression melted into a smile when she finally spotted Helen. Susan looked worn, as though she had aged several years since the trial began on 7 March. Still reed-thin and wobbly, she stood before Brady in the same dark floral blouse and brown dress she had worn to court the day before. Her tousled salt-and-pepper hair was now mostly gray and her skin was pale and drawn.

It was 9.05am when the proceedings got underway. As the prosecution can both open and close the final arguments, jurors heard first from ADA Sequeira that morning. Susan would step before the court that afternoon to deliver her final remarks – after informing Judge Brady she didn't want her photo taken after the reading of the verdict.

Jurors sat stone-faced as a weepy Susan walked to the podium just after the lunch break. Despite repeated admonishments from the judge, she had objected no less than sixteen times during the prosecutor's closing remarks that morning.

'Imagine for a second there's a man on top of you,' Susan began. 'What would you do? I kicked him in the groin.'

Susan listed seven reasons why she could not have killed Felix: her arms are not long enough, she's not big enough to throw Felix to the floor, she had injuries herself, the distribution of the stab wounds, the nature of the head trauma, the physical improbability and a lack of intent to kill.

Compounding her physical inability to murder Felix was the fact that, according to her, a proper investigation never took place. 'Anything they found that didn't fit with murder, they erased.' She contended that police never subpoenaed Felix's naval records. 'I wrote the navy for them and they sent them within two weeks.' In addition, she argued that they didn't want to locate Felix's computer 'because theoretically it could have shown that Felix was trying to kill me.'

'I made up my husband's history of violence?' she posed. 'Come on.

'According to the D.A., I'm delusional. According to my husband, I was delusional, but I was in charge of our stock portfolio . . . This trial has become a witch hunt,' she insisted, anxiously watching the clock in the rear of the courtroom to stay within her time limit. 'Am I on trial for saying I predicted the 9/11 terror attacks or am I on trial for murder?'

Susan insisted that even if jurors believed she 'is as guilty as a bedbug' they should vote to acquit her because she killed her husband in self-defence.

'Please use your common sense and do not be swayed by the misrepresentations of the district attorney,' she concluded.

And with that, Susan Polk rested her case.

She looked glum as she shuffled back to her seat at the defence table, where a framed photo of a young Eli Polk was propped in front of her. Valerie Harris was seated next to her at the table in a chair traditionally reserved for lawyers. Throughout the proceedings, local lawyers tending to matters in the courthouse had voiced surprise over the court's decision to allow Harris to sit in that seat. Judge Brady even softened and gave Susan an additional ten minutes to finish her closing remarks that day. But there had been almost nothing traditional about the way Susan's case had played out over the thirteen weeks. It was on this note that the prosecutor began his last argument to the jury.

'There's two sets of rules,' Sequeira said during his rebuttal remarks. 'There's one set for Susan Polk and one set for the rest. She lives by her own rules and always has.' He noted that Susan had originally claimed that the sexual relationship with Felix began when she was sixteen. On the stand, she now realised that she was actually fourteen at the time. 'The problem is, it's just like everything else in this case. Sixteen wasn't good enough. Then fifteen wasn't good enough. Now it's fourteen.

'And now she's being raped and drugged.

'It doesn't matter, if it was twenty, it's still wrong.' Sequeira maintained. 'But it's never good enough.'

Walking to the overhead projector, the prosecutor replaced Susan's childhood photo with a photo of the crime scene. He told jurors, 'Susan was not a captive. She was free to leave whenever she wanted. Felix even made arrangements for travel out of the country.'

Reading from Susan's statements to police during her interview at headquarters that first night, Sequeira strode around the courtroom and replayed her repeated claims of innocence. He also discussed her suicide attempt at Yosemite National Park, her revelations about her marriage at her fortieth birthday party and her theory about Felix's death.

As he spoke, Susan could not quell the urge to jump up and object to his remarks, but the judge threatened her with sanctions if her protests continued. Once she settled back in her seat, Sequeira laid out his theory of how the murder unfolded. 'She did it by surprise,' he said, charging that Susan had the knife with her when she went to speak with Felix in the guesthouse that night. The prosecutor noted that defence pathologist John Cooper had contended the knife used in the assault would not be the weapon of choice to commit a murder. It was too small.

'Oh really?' Sequeira said, raising his arm in the air with dramatic flourish. Standing beneath the judge's bench, he rapped three times on the ledge of the desk, pretending he was gripping a large knife as Felix answered the door. 'Can I come in?' ' he said, mimicking Susan. 'And she's standing there with a kitchen knife this long?'

Laughter engulfed the courtroom.

Despite the previous warnings from Judge Brady, Susan continued to object, calling for a mistrial no less than five times during the forty-six-minute rebuttal presentation. Nevertheless, Sequeira was not deterred, and when referring to Susan's accusation that police had 'staged' the crime scene, he asked 'How did they do it? Couldn't they have done a better job?

'Felix had blood on his knees. Why would he have blood on his knees if he fell backwards? The car, she moved it. Why? The knife, where did it come from? Did it come from his underwear? Susan took the knife from the house. This is evidence of premeditation. The torch, if she did not use it as a weapon, then why did she need to wash it off?

'I can only ask you to do the right thing,' Sequeira concluded. 'Justice for Dr. Polk and his children is now in your hands.'

Judgment day for Susan Polk was near.

On Tuesday, 12 June, jurors got the case – but not before Judge Brady informed Susan that she had failed to enter many of Felix's naval records into evidence, meaning that jurors could not consider them in their deliberations. Susan was uncharacteristically subdued. Realising the error was hers, she barely argued with Brady over the pronouncement. She requested only that the judge greet jurors each morning. She wanted to be sure that they were properly admonished not to read or listen to the news or talk outside the jury room about the case. She also wanted them to have a plastic magnifying device that Valerie Harris had purchased for her at Staples to be able to examine crime scene photos and other evidence carefully.

The judge agreed and then directed jurors to begin deliberations in the jury assembly room on the first floor after lunch.

CHAPTER TWENTY-NINE

THE JURY'S VERDICT

Jurors had been deliberating for four days when the announcement came that they had reached a verdict on Friday, 16 June.

That morning, Susan, dressed in a black, long-sleeved shirt, sat alone at the defence table awaiting their decision. Her mother and brother were in San Diego and had asked that someone phone if there was an acquittal. Eli, the only son who had supported her at trial, was still in jail serving his sentence for assaulting his girlfriend.

Outside the courtroom, there were four uniformed deputies posted to handle the crush of trial watchers anxious to hear the decision. Prosecutor Paul Sequeira and Contra Costa District Attorney Robert J. Kochly seemed in good spirits as they stood in the hallway. Sequeira entered the courtroom first, with Adam, Gabe, and the Briners in tow. Susan's two sons were dressed casually in jeans and short-sleeve, collared shirts.

It was 11.25am when a hush fell over the courtroom.

Fighting back tears, Susan turned to look for her sons in the gallery. Adam and Gabe were sitting shoulder-to-shoulder in the front row, the Briners by their side. Valerie Harris was in the courtroom, but not yet in her usual chair.

'Turn off all cell phones and Blackberrys,' the bailiff instructed. 'No one is permitted to leave before the jury.'

'Count one,' clerk Nancy Chertkow read aloud from the verdict sheet. 'Not guilty on the charge of murder in the first degree.

'On the count of "use of a deadly weapon",' the clerk said 'Not guilty.'

Susan looked astonished and just a bit hopeful. Then the clerk continued.

'Lesser count one, guilty of murder in the second degree,' Chertkow announced. 'Use of a knife, true.'

Susan sat expressionless as the guilty verdict resonated in the courtroom. After three months of testimony, jurors had convicted her of second-degree murder and found that the special enhancement, using the knife in the act of murder, applied.

Adam Polk let out an audible sigh when the guilty verdict was read. From his seat in the gallery, he addressed the court. 'Susan had no right to take him from us,' he said, thanking jurors for enduring the lengthy trial. Gabe was silent.

Susan Polk was impassive, revealing no emotion as she sat alone with her chin resting in her hand.

Members of the media were on the edge of their chairs, gathering up their belongings as jurors were individually polled and then led from the courtroom. The jurors' exit prompted a mad dash to the first floor for the much-awaited press conference. After four months of testimony, everyone was anxious to hear what jurors had to say.

'We didn't think Susan was credible,' jury foreperson, Lisa Cristwell, told the media. 'We didn't believe it was self-defence in any way.'

Picking up on the language of the trial, another juror, Kathy Somesse, described Susan as 'delusional', saying that while jurors didn't believe the murder was premeditated, they also didn't believe Susan's version of events. In a one-on-one interview with Court TV's Lisa Sweetingham, Somesse said jurors first ruled out self-defence with their own reenactment of the killing as Susan claimed it occurred.

'We actually reenacted the events that Susan said happened, and after doing that, we determined it wasn't possible for her to inflict those stab wounds the way she said she did.' she said.

During the deliberations, she continued, jurors were 'split between murder one and murder two, with some strong murder ones and some strong murder twos.'

'The evidence was pretty clear,' added juror Pat Roland.

Roland noted that Susan hid her husband's car at the commuter station and initially denied any role in the killing. But, unable to find premeditation beyond a reasonable doubt, the panel ruled out first-degree murder.

Roland also said jurors found testimony from Susan's middle son, Eli, unconvincing, noting there was 'a lot of coaching' going on between Susan and her son. In contrast, all twelve panellists agreed that Gabriel Polk's testimony was 'pivotal' to the case. 'He was the first one on the scene,' said juror, Bob Borkenhagen.

'He was fifteen at the time of the murder, and his first reaction after finding his father's body was not to go and tell his mother, but to hide from his mother and call 911 and say "my mother shot my father"', Somesse added. 'That was very telling.'

Somesse admitted that jurors remain perplexed as to Susan's motive for the killing. 'I think we all speculated what the motive was and wondered about it a lot,' she said. 'But we really don't know. I think it was a controlling thing.'

Remarkably, jurors said that Susan's provocative behaviour in court did not sway their opinion of the evidence in the case – though they did find it 'painful' at times. 'Good or bad, I got to know who Susan Polk is, as a person, and there was a point where I looked at all the facts in the deliberation room, and I asked, Could Susan Polk have killed someone? and because I knew her, I felt the answer was yes.'

'Oh, my God, my life is over.'

Susan's voice rang through the empty courtroom, as she comprehended the jury's verdict. She had waited until the last spectator had filtered out of the room before reacting, and now, with Valerie Harris at her side, the outcome hit home.

'We're just starting another phase of the fight,' Valerie Harris assured her, but her words seemed lost on Susan.

Once she regained her composure, Susan asked that Harris talk to the jurors on her behalf. She wanted to know their responses to two questions: how they addressed her credibility as her own attorney, and what she did or said that suggested she should not be believed?

Continuing to look at the situation with an element of pragmatism, she asked Judge Brady to advise her about legal options. Brady responded by informing Susan that she would need to file supporting evidence to be eligible for an appeal, prompting Susan to charge anew that county officials could not be objective in her case. 'Throughout this trial, there has been fabricated and suppression of evidence by county officials,' she complained. 'It would be preferable to appoint the state public defender's office.'

Outside the courtroom, Sequeira said he was 'ecstatic' with the verdict, although he admitted that facing off against Susan 'wore me down'. Prosecuting her had been the most difficult task of his career, he said, adding that his courtroom opponent was 'the most hateful' person he ever met. Sequeira said his only regret was that he had been unable to counter Susan's punishing character assassination of her husband. While he had potential witnesses who would have painted a 'better perspective' of Felix's character, the district attorney's office had chosen to centre its case around Susan's role in the killing – and not on the couple's relationship.

Over the course of the summer, Susan's sentencing date was postponed several times. In July, she announced her desire to be represented by counsel Charles Hoehn at her pre-sentencing hearing, but when Judge Brady declined to grant Hoehn's request for an immediate transcript of the trial, the lawyer stepped down, leaving Susan with no representation. To further complicate matters, the Contra Costa County Bar Association's Conflict Panel that assigns lawyers for defendants was unable to find anyone willing to take Susan's case. Nineteen lawyers with homicide experience refused to represent Polk, citing conflicts of interest or jam-packed schedules.

In August, Valerie Harris requested a two-day delay to allow attorney Dan Russo to confer with Susan. But when the parties returned to court on Tuesday, 15 August, the judge was informed that Russo was declining the case. He told Brady that Susan was 'not completely comfortable with me'.

The lawyer told Brady that Point Richmond attorney Linda Fullerton, a member of the county bar association's conflict panel, was interested in representing Susan, and the judge scheduled another hearing date. Outside court, Harris said Russo was 'fabulous', but that Susan needed a lawyer who could be available on a full-time basis to 'hit the ground running'. They must also be open to the possibility of asking for a new trial, she said. As Harris said, 'I've got a little laundry list of items to give to the next attorney.'

Meanwhile, Prosecutor Paul Sequeira accused Susan of stalling. He noted that almost two months had passed since her conviction and still there was no sentencing date.

'I'm going to ask for a reasonable date to be set,' he said. 'The victim's family has the right to a judgment entered.'

Susan faces incarceration at the Central California Women's Facility in Chowchilla for a period of sixteen years to life. Opened in October 1990, the facility is located on 640 acres in Northern California and is the largest women's prison in the United States. Susan would be sixty-two years old before becoming eligible for parole in 2020.

Sequeira raised doubts as to whether authorities would ever release Susan. 'The parole board will only let you out after you acknowledge your guilt, say you're sorry, and go through some therapy in prison,' he told reporters at a press conference. 'I'll let you figure out if any of those three things are ever going to happen.'

EPILOGUE

As this book goes to press, Susan awaits her sentencing by Judge Brady. Having found lawyer, Linda Fullerton, currently willing to handle her appeal, she received a six-month extension in August to obtain a transcript and file necessary motions for a new trial. While Susan's decision to represent herself was a disastrous misstep, it is unlikely that the trial judge will determine that this obvious 'ineffective assistance of counsel' will compel a retrial. The old adage, that anyone with himself as a lawyer has a fool for a client, may be true, but this poor decision is not legal grounds for a new trial. Despite the unorthodox proceedings, there does not appear to be any glaring errors that will ensure Susan receive another shot at an acquittal.

Susan has already been behind bars for several years. Interestingly, she seems to have adapted well to her regimented environment. Despite her assertions that Felix was an oppressive, controlling spouse, it may be that years of this relationship prepared her for her time in prison. She spends her time reading and writing, often isolating herself from the other inmates. Ironically, now she has plenty of time for the contemplative life she imagined leading in the wilds of Montana.

As tragic as her circumstances may be, they do not compare with the burdens her three sons may carry throughout their lives. The long-term psychological effects of their upbringing will manifest in myriad ways in the coming years. Ironically, eldest son Adam told me that he is contemplating a career in law. He should be able to get into a good programme, having excellent grades as an English major and many accolades as one time student body president and head of the university's honour society. He held down a job while achieving all of this and, at least outwardly, seems to be creating a semblance of normalcy in his world. Professing love for his mother, he nevertheless refuses to get sucked into an ongoing family drama now that the trial has concluded. However, he is the 'father figure' now, and his two younger brothers will need his guidance.

The youngest son, Gabriel, was very lucky to have the Briners enter his life. A well-adjusted couple with big hearts, this duo is determined to help Gabe survive the trauma of his childhood. Their guidance and support will be critical, as he must have a healthy blueprint for families and relationships to heal these scars. As with the other boys, he is bright and capable, and with serious work, he may succeed in processing the emotional violence of his youth.

The one most in danger, I believe, is the middle child, Eli. Throughout the trial, he seemed to have adopted his mother's delusions of conspiracy and her rebellious actions against anything that smacked of authority. He willingly chronicled a history to conform to her world despite so much evidence pointing to another reality. His own choices since Susan's incarceration have been consistently bad, from his relationship with the much older girlfriend that produced repeated charges of abuse, to his acting out in ways that virtually assured that authorities, especially the police, would have to step in and control his behaviour. This vicious circle – paranoid beliefs about authority, acting out so that he becomes a target and the inevitable clamping down on his freedom – will not be broken unless Eli gains personal insight that, thus far, does not seem to exist.

After many years at the hands of two people well-educated in psychology, it is ironic that more counselling and therapy may be the only hope for Eli's salvation. Some people are capable of working through emotional troubles on their own or at least compartmentalising the past such that they appear to function well in their daily lives. I am not optimistic this will occur for Eli. Despite his physical appearance, time spent around this young man made me acutely aware of his frailties. Coupled with the detrimental impact his recent imprisonment has had, and the essentially life-time incarceration of his only living parent, I do not believe the prognosis for Eli's future is a good one.

At present, Eli has been released from jail. His grandmother, Helen, a figure virtually unknown to him until Susan's arrest and one who reinforces her daughter's skewed world view, has a condominium waiting for him in San Diego, but Susan is objecting to this arrangement. She wants him to stay in the Miner Road house completely alone, despite the planned sale of that home. Sadly, Eli continues to listen to such irrational advice from his mother.

He dreamed of entering the military. Maybe the discipline would have been a good balance for him, but I believe that insubordination would have been his likely reaction to that environment. Nevertheless, his criminal record has now foreclosed this career path. Will he reconcile with Adam and Gabe such that his remaining family can form a support unit? Again, that does not seem likely in the immediate future. Can Eli manage any remaining monies from his parent's estate as he tries to get his feet on the ground? I fervently hope that alternatives present themselves for this troubled young man, but I cannot conjure such a scenario at present. I worry that, without extraordinary intervention, the Polk story has more tragedy in store for him.

In stories such as this, I am always searching for the larger meaning. Obviously, the issue here is recognising the enormous repercussions that flow from dysfunctional families. Both Susan and Felix were set on a path in their early years that propelled them toward pain and grief in their lives. That the two would find each other is not so unusual. Society has learned much about codependent relationships in recent decades. Yet there were many warning signals ignored along the way. Many people in positions of responsibility were aware of the improper, unethical beginnings for the Polks, yet did nothing to address this.

Even more evident were the rampant behavioural problems exhibited by the Polk sons at relatively early ages. School professionals, members of law enforcement, jurists, and psychologists – all could see that these boys were having grave troubles, but they did little to challenge the underlying conditions at home. With the benefit of hindsight, it is easy to criticise, but the incidents were too numerous to chalk them up to minor difficulties in an otherwise normal family.

The literature on dysfunctional families has grown astronomically in recent years. The requirements that officials at school and elsewhere report and react to such events exist for a reason. More aggressive behaviour by these authorities had no assurance of success, but much more could have been done.

Ultimately, the Polk family seemed to be on a runaway train barrelling toward a cliff with no way to halt the looming tragedy. If Susan had not killed Felix, I believe another catastrophe would have presented itself. I cannot fathom that a divorce between these two people would have ended their dangerous dance; nor would a legal dissolution have repaired the younger boys, Eli and Gabriel. Adam simply removed himself from the family unit, exhibiting enough inner strength to reject the poison that was still infecting his siblings. What might have occurred had the younger boys continued as players in their parent's drama will never be known. But it is not hard to imagine that some sort of violence would have occurred – an outcome that still threatens Eli.

Our families are the most formative influence on the human psyche. For better or worse, a childhood forever shapes attitudes, outlooks, and more subtle perceptions about the world. Felix brought enormous trauma and inner turmoil to his relationship with a very troubled young woman and, instead of healing her wounds, exacerbated her serious psychological problems. The couple then projected their disastrous mix onto three helpless children.

This is the story of so many of the people who fill our prisons today. Whether rich or poor, smart or simple, this group usually has been damaged long before they act out. Society cannot simply empathise and open prison doors because of a bad childhood, but it should understand that without addressing this insidious damage, incarceration will do little to affect what makes such people dangerous to others or themselves. Prison therapy is often seen as a weak, 'liberal' response to criminal behaviour, but it is one of the few measures that might actually rehabilitate those who will one day walk our streets again.

As you read this, adults and children all over the country are being subjected to mental and physical violence in a place that should be the most safe – their homes. Their personal traumas regularly become bigger problems for our schools, our workplaces, and the criminal justice system. We must better address this reality to save not only these tragic souls, but our larger family – the human race.

APPENDIX

A copy of Felix's naval records, which Susan used during the trial.

2NG-NH59-6216/1

U. S. NAVAL HOSPITAL
ST. ALBANS L. I. 25. N. Y.

IN REPLY REFER TO:
NH59-4PP-am
6 September 1960

From: Board of Medical Examiners
To: Physical Evaluation Board, Third Naval District

Via :   Commanding Officer

Subj: POLK, Frank F., 575108/1109, LTJG, USNR, RET.
        Report of Final Periodic Physical Examination

Ref: (a) BUPERS ORDS Pers-B51/wmd Ser.PF61/6:356 of 9 May 1960

Encl: (1) Original Medical Board

In accordance with reference (a), subject named temporary disability retired
member was seen at this command on 14 July 1960 for a periodic physical examination. This member was placed on the Temporary Disability Retired List on 1 March
1956 by reason of SCHIZOPHRENIC REACTION, n.e.c. (3007).

The evaluee and his medical records were examined in detail by the members of the
Board,

Interval history revealed that this 28 *year* old temporary retired officer has been
gainfully employed continuously since his last periodic physical examination in
December 1958. Since September 1959 he has been employed as a social worker at
Cedar Knolls School, Hawthorne, New York and his income there is $4,780.00 per
year. Since retirement the patient has obtained a Master's Degree in social work,
He has continued on treatment consisting of psychotherapy which he receives twice
per week. He has continued to experience recurrent bouts of depression and anxiety
but these have never been really disabling. The patient's social adjustment has
been slightly impaired due to his irritability when he feels anxious or depressed.

The physical and neurological examinations were within normal limits. On mental
examination the patient appeared quiet, passive and showed slight depression and
slight blunting of affect. He was friendly, alert and cooperative and showed no
overt evidence of psychosis. He apparently had developed considerable insight
into the psychological difficulty that led to his retirement from the service.

This is the Final Periodic Physical Examination in this case and at this time the
patient's psychosis is in *a* state of complete remission. He is mentally competent
and capable of managing his own affairs. He may appear before a Physical Evaluation Board in person but disclosure to him of information relative to his mental
health may adversely affect his mental' health.

J. H. HOLMES
CDR MC USN
Senior Member

A. SILVERSTEIN
LT MC USNR
Member

C. WEINSTOCK
LT MC USNR
Member

The letter written by naval doctors that details their diagnosis of Felix's suicide
attempt as a schizophrenic reaction

I have done what for a long time I know I must do. When a rock is thrown into water it sinks. It must sink as now must I. My minds is so heavy with wretchedness, with utter loneliness, with an unknown past, a frightening future and an intolerable past present that no choice remains.

I don't fear death at all. What it is but non-life and what is life but a continuous torture?

This final act is not sudden or impetuous. I have known that some day it would take place. The question has only been where, when and how. Until a few weeks ago there has always been some spark some hope which prevented me from the obvious. This night there is no hope. There is nothing; and tomorrow and tomorrow.

Of regrets I have few. It would be folly for anyone to assume the blame for something of which I myself and no one else is responsible.

I say goodbye to a hateful world with a smile. In life I hated pity and in death I want none.

Had I not come this far in life my loss would perhaps have been easier. I have forgotten the world and now the world much forget me.

Felix's 1955 suicide letter

Susan, younger, at one of the Polk's earlier houses

Susan and Felix on a trip to Europe

Susan and her children on a trip to a California vineyard

IN THE SUPERIOR COURT OF THE STATE OF CALIFORNIA
IN AND FOR THE COUNTY OF CONTRA COSTA

In re the matter of:

PETR/PLTF: SUSAN MAE POLK

and

RESP/DEFT: FRANK FELIX POLK

CASE NO.: Do1-01732

DECLARATION RE: NOTICE UPON
EX PARTE APPLICATION FOR ORDERS

I, STEVEN LANDES _____ , declare:

1. That I am (counsel for) (Petr/Pltf) (Resp/Deft) (other: RESPONDENT _____)
   in the within action.

2. That pursuant to Local Rules of Court, I have given notice of the present ex-parte
   application (WHICH INCLUDES HAVING DELIVERED COPIES OF THE PROPOSED
   ORDER) to DAN RYAN, PETITIONERS ATTORNEY _____
   in the following manner:

   __X__ (a)   By telephone call at _____ 12:00 a.m./p.m. on _7/31/02_
              (Describe message left or conversation below.)
   _____ (b)   By letter (mailed) (personally delivered) at _____ am/pm
              on _____ . (Copy of letter attached)
   __X__ (c)   Other (describe): FAX AT 925/682-8192 _____

3. The opposing party has responded to my notice in the following manner:
   N/A _____

4. I have not given notice of the present Ex Parte Application for Orders for the following
   reason(s) indicated:
   _____ (a)   Notice of this application would frustrate the purpose of the order(s)
              sought herein (EXPLAIN BELOW).
   _____ (b)   The applicant would suffer immediate and irreparable harm before the
              other party could be heard in opposition. (EXPLAIN BELOW)
   _____ (c)   No significant direct burden or inconvenience to the other party is likely
              to result from the orders sought (EXPLAIN BELOW).
   _____ (d)   I made the following reasonable and good faith efforts to notify the other
              party and further efforts to give notice would probably be futile or unduly
              burdensome (EXPLAIN BELOW).
   _____ (e)   Other: _____

   I declare under penalty of perjury that the foregoing is true and correct and that
this declaration was executed on 7/31/02 _____
at VENICE _____ , California.

Sign: _____

STEVEN R. LANDES

A page from the legal case of *Polk v. Polk*

Always an avid outdoorsman, Felix loved hiking with his boys.

The police report from Felix's death scene

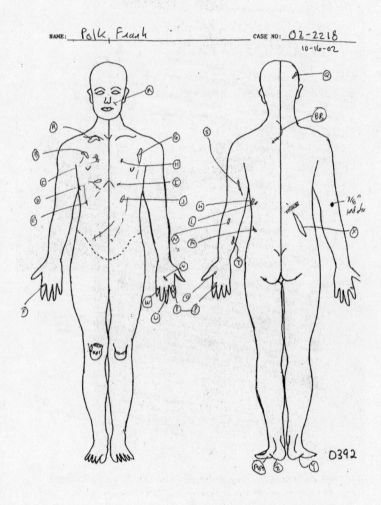

Dr. Peterson's wound chart from Felix's autopsy. This diagrams each of the places where Susan's knife hit Felix.

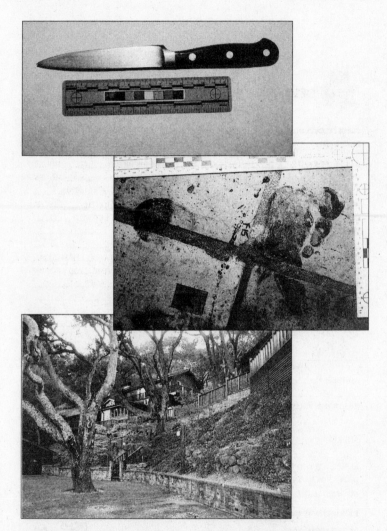

Top: The knife that Susan claimed she used when she killed her husband
Centre: A bloody footprint on the floor of the Miner Road pool house taken
by Costa County Police Department. The footprints would prove a subject of
great controversy during the trial as Susan used them to demonstrate
procedural errors on behalf of the police department.

Bottom: A police photo of the Polk's Miner Road estate

CONTRA COSTA COUNTY
OFFICE OF THE SHERIFF - CORONER
CORONER'SREPORT

CLASSIFICATION: _____ Homicide/Other _____ **CASE:** __02-22 18__

DECEDENT: _____ POLK _____ FRANK _____ FELIX _____
                  Last   *First*   *Middle*

DATE REPORTED: _____ 10/15/2002 _____ **TIME REPORTED:** __1600__ HOURS

DATE OF DEATH : _____ 10/14/2002 _____ **TIME OF DEATH :** _Unknown_ HOURS

AKA: _____ **Other I.D.:** _____ CDL# K0182705 _____

DOB: __06/30/1932__ **AGE:** _70_ YEARS (UNDER 1 YEAR: ____ MONTHS ____ DAYS)

SEX: _Male_ **RACE:** ____ Caucasian ____ **EST HGT:** ___5-9___ **EST WGT:** __175__

HAIR: ____ Brown ____ **EYES:** ____ Brown ____ **SOCIAL SEC#:** _____

IJSUAL ADDRESS: _____ 728 Miner Road _____

CITY STATE ZIP: _____ Orinda, CA 94563 _____ **PHONE#:** _(925)254-3124_

IDENTIFIED BY: _____ Family _____ **DATE:** _10/14/2002_ **TIME:** _TOD_ HOURS

ADDRESS and PHONE#: _____ 728 Miner Road, Orinda, CA 94563 _____
_____ (925)254-3124 _____

OTHER INVESTIGATING AGENCY: _____ CCCSO _____

AGENCY FILE#: __02-29182__ **ASSIGNED OFFICER:** _____ Det. M. Costa _____

NEXT OF KIN

_____ Susan Polk _____   Wife _____
     NAME OF LEGAL NEXT OF KIN   *RELATIONSHIP TO DECEASED*

ADDRESS: _____ 728 Miner Road _____
_____ Orinda, CA 94563 _____

RESIDENCE PHONE #: ____(925)254-3124____ **BUSINESS PHONE#:** _____

_____ Adam Polk _____   Son _____
     AUTHORIZED ALTERNATE NEXT OF KIN   *RELATIONSHP TO DECEASED*

ADDRESS: _____ 611 Gailey Avenue _____
_____ W. Los Angeles, CA 90024 _____

RESIDENCE PHONE #: ____(925)330-0608____ **BUSINESS PHONE#:** _____

LEGAL NOK NOTIFIED BY: _____ Present _____ **AGENCY:** _____

NOTIFIED DATE: _____ **TIME:** ____ HOURS **HOW:** _____

REPORTED BY DEPUTY CORONER: _____ L. Martin _____

CCC SHERIFF CORONER'S REPORT   0380   Page 1

The coroner's report from Felix's autopsy

Felix Polk's death certificate

Taken by the police, this photo shows the edge of the pool house and the pool.

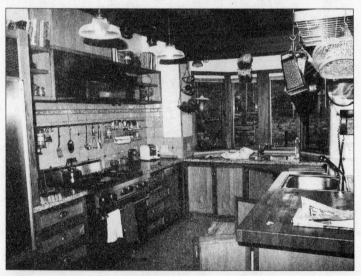

The interior of the main house kitchen photographed by police during their sweep of the premises on 15 October.

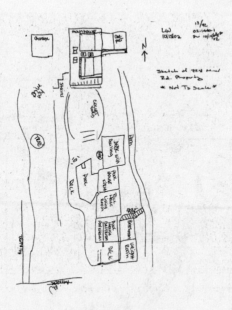

An alternate police sketch of the Miner Road estate

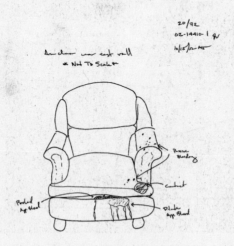

A police sketch of the bloodstained chair in the living room of the pool house

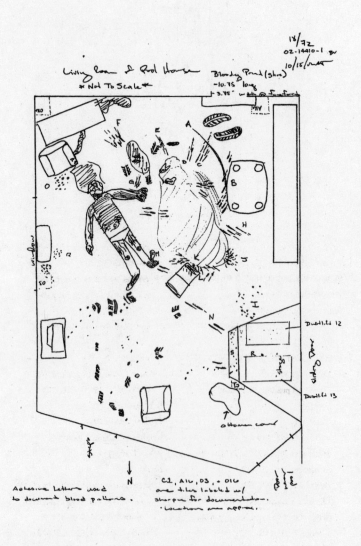

A police sketch of the crime scene from overhead

INDEX

ACKNOWLEDGEMENTS

A nonfiction book is always the work of many dedicated individuals; those who research, compile, review, and of course, those who give their time and recollection to help develop a meaningful narrative. Cole Thompson again took the lead in uncovering and gathering critical information, while Lisa Pulitzer spent countless hours organising and structuring material that covered several generations. Dr. Keith Ablow generously reviewed the relevant histories of the Polk family members and shared his psychiatric insights. Lisa Sweetingham was often my eyes and ears in the courtroom during Susan Polk's trial and offered her own invaluable reflections on the proceeding. Without the generous time offered by many of the people integrally involved in these events, it would have been impossible to examine the very personal details necessary to fully present this story.

Jan Miller, my friend and agent for many years, shepherded the project. Judith Regan and my editors Cal Morgan and Matt Harper had faith, once again, in the relevance and fascination of a true crime story that seeks to go beyond the 'who' and delve into the complex 'why' behind family violence. I want to acknowledge my wonderful staff at Court TV for their support. Very special thanks to my assistant, Barbara Stansell for being there twenty-four/seven and D. J. Haverkamp for keeping the trains running on time. Finally, love and gratitude to Scott Carney, who kept me focused and grounded throughout this project.